The World of the Weaver in Northern Coromandel c.1750 – c.1850

The World of the Weaver in Northern Coromandel c.1750 – c.1850

P. Swarnalatha

Orient Longman

ORIENT LONGMAN PRIVATE LIMITED

Registered Office
3-6-752 Himayatnagar, Hyderabad 500 029 (A.P.), India
e-mail: hyd2_orlongco@sancharnet.in

Other Offices
Bangalore, Bhopal, Bhubaneshwar, Chennai,
Ernakulam, Guwahati, Hyderabad, Jaipur, Kolkata, Lucknow,
Mumbai, New Delhi, Patna

First Published 2005

ISBN 81 250 2868 4

Typeset in 10.5/12.5 point Elegant Garamond

Typeset by
Bukprint
Delhi

Printed in India at
Sai Printopack Private Limited
New Delhi

Published by
Orient Longman Private Limited
1/24 Asaf Ali Road
New Delhi 110 002
e-mail: olldel@del6.vsnl.net.in

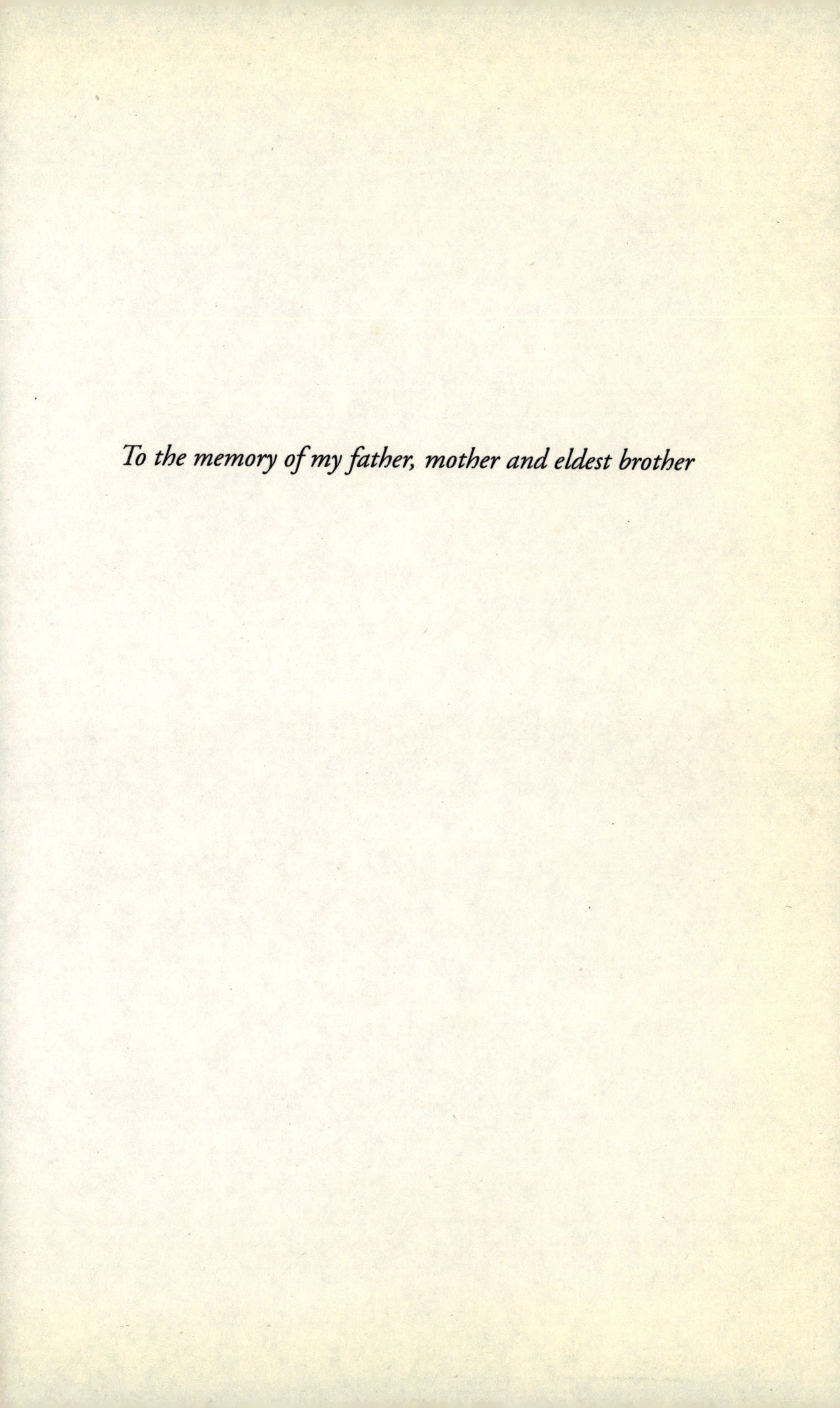

To the memory of my father, mother and eldest brother

Contents

List of Tables in Appendix

Acknowledgements

The research that served as the basis for this book was conducted as my Ph.D thesis at the University of Hyderabad. I am grateful to my research supervisor Dr P. Sudhir for his valuable suggestions and guidance. I extend my gratitude to the members of the Department of History for providing me with all the necessary facilities and help for carrying out this work.

In the course of carrying out the research, I have received help and support from several individuals and institutions, all of whom I acknowledge with gratitude. In particular Professor Ratna Naidu, Professor V Ramakrishna, Professor G.N. Rao, and Professor D. Narasimha Reddy have extended their encouragement and offered valuable suggestions. As one of my thesis examiners, Professor G.N. Rao was particularly helpful in offering detailed criticism and suggestions.

I gratefully acknowledge the kind cooperation of the staff of several libraries and archives across the country without whose help and cooperation this work could never have been complete. These include the Andhra Pradesh State Archives, Hyderabad, the Tamil Nadu State Archives, Chennai, the National Archives of India, New Delhi, the Indira Gandhi Memorial Library of the University of Hyderabad, Hyderabad, the Nehru Memorial Museum and Library, New Delhi, Weavers Service Centre, Hyderabad, National Museum, New Delhi, and Osmania University Library, Hyderabad.

I thank the University Grants Commission for awarding me the Junior and Senior Research Fellowship, with which the preliminary research on the book was completed. I also wish to thank the University Grants Commission for awarding me the Part Time Research Fellowship for women from 1999–2002, during which I got an opportunity to work on the final drafts of the book. I am also indebted to the Department of History, Mumbai University, its faculty members, and the authorities of the University of Mumbai for providing me a chance to pursue my post-doctoral research. In particular, I express my gratitude to Professor Mariam Dossal. I am grateful to the Dhirubhai Ambani International School for providing an environment in which I could finish work on this book.

Several people responded readily to requests for material and references. I owe special thanks to Sri Akurati Venkateswara Rao, Sri Pinjala

Somasekhara Rao, Dr John Akkidas, and the late Sri Tekumalla Viswanatha Rao for their valuable inputs on the socio-cultural aspects of the weaving community.

Many friends have extended their unstinting help and cooperation throughout the course of my research and studies, and I owe special thanks to Vasanthi, Nirmala, Uma and Sujatha, Padmavathi, and Subhalakshmi.

Nothing will suffice to express my indebtedness to my family members, who gave me immense support during the entire course of my study. This book would not have seen its final shape but for the support and assistance given by Parathsarthy, Pavan, Anognya, and Rohil, who provided the needed relaxation from long hours of work and also had the patience to bear with my academic preoccupations and consequent inability to spend quality time with them.

The anonymous referees of Orient Longman substantially improved the quality of the final output as did the editorial staff of Orient Longman. A part of chapter six of this book was earlier published as "Textile Trade and Territorial Imperatives" (with P. Sudhir) in the *Indian Economic and Social history Review*, Vol. XXIX, No.2, 1992. The Oriental and India Office Collections of the British library in London kindly consented to the reproduction of the picture used on the cover of this book with waiver of copyright fee.

ONE

Introduction

This book is a study of the fluctuating fortunes of handloom weavers in the northern districts of coastal Andhra between A. D. 1750 and 1850. The process of incorporating India into global trade in the course of these hundred years transformed the world of the Coromandel weaver in many significant ways. However, by the end of the period, the weaver remained an integral part of the economy, continuing to produce and, to a limited extent, export textiles, surviving thus into the 1850s, when the flood of industrial products from Lancashire was to radically alter his domain. The study contributes to a better understanding of the position of the handloom industry at a time when foreign markets for Indian cloth were slipping away and the English penetration of Indian markets was just beginning. These changes affected the weavers in many complex ways, directly and indirectly, and had an impact on the intricate matrix of merchants, moneylenders, artisans, and peasants in which they were situated.

The book traces the fate of the weaver and the textile economy of the northern Coromandel during the period in which the political ascendancy of the East India Company was followed by the consolidation of the colonial system. While attempting to do this, it also explores the ways in which the social and political affiliations of the weaving world interacted with the objectives of colonial rule.

The aim, therefore, is to reconstruct, at the level of locality, a "total history" of the weaving community in the northern Coromandel region. The concept of totality is invoked here not in the Rankean sense of collecting all the "facts", but rather, in the Annaliste method of recognising the necessity of adopting a holistic perspective and of perceiving the integral nature of the several intersecting spheres in which the weavers functioned, namely, cultural, economic, political, and social.

Next only to agriculture, weaving was the most important artisanal activity of rural India. Apart from providing necessary clothing to the people of India, the numerous weaving communities scattered across the land produced textiles for export to distant countries.[1] Not

1 For more details on this, especially with reference to the pre-modern (medieval) period, see Vijaya Ramaswamy, *Textiles and Weavers in Medieval South India* (New Delhi: Oxford University Press, 1985), xi – xvii.

surprisingly, when European companies began to trade in India, one of their primary interactions was with the weaving community. A survey of this community would, therefore, be useful for two reasons. First, it would help in the reconstruction of the history of an important segment of Indian society. Second, it may enable us to find answers to some fundamental questions regarding the way in which colonialism worked with a peripheral occupation.

Although weavers contributed substantially and significantly to economic activity, very little research work has been done on their history.[2] Scholars tend to focus on the rural economy as a whole and emphasise the agrarian dimension, ignoring an important element of that economy—the weavers. Reconstructing the history of the weaving community, therefore, will permit us not only to return the weaver to history, so to speak, but also make explicit certain aspects of the economic history of the past. The weaver was, after all, one component in an

2 Several works on the textile trade do exist. For instance: Joseph Brennig, "The Textile Trade of Seventeenth Century Northern Coromandel: A Study of a Pre-Modern Asian Export Industry" (Ph.D. diss., University of Wisconsin, 1975); Joseph Brennig, "Textile Producers and Production in late Seventeenth Century Coromandel", *Indian Economic and Social History Review* (*IESHR*) 23, no. 4, 1986, 333–53; Sinnappah Arasaratnam, *Merchants, Companies and Commerce on the Coromandel Coast 1650–1740* (New Delhi: Oxford University Press, 1986); K. N. Chaudhuri, "The Structure of Indian Textile Industry in the Seventeenth and Eighteenth Centuries", *IESHR* 11, no. 2, 1974, 127–82; Irfan Habib, "Notes on the Indian Textile Industry in the 17th Century", in Barun De (ed.) *Essays in Honour of S. C. Sarkar* (New Delhi: People's Publishing House, 1976), 180–92; John Irwin, "Indian Textile Trade in the Seventeenth Century; South India", *Journal of Indian Textile History* (*JITH*) 2, 1956, 24–39; John Irwin and P. R. Schwartz, *Studies in Indo-European Textile History* (Ahmedabad: Calico Museum, 1966); Konrad Specker, "Madras Handlooms in Nineteenth Century", *IESHR* 26, no. 2, 1989, 131–66.

Studies of the weaving community itself are very few. For example, after H. Dodwell, "The Madras Weaver under the Company", *Proceedings of* the *Indian Historical Records Commission* (Calcutta: Government Press, 1922), 41–47, the few major works to appear are Ramaswamy, *Textiles and Weavers*; S. Arasaratnam, "Weavers, Merchants and Company: The Handloom Industry in South Eastern India, 1750–1790", *IESHR* 17, no. 3, 1980, 257–81; Debendra Bijoy Mitra, *Cotton Weavers in Bengal* (Calcutta: Firma KLM, 1978); Hameeda Hossain, "The Alienation of Weavers: Impact of the Conflict between the Revenue and Commercial Interest of the East India Company, 1750–1800", *IESHR* 16, no. 3, 1979, 323–45; Hameeda Hossain, *The Company Weavers of Bengal. The East India Company and Organization of Textile Production in Bengal, 1750-1813* (New Delhi: Oxford University Press, 1987); A. K. Sinha, *Transition in Textile Industry (A History of Textile Industry in Bihar 1783–1833)* (New Delhi: Capital Publishers, 1984).

integrated economic system in which several elements such as merchants, markets, peasants, money-lenders, artisans, technology, trade, and the environment, interacted with one another. It thus becomes necessary to situate the weaver in this complex matrix, and consequently, it can be argued, any study of the weaving community must also contribute to a clearer understanding of the economic structures of the past.[3]

In geographical terms, the space covered under this study is the northern part of the Coromandel coast. It extends primarily between the Godavari and the Pennar rivers, and includes Visakhapatnam district. All the five districts that were ceded to the Company under the name 'The Northern Circars' also fall within the boundaries of this region.[4] Defining and mapping a region has been a problem for historians as well as geographers and cartographers. This is further complicated for the economic historian since spheres of economic activity rarely match political, cultural, or linguistic zones. Apart from the linguistic-cultural unity characterising the northern Coromandel region, there were specific economic parameters that also provided a degree of cohesion.[5] Whether in market transactions or in production processes, the region displayed strong indications of being bounded, of being a definable region. It is true that very often these economic operations overflowed the confines, linking the region to a much larger economic world. However, there were specific activities that marked off the contours of the space quite clearly. For example, in the production of *chintz* (hand-painted or block-printed cotton fabric), the painters of Masulipatnam depended on the weavers of the immediate neighbourhood as well as on those in more distant Nellore. In the marketing arrangements also, the weavers of Guntur district looked to the neighbouring districts as well as distant markets. Similarly, the occasional migrations of weavers within the region also helped to create its boundaries.[6] Cultural factors like caste

3 As K. N. Chaudhuri has pointed out: "...the fortunes of the weaver and the textile industry would be tied to the state of regional agriculture, density of population, transport facilities and the quality of political rule..." "Indian Textile Industry", 130.

4 Sarojini Regani, *Nizam-British Relations 1724–1857* (1963; reprint, New Delhi: South Asia Books, 1988).

5 For a discussion of the ways in which cultural factors shape a region, see Burton Stein, "Circulation and Historical Geography of the Tamil Country", in his *All the Kings Mana: Papers on Medieval South Indian History* (Madras: Oxford University Press, 1984), 90–117.

6 C. I. Bird, Collector to Board of Revenue, 15 January 1845, *Proceedings of the Board of Revenue (PBR) 1950*, 1148, provides information on this aspect.

and kin networks of the weaving communities and textile merchants were other particulars that defined the region.

By the early seventeenth century, the ports of the northern Coromandel had become major emporiums of textiles for European traders.[7] This, in turn, meant that a regular network of economic relationships emerged between the places of production in the hinterland and the coastal centres of international export exchange. For instance, various cotton piece-goods produced in the vicinity were being purchased by the Portuguese at the port of Masulipatnam.[8] Not surprisingly, by the late eighteenth century, this region became the most important and valuable area for investment by the East India Company.[9] Focussing upon this region will enable us, therefore, to investigate the methods of production and distribution of textiles and, in the process, understand how the East India Company acquired economic control over the weavers.

As the Company extended its political control of, and economic penetration into, India, several far-reaching changes occurred in various sectors of the economy and society.[10] Scholars have investigated in some detail the interaction between the European companies and the Coromandel economy prior to 1750.[11] The recent work of S. Arasaratnam analyses the impact of the political control of the English East India Company on the textile economy of the region further, till 1800.[12] It was

7 Dettaze at Masulipatnam to Coen at Bantam 1 September 1617, cited in Om Prakash, *The Dutch Factories in India, 1617–1623: A Collection of Dutch East India Company Documents Pertaining to India* (New Delhi: Munshiram Manoharlal, 1984), 36.

8 S. Arasaratnam, *Maritime Commerce and English Power: Southeast India 1750–1800* (U.K.:Varorium and New Delhi: Sterling Publishers, 1996), illustrates how the demand for the region's textiles generated competition among European companies, company officials, and private merchants during this period. A. Sarada Raju, *Economic Conditions in the Madras Presidency 1800–1850* (Madras: Madras University, 1941), 146.

9 For a discussion on this view, see Immanuel Wallerstein, "Incorporation of Indian Subcontinent into Capitalist World-Economy", *Economic and Political Weekly* (*EPW*) 21, no. 4, January 25, 1986, 28–39.

10 T. Raychaudhuri, *Jan Company in Coromandel 1605–1690: A Study in the Interrelations of European Commerce and Traditional Economies*, Verhandelingen van het Koninklijk Instituut voor Taal-, Land- en Volkenkunde 38 ('s-Gravenhage 1962) (The Hague, 1962). More recently, S. Arasaratnam, *Merchants, Companies and Commerce*.

11 Sanjay Subramanyam, *The Political Economy of Commerce: Southern India 1500–-1650* (Cambridge: Cambridge University Press, 1990).

12 S. Arasaratnam, *Maritime Commerce and English Power*.

only after 1750, once the East India Company had acquired political dominance over the northern Coromandel region, that many changes were brought about by the colonial state in the economic institutions of the weaving world. These changes greatly facilitated its commercial transactions, although at times the Company's revenue/political functions clashed with its commercial objectives.[13]

The hundred years from 1750 to 1850 is of particular significance for the study of the history of these weaving communities for three reasons. First, this was the period during which the East India Company acquired dominance and control over the textile economy. Second, this was also a period in which the Company began to withdraw from the textile trade, a process that had important consequences for the weavers. Third, this period was one in which the massive influx of mill-made fabrics had not yet occurred in the region.

The broader transformations occurring in the textile economy can be said to have taken place in two phases during this century. The first was from 1759 to 1790, when the Company tried in various ways to cope with competition from other European companies like those of the Dutch and the French and also from private traders. In its attempts to establish control over the weavers, the Company had necessarily to depend on indigenous groups such as merchants and landed elites. During the second phase, 1790 to 1830, the English East India Company emerged as the single largest buyer of certain varieties of textiles. As such, the Company undertook more direct methods—for instance, the organisation of administrative units, elimination of certain varieties of taxes, reducing the control of *zamiṇdar*s (landholders who collect revenue on behalf of the government) over weavers, legal provisions and other measures to exercise control. More importantly, it was in the second phase that the role of caste and community leaders in the weaving economy was recognised.

Existing studies indicate a complex socio-economic structure among the weavers governing not only their social but production relationships as well. The structural organisation of production was subjected to many pressures, mainly to eliminate middlemen and reinforce caste identity.[14] One of the major aims of this study is to delineate in detail the structure of the community and to examine the changes that took place. For this, the social dimensions of the community have to be particularly highlighted, especially the role of caste. It would appear that even when

13 See, for example, Hameeda Hossain, "The Alienation of Weavers".

14 S. Arasaratnam, "Weavers, Merchants and Company", 257–81.

seeking to alter the network of relations among the different segments of the weavers, the Company was often forced to recognise the importance of the traditional elites. To illustrate this, mention may be made of the appointment of the *senapati* (leader or headman) as the head of an administrative unit for the weavers.[15]

Economic crises and famine conditions also deeply affected the weavers during this period. Social tensions, usually latent, came to the surface in such troubled times.[16] Some of these tensions were rooted in the 'left hand–right hand' caste divisions and others were related to economic problems such as oppression by the *gumastahs* (agents / clerks) of the zamindars or merchant groups.

Further, location of weaving centres in various revenue-collecting zones— zamindari, proprietary, and government villages—seemed to have affected not only the production process but also economic aspects of the weaver's life. This was particularly so because of different taxation policies enforced over the artisans of the region.

Studying these social and economic conflicts will lead to a better understanding of the ways in which different strata of the weaving community related to one another and to the society around them.

The complex process by which raw cotton was transformed into a finished marketable fabric can be examined in two ways. One is to look at the organisational aspect and the other, to study the technical. The organisational aspect throws up several pertinent questions related to the procurement of raw materials such as cotton, indigo, *chay* root, and thread. The production process necessarily includes the supply of raw material. How did the weavers secure the required yarn? It is known, for instance, that 'thread markets' existed, and that their maintenance was deemed vital.[17] How was the network of production and supply of thread to these markets as well as the supply of cotton to the spinners organised? Who controlled this part of the production process? What was the socio-economic nexus that governed the transformation of raw cotton into thread and then into fabric? The entry of the Company into the scene

15 Letter dated 25 June 1820, GDR 832, 203–32 in *Guide to the Records Godavari District* (*GDR*) 1, Madras, 1935, 35; See Ramaswamy, *Textiles and Weavers*, 14, "...the leader of the Sale or Salapa was called the sanapati" [sic], ibid. 16.

16 For details of social tensions in the early nineteenth century, see John Rowley (Commercial Resident, Ingeram) to Benjamin Branfill (Collector, 3rd Division, Rajahmundry and Ellore Circars) 30 April 1795, *GDR* 921, 249–50; Rowley to Branfill, 11 May 1795, *GDR* 921, 267–68.

17 Letter dated 8 April 1796, *GDR* 926, 79–80.

affected traditional modes of investment and production of raw material and caused the marginalisation of some communities. Questions concerning the technical process of production are related. What, for example, distinguished the technological features of spinning, weaving, dyeing, and printing? Did the rise in the demand for textiles impact technology?

Among the fundamental institutions which linked weavers to the external world were the markets for their products. These markets operated at several levels—local, regional, and international. At all three levels, the markets were social spaces in which the various segments of the weaving community interacted directly or indirectly with others, including merchants, middlemen, and East India Company traders. A detailed examination of the specific textile goods marketed at different levels and of the modes of business throw light not only on market mechanisms but also on the nature of the different elements of the communities participating in the transactions. Another question that arises in this context is what changes, if any, occurred in the system, especially in local and regional markets, as a result of the rise and fall of the European demand for Indian textiles.

The superimposition of a new and changing order on the world of the weaver caused tensions. It is generally assumed that artisans, in distinction to the peasantry, are not militant. Weavers in the region were conscious of the possibilities of collective political and legal action opened up by the new institutional structures. From about the mid-eighteenth century, they launched a series of 'agitations' and 'mutinies' protesting the state's increased control over the production process as well as its attempts to de-skill them.[18] Using a variety of means to organise themselves and displaying remarkable skill in manipulating the caste network to expand their movements during periods of unrest, weavers kept changing their alignments with colonial institutions and local elites in their struggles.

A major controversy in Indian economic history has centred around the decline of the handicraft industry, particularly that of the weavers. At the beginning of the nineteenth century, the demand for Indian textiles remained very high and the East India Company itself had several flourishing weaving factories. Yet, by 1829–30, the Company had decided to close its factories, and quite soon thereafter, British

18 Anthony Sadleir to Board of Trade, Fort St. George, 19 February 1775, *Public Department Consultations* (*PDC*) 113A, 196–200.

manufactured textiles began to flood the Indian market. How did the weavers respond to the changing situation? Also, did the import of textiles affect weavers manufacturing different assortments, for instance, weavers of coarse cloth as opposed to those producing finer varieties?

One of the basic issues that need to be examined is the relationship of the weaver to the various other elements around him. That between the agrarian economy and the weaver was the most important one. Although several weavers worked as both peasants and artisans, or shifted easily from one occupation to the other, large numbers remained disassociated from agricultural production. This often enabled landlords to force grain on them at inflated rates, a practice abolished by the colonial state in the 1790s.[19] Further, with the introduction of land revenue systems between 1802 and 1804, the interaction between the zamindars and the weavers slowly dwindled.

The impact of colonialism on a particular socio-economic group at the level of a region merits consideration. It is argued that imperialism operates at different levels and with different focal points. In India, its political edge was expressed through battles, wars, and the institutions and policies of the colonial state. In one sense, the two facets of imperialism converged at and found their sharpest expression in the locality, whether it was the village or the district. It was here that the British rule manifested itself directly and in a naked fashion. Yet, as has been argued, for all its pomp and power, imperial authority had to bow before and yield to local influence.[20] We are not concerned here with the question whether colonialism operated to preserve a pre-capitalist mode of production, or whether it generated a colonial mode of production, or whether it created conditions for the emergence of capitalism. What we do need to examine, however, is the related issue of how the colonial state and the world of the weaver interacted.

In this context, it is necessary to make certain assumptions about the state. That it was exploitative is perhaps a truism. Nevertheless, it has to be recognised that the power of the colonial state was tempered and limited by the conditions of the locality. Although the purpose of the state ultimately might have been the appropriation of the surplus product, the changes which it introduced themselves generated contradictory forces. These often created resistance and thus impeded the colonial

19 See Chapter 8 for details.

20 R. E. Frykenberg, "The Administration of Guntur District with Special Reference to Local Influences on Revenue Policies, 1757–1848" (Ph.D. diss. University of London, 1961).

state in achieving its objectives. However, despite the inertia of traditional society and its ability to resist change, the British were able to envelop the local economy and society in larger global structures that were essentially created in the interest of the metropolis. Through a study of these aspects we would then be able to form a clearer picture about the way in which British rule led to alterations in the Indian economy in general and the textile economy in particular.

This book adopts a materialist approach. This does not mean, however, that the cultural dimension is ignored or relegated to the margin. On the contrary, it is accepted that the material and the cultural are but two interdependent sides of the historical process. This is particularly true of the weaving economy, since the end product of the material, economic process of weaving is very much a cultural artifact, a piece of cloth. Clothing styles, fashions, and varying tastes in distant markets were all essentially cultural factors that shaped the contours of textile production in the northern Coromandel area. Equally important as cultural determinants of textile production would be rituals and rites in the society, with their own associated clothing prescriptions. An examination of the role played by these factors will help clarify the relationship between the cultural and the material factors in the textile economy.

The complex nature of the weaver's world precludes a truly 'total' reconstruction of his history. However, in attempting to answer the questions set out, it is hoped that this work will contribute to the process of unravelling the tangled threads of the past, even if the exegesis remains incomplete.

Two

The Northern Coromandel Region, 1750–1850

From 1750 to 1850, the northern Coromandel region was the theatre of several contending forces and influences. Till the turn of the eighteenth century, the colonial state tried hard to give political cohesion to the conflict-ridden society of the area. Through the adoption of various administrative systems, the East India Company penetrated deeper into the hinterland's societal activities, tied up with agrarian, trade, and other operations, and thus completed its process of consolidation. As R. E. Frykenberg has suggested, the Company was able to establish colonial hegemony over the region, as it comprehended its role "within the inner logic and dynamics of traditional society."[1] The colonial frontier included not only geographical extent in terms of distance but also social space through which the indigenous civil and economic structures could be entered.[2] Such attempts effected changes in the weaving world of the region because of its direct linkage with the state and political economy.

The Northern Circars constituted an important part of the Vijayanagara kingdom till 1565, when these territories came under the control of the Qutb Shahi rulers of Golconda. In 1687, after the Mughal conquest of the Deccan, they became an integral part of the Mughal empire under the *subedar* (provincial governor) of the Deccan. Some prominent zamindars took advantage of the chaotic situation that followed the death of Aurangazeb and usurped the power of the Mughal collectors.

1 R. E. Frykenberg, "Company Circari in the Carnatic, 1799–1859: The Inner Logic of Political Systems in India". In Richard G. Fox (ed.), *Realm and Region in Traditional India* (Duke University Program in Comparative Studies in Southern Asia. Monograph and Occasional Paper Series. Monograph No. 14, Durham, 1977), 117–59.

2 Fernand Braudel, *Civilization and Capitalism 15th–18th Century. Vol.1 The Structure of Everyday Life: The Limits of the Possible*. Translated, Sian Reynolds. (London: Fontana Press, 1985), 98.

In 1724, these districts came under the rule of the Nizam of Hyderabad. Nizam-ul-Mulk tried to establish his authority over the region by appointing *nawab*s (viceroys/governors) to rule over the *pargana*s (parts of a district, comprising many villages). In 1753, the four Northern Circars of Eluru, Mustafanagar (Kondapalli), Rajahmundry and Chicacole were granted to the French by Salabat Jung. In 1759, these territories fell into the hands of the English.[3]

The Northern Circars, however, were formally acquired by the English Company through the Mughal grant in 1765, which in turn was confirmed by a treaty with the Nizam of Hyderabad in 1766. The Palanadu *taluk* (district), lying in the extreme west of the Kistna district, was mortaged by the Nawab to the Company in 1787, and in 1790, the Company assumed its direct management. Finally, in July 1801, a treaty was concluded ceding Palanadu to the Company. Until 1823, it paid an annual tribute to the Nizam for the Northern Circars. In 1823, this was commuted for a single payment of Rs. 11¾ lakh.

Up to 1794, the Northern Circars were administered by a Chief and Provincial Council. In 1794, a system of collectorates was adopted. Till 1859–60, the northern Coromandel region contained four such revenue districts: Visakhapatnam, Rajahmundry (Godavari), Masulipatnam and Guntur (Kistna).

Although the Company acquired political power in 1765, it took forty years for it to establish its hegemony over the region. As a first step, it recognised the need for pacification programmes as part of a cautious

3 See *Madras Despatches*, 13 January 1755, Para 26, I, 362; *Madras Despatches*, 12 May 1758, Para 13, I, 921; for instance, the *Despatch* of 12 May 1758 emphasised the necessity of doing everything for the recovery of the Northern Circars. Quoted in Lanka Sundaram, "The Revenue Administration of the Northern Sarcars, 1769–1786", *Journal of the Andhra Historical Research Society* 7–15, Rajahmundry, 1946.

Prior to the organisation of the Northern Circars into revenue districts in 1794, there existed Provincial Chiefs and Councils at Masulipatnam and Visakhapatnam, and the Residency at Ganjam. In 1794, four divisions were created and Collectors were put in charge of management and superintendence of revenue. These four divisions were: Ist Division of the Rajahmundry Circar; 2nd Division of the Eluru and Rajahmundry Circar; 3rd Division of the Eluru and Rajahmundry Circar; 4th Division of the Condapalli and Mustafanagar Circar. A Collector was appointed separately in the Guntur Circar. For the jurisdictional limits of each of these revenue districts and the placement of particular zamindari and *haveli* lands within the territoriality of these districts, see letter from Lord Hobert, Governor-in-Council, Fort St. George, (circular) December 1794, *GDR* 920, 21–28.

policy in its relations with the zamindars. This recognition derived from the belief that the powers of the zamindars and lease-holders essentially stemmed from their military force. In its initial period of administration, the Company, therefore, enjoined many zamindars to dismiss a great part of their armed strength, allowing them to keep only a minimum for revenue management.[4]

Local elites and zamindars, unable to clear the revenue demands of the new state and unwilling to accept the emerging hegemonic control over their territorial possessions, created a disorderly situation and deterred the Company's attempts to penetrate into the hinterland. Alongside its pacification policies, the Company had to subdue such unrest. For instance, frequent disturbances occurred between 1785 and 1790 in the Polavaram and Gutala zamindari, with the zamindar being supported by the hill zamindars also.[5] Particularly significant was the stiff opposition of the Vizianagaram zamindar to colonial intervention in the internal affairs of his zamindari between 1760 and 1794. The Company's defeating him in 1793 was of importance for the textile economy as the zamindar wielded enormous power over the weavers resident in his territories.[6] A similar situation prevailed in Guntur district. As per the *firman* (royal order) of 1766, the Guntur Circar was to be retained by Basalat Jung, the brother of the Nizam, and be placed under the Company's authority after him. Though Basalat Jung died in 1782, it took nearly six years for the Company to secure its possession. It finally acquired the district on 18 September 1787, not by military strength but through "protracted negotiations".[7]

The colonial state's involvement in the political affairs of neighbouring states—the Carnatic and Mysore wars and clashes in the Nizam's dominions—was part of its consolidation of power. The fluid

4 For a detailed description of the way in which the Company carried out the pacification programmes, see Sundaram, "The Northern Sarcars" and Burton Stein, "Integration of the Agrarian System of South India" in his *All the Kings Mana*, 128.

5 Henry Morris, *A Descriptive and Historical Account of the Godavary District in the Presidency of Madras*, generally called *Godavari District Manual* [hereafter *GDM*] (Madras: Government Press, 1878), 254.

6 This power is reflected in the proposal the zamindar made to the East India Company to commute his revenue payment into cloth to be supplied by him. See General Letter to England, 28 April 1791, *Commercial Department: Despatches to England* [hereafter *CDDTE*] 1B, 319–21.

7 Sarojini Regani, "Anglo-Nizam Relations Pertaining to the Northern Sarkars", *Journal of Deccan History and Culture* 4, no. 2, 1956, 21–58; see also her *Nizam-British Relations*.

situation caused by this had repercussions not only on the agrarian economy, it also affected the weaving world of the region. The production, trading, and, to some extent, even the social activities of the weavers depended on the Company's relationship with its neighbours.[8]

The area falling within the jurisdiction of the northern Coromandel region comprised essentially three zones in which local ruling groups had arrogated enormous power to themselves. These were the zamindari lands, the *haveli* (under immediate government control) lands, and the hill areas.

The predominant portion consisted of zamindari lands. Some of the zamindars, such as those of Vizianagaram, Bobbili, Pitahpuram, Peddapuram, Cotah and Ramachandrapuram, Mogulturu and Nuzividu, were hereditary landowners tracing their ancestry to comparatively remote periods. Others were self-created territorial proprietors who came into existence during the turbulent times that followed the break up of the Bahamani kingdom and the Mughal empire.[9]

The lands that were under the immediate management of the previous government without the intervention of zamindars or *jagirdar*s (holders of land given by government as reward for services) were called haveli lands and these became direct possessions of the Company.[10]

Some tracts of the northern Coromandel region were under the control of "unsettled" power groups like the hill chiefs, who were referred to as hill zamindars in the eighteenth century. The colonial presence was not very evident here owing to their insubordination.[11]

8 C. D. Maclean, *Manual of the Administration of the Madras Presidency in Illustration of the Records of Government and the Yearly Administrative Reports* 2, (Madras: Government Press, 1885; reprint New Delhi, 1987), 9–35.

9 William Orams, *Report on the Zamindari Lands*, 1787, generally called *Circuit Committee Report*, 15 February; *Masulipatnam District Records* [hereafter *MDR*] 3009, passim; W. K. Ferminger (ed.), *Fifth Report of the Parliamentary Committee on East India Affairs* (London: Stosius Inc., 1813; reprint Delhi, 1984) 3; W. Robertson, Collector, Rajahmundry to BOR, 25 June 1823, *GDR* 4637, 156–57; Tomati Donappa, *Andhra Samsthanamulu: Sahitya Poshana* (Waltair, 1969; reprint Hyderabad: Navayuga Books, 1987); Gordon Mackenzie, *A Manual of the Kistna District in the Presidency of Madras*, generally called *Kistna District Manual* [hereafter *KDM*] (Madras: Government Press, 1883), chapter 10.

10 See *Report of the Farms and Haveli Lands Dependent on Masulipatnam*, 18 December 1786, *GDR* 4632, 93–96.

11 For a sketch on special agencies created by the Company in the northern Coromandel region, see Maclean, *Manual of Madras* 1, 68–77; For details of the assistance provided by the hill chiefs to the Polavaram zamindar, see Morris, *GDM*, 249–51.

Agrarian Economy

The Company's entry into the economic and social activities of the region began with its attempts to strengthen its hold over the agrarian economy.

The zamindars of large estates appropriated a substantial part of the surplus produced by the peasantry and remitted the remaining portion to the state. Their rights were so absolute that they not only levied land and *sayer* (transit) duties but also collected *moturpha* (tax levied on artisans, traders, and other mercantiles groups) and other informal taxes from the various social groups of the region.[12]

The elucidation of old systems of land holdings gives clear evidence about the structure of the agrarian economy. The land-holding patterns of Godavari district, for instance, presented a complex picture, especially of the nature of proprietary rights. These rights at the village level seemed to have been vested in the hands of primary zamindars. *Mirasi* (hereditary privileges) rights appeared to have been the prerogative of hereditary landholders called *kadeem*s (tenant cultivators) in those villages where sole proprietorship (*ekabhogam*), joint proprietorship (*palabhogam*), and communal ownership (*samudayam*) prevailed.[13] Kadeems were described as cultivators who were the descendants of the original settlers in the village.[14] They were possibly landowners enjoying either the possession or the usufruct of tenures that were confirmed by hereditary succession.[15]

Under the right of possession of land claimed by *mirasidar*s, there existed the right to cultivation often claimed by people called *payakari*s. They comprised two groups: *ulparakudi* payakaris or resident cultivators and *ururkudi* payakaris or non-resident cultivators. The ulparakudi payakaris (also called *ulkudi* payakaris) were regarded as the permanent tenants of the mirasidar residing in the same village.[16] Their rights to

12 Letter from Wynch, 9 December 1770, *General Report of BOR*, [hereafter *GRBOR*] I, 1871, 4; Also, for a detailed description of the nature of zamindari rights over revenues from artisans and weavers, see Chapter 8.

13 BOR to A. D. Campbell, Acting Collector, Rajahmundry, *GDR* 909, 27; *GRBOR* 2, 86, 87; also extracts from *Reports Respecting Land Tenures in the Carnatic and Mysore Territory*, 26 February 1807, Appendix 36; Ferminger (ed.), *Fifth Report* 3, 344; Sarada Raju, Presidential Address, 37th Indian History Congress [hereafter IHC) at Calicut, 1976, 4.

14 BOR to Campbell, *GDR* 909/A, 27, 28.

15 Maclean 3, 113.

16 BOR to Campbell, *GDR* 909/A, 13–28.

land were defined by local usage which made tenure transferable. Thus, usually falling under the category of occupancy tenants, they could also at times enjoy conditional proprietary rights.[17] Ururkudi payakaris were temporary tenants invited from a neighbouring village by the mirasidar to cultivate his land under an agreement for a given period.[18] They were normally tenants at will, working under contract, who would have no proprietary rights.[19]

In the pre-colonial village economy, these three groups of cultivators—kadeems, ulkudi payakaris, and ururkudi payakaris—belonged to the Vellalar caste.[20] The first ever census statement of the Guntur Circar drawn up by colonial officials in the late eighteenth century mentions that "Brahmins, Rajahs, Velamas, Cumma and Gentoo were the main categories of tribes that were conducting agriculture" and the total number of their families was 10923,[21] whereas in the 1813 census of Visakhapatnam, the cultivators of the district were placed under the single category of Caupoos (same as Kapu) or farmers.[22]

A number of other groups involved in the maintenance of the village administration also occupied a prominent position in the agrarian structure of the Guntur and Masulipatnam districts. These included Brahmins, Deshpandis, Karnams and others, who received a large proportion of produce from the cultivated lands.[23]

At the bottom of the agrarian structure were agricultural labourers, the actual cultivators of the soil, essentially belonging to the lowest castes. In the case of alienated lands of all types, i.e., *inam* lands and *manium* lands (land held rent free and in hereditary and perpetual occupation) as well as lands assigned for the support of temples and mosques or other endowed institutions, cultivation was carried on with their help.[24]

17 Skinner, Collector, Rajahmundry, to BOR, *GDR* 857, 154–87.

18 BOR to Campbell, 23–29.

19 Sulekha Chandra Gupta, *Agrarian Relations and Early British Rule in India: A Case Study of Ceded and Conquered Provinces, U.P. 1801–1833* (Bombay: Asia Publishing House, 1963), 53–9.

20 Census Report of 1871, quoted in Morris, *GDM*, 331.

21 Smith, Collector, Visakhapatnam, to BOR, 20 September 1814, *PBR* 656, 12293–308.

22 Andrew Scott, Collector, Masulipatam, to John Chamier, Secretary to Governor-in-Council, Madras, 12 February 1789, *MDR* 2995, 208.

23 John Reed, Collector, Masulipatnam, to BOR, 11 November 1800, *MDR* 2998.

24 H. Oakes to MBOR, 25 April 1917, *GDR* 878, 64–70; Dharma Kumar, *Land and Caste in South India: Agricultural Labour in the Madras Presidency during the Nineteenth Century* (Cambridge: Cambridge University Press, 1965), provides a detailed account of the composition of agricultural labour in South India.

The two groups of workers responsible for the actual cultivation of the soil were the farm servants and the field labourers or *coolies*, who worked for wages. The farm servants (bonded labour called *palikapus* or *paleru* in this region) worked throughout the year for the landholder, who had the exclusive rights to their service.[25] The coolies or field labourers were employed seasonally for harvesting and other work and were paid wages ranging from two to four annas a day.[26] In the villages, cultivators exercised a form of coercion on these agricultural labourers. In Masulipatnam, a great number of the more substantial cultivators had slaves, or rather they engaged men whose families had been in the employment of their ancestors from time immemorial and whose services they had a right to enforce.[27]

Prior to the introduction of the Permanent Land Revenue Settlement in 1802, the principal modes of revenue collection in zamindari areas were those from *asara* lands (wetlands dependent only on tank or canal irrigation), the *visabadi* system (lands or profits allotted among hereditary owners), and the renting systems.[28] In all these, the division of the surplus produce among the different cultivators was based on the system of share cropping. The rates of assessment and shares apportioned to the different constituting elements of the economy varied, depending on the nature of the crops—wet grains or *nunjah* crops and dry grains or *punjah* crops—and also on the status of the persons who held those lands.[29]

The Company introduced the Permanent Settlement of 1802 in the northern Coromandel, similar to that of the Bengal Settlement of 1793.[30] By this, not only were the existing zamindars of the region recognised, new proprietary estates were also created in haveli lands. In reality, though, these estates were only bought by those belonging to the traditional zamindari families.[31]

25 Hemingway, *GGD*, 90–91.

26 Ibid.

27 Census Report of 1871, quoted in Morris, *GDM*, 331.

28 For a discussion of the pre-Permanent Revenue System in Godavari district, see P. Swarnalatha, "Agrarian Structure of Godavari District, c 1800–1840" (M.Phil diss., University of Hyderabad, 1986).

29 See Branfill, Collector, Rajahmundry, to MBOR, 29 February 1796, *GDR* 842, 309.

30 Letter to MBOR, 15 October 1799, *GDR* 890, 389–504.

31 For details, see Nerallapalli Vasanthi, "The Agrarian World of Masulipatnam District, c1750–1850" (Ph.D. diss., Department of History, University of Hyderabad, 1993).

Within a decade of its operation, the Permanent Settlement of 1802 showed signs of decay—in Godavari district by 1810 and in Guntur and Masulipatnam districts by the 1820s and 1830s respectively.[32] This was followed by the village lease system of revenue collection. Indeed, this period came to be called "transitional" in the revenue history of the region.[33]

The socio-economic matrix in which the weaver of the northern Coromandel lived and operated was thus many layered and complex. The rural elites, who wielded various kinds of power, were focal points around which the society and the economy were structured. Not all of these people encroached upon the lives of the weavers. If the money-lender played no direct role in the textile economy, the zamindar did. Similarly, even if the karnam as a village official had only a shadowy presence in the weaver's world, he could, in times of crisis, assume a sudden significance. More than anything else, all of them were consumers of the textiles produced by the weavers.

Famines and fluctuations

Most of the zamindari areas, and a few haveli lands, were situated in the three major river basin areas—the Godavari, the Kistna and the Pennar. The Kistna and the Godavari are perennial rivers, because of their origin in the humid Western Ghats. The major direction of these rivers and the seasonal fluctuations caused by the rains with the onset of the south-west and north-east monsoons not only determined agricultural operations, they decided the entire pattern of socio-economic growth in the region. The disequilibrium caused by weather uncertainties created severe conditions in the agrarian economy and affected societal activities, especially by reducing the density of population. Between 1750 and 1850, famines were so frequent that they became instituted into the economy of the region.

A prolonged food crisis occurred along the coast from 1772 to 1776 owing to crop failures and some parts of the region were affected by famine conditions. This resulted in rise in the prices of foodgrains and cotton. Failure of rains in 1783 led to shortage of food and the consequent problem of collection of land revenue.[34] The famine of 1790–92 was the worst, engulfing almost all the four districts and all sections of society.

32 Ibid.

33 Maclean 1, 9–35.

34 Arasaratnam, *Maritime Commerce and English Power*.

Masulipatnam district was affected by another famine in 1807. In 1823–24, there was a minor famine in Godavari district. In 1833, a succession of unfavourable seasons culminated in the great Guntur famine that devastated the population in the districts of Guntur and Masulipatnam.[35] These drastic demographic changes affected the weavers too, both by reducing their markets and by pushing up the prices of raw materials.

Natural disasters that occurred in the region also altered the normally sedate rhythms of the textile economy. Inundations of the coast by the sea (called *uppena* in the local language) and cyclones were, for instance, other natural calamities that occurred during these years. Many of the coastal areas around the port towns of Coringa, Ingeram, and Nursapur were disastrously affected by the inundation of 20 May 1787. In Guntur district, a great loss was sustained by the villages lying on the coast by a cyclone in December 1800. In 1839, another cyclone raged all along the coast from Visakhapatnam to Nursapur.[36] Such storms and cyclones disrupted production of textiles, affected shipping and river transportation, and had a drastic impact on the marketing of fabrics.

Administrative Organisation

All French, Dutch, and Danish possessions were taken over by the British during various wars involving those powers from 1765 to 1815. At each of the succeeding peace settlements, most, if not all, of those possessions or rights to their use were formally restored to their respective former occupants.[37] During the second half of the eighteenth century, there was a marked decline in the participation of the Dutch in the Coromandel trade, their activities being limited to Jagganathapuram (Cocanada), Palakollu, and Masulipatnam. The French East India Company enjoyed considerable trading privileges with brief intervals at Visakhapatnam, Yanam, Ingeram, Maddepollam, and Masulipatnam; at Yanam, the French retained their prime position right from 1816 well into the twentieth century. By the 1790s, the East India Company emerged as the sole power in controlling the entire long-distance trade networks. It had consolidated its political power in all the port settlements of the northern Coromandel, namely, Visakhapatnam, Jagganathapuram, Ingeram,

35 For a note on the history of famines in eighteenth- and nineteenth-century Andhra, see Raju, *Economic Conditions*, 283–91.

36 Hemingway, *GGD*, 376–77.

37 Arasaratnam, *Maritime Commerce and English Power*.

Maddepollam, Palakollu, and Masulipatnam.[38] The presence of diasporic communities like the Armenians and the Persians further increased the intense competition among the Europeans for a share of the Indian trade.

The entire commercial organisation was broadly divided into three parts: the Court of Directors in England, the Board of Trade in Madras, and the Company's establishment at the factory with the Commercial Resident as chief. The Court of Directors generally despatched the yearly list of investment by January or February of each year. Lists were prepared about two years ahead of the arrival of goods in England, to allow sufficient time for the despatch of the order, the negotiation of contracts, the collection of goods by the merchants, and their shipment to England. Such consolidated dispatches on investment were forwarded to the Board of Trade in Madras, which again was responsible for sending out individual lists to the particular factories concerned. The crucial role of the Board of Trade lay in determining not only the probable quantity to be provided at the various factories but also deciding the amount of money to be spent on packing, washing, beating, and transporting of goods. The Board of Trade also specified the salaries to be paid to the Commercial Resident and other high European officials, and to the native staff at each of these factories.[39]

A typical factory like the one at Ingeram in Rajahmundry district occupied a vast area extending to about a few hundred acres. This included large buildings like bale godowns, sorting godowns, cash godowns, *cutsherry* (revenue or police office), record rooms, and small buildings used for making wax cloth (for wrapping). Washing greens containing wells and tanks, but no buildings, were also located within the factory area.[40]

38 Based on details provided in Joseph Schwartzberg (ed.), *A Historical Atlas of South Asia* (Chicago: Chicago University Press, 1978). Map dealing with European/ South Asian Commercial Contacts, 16th–18th centuries, provides exact dates during which the Dutch, French, and British enjoyed the possession of the northern Coromandel ports.

39 R. N. Banerji, *Economic Progress of the East India Company on the Coromandel Coast (1702–1746)* (Nagpur: Nagpur University, 1974), chapter 7, describes the commercial organisation of the Company in the early eighteenth century; Advertisement given by I.H. Bell, Head Assistant Collector-in-Charge, Collector, Circuit cutcherry, Nursapur, 5 April 1837, *Commercial Department Consultation* [hereafter *CDC*] 62, 40–46, where details of the spatial location of the Maddepollam and Ingeram factories are given.

40 Banerji, *Economic Progress*.

The factory, under a Commercial Resident assisted by a Deputy Commercial Resident, was considerably restructured by the end of the eighteenth century. The Commercial Resident was responsible for channelising all the Company's investment in the entire zone that came under the purview of the factory and enjoyed considerable judicial powers in deciding matters related to its affairs.[41]

There was a native establishment as well, with a number of assistants to run its affairs. By 1828, at the Visakhapatnam factory, for instance, the proposed establishment consisted of 30 assistants with different functional operations. These included head servant, accountant, record keeper, writer, warehouse keeper, *shroff* (money-changer or broker), beating *kanakapillai* (native accountant), washing kanakapillai, *gentoo* (Telugu) assistants, *lascars* (member of an army camp or cantonment) and a host of others. They received fixed monthly salaries.[42]

Among the multitude of mediators, merchants, revenue officials and others who facilitated commerce, one of the most significant was perhaps the *dubashi* (interpreter or translator). By definition, looking both ways, speaking two tongues, the dubashi was a necessary bridge between the two commercial spheres, and thus became a key element in the construction of the new world of mercantile activity in the Coromandel.[43]

The role of the dubashi as an interpreter between the new merchants and the indigenous groups covered all aspects—in political situations, in district revenue administration, and in organising the commercial interests of the Company. Not surprisingly, corruption and mismanagement at various administrative levels came to be attributed to this powerful figure. In fact, it was this alarming influence that

41 For details on the role of the Commercial Resident and the judicial powers he enjoyed, see section on Law in Chapter 5.

42 "Proposed Establishment of Servants for Maddepollam Factory", F. A. Savage, Commercial Resident, Ingeram to the Commercial Superintendent and Warehouse Keeper, 26 December 1827, *CDC* 50, 61–65; List of Department of Visakhapatnam for the year 1828–29; H. Taylor, Resident, Visakhapatnam, to the Commercial Superintendent and Warehouse Keeper, 19 February 1828, *CDC* 50, 316–19.

43 For a recent discussion on the role of the dubashi in the Madras Presidency, see Susan Neild Basu, "The Dubashes of Madras", *Modern Asian Studies* (*MAS*) 18, 1, 1984, 1–31.

necessitated district revenue officials' learning the local language—an instrument of colonial control through cultural conquest.[44]

Weaving Centres

It was in this historical context where the political, social, economic, and others forces added complexities to the existing political economy of the region that the weaving world of the northern Coromandel was situated.

The location and distribution of weaving villages were conditioned by many details such as availability of raw materials, proximity to nearby market centres and port towns, means of transport, and ecological factors.[45]

In the northern Coromandel region, the chief centres of textile manufacturing were mostly located within the territories of the zamindars, with only a few in the haveli possessions of the Company.

In Visakhapatnam district, nearly 50 per cent of the weaving population was situated in the area falling under the jurisdiction of the Vizianagaram zamindari. Other locales such as Bobbili, Salloor, Sharemahapnedapur, Belgaum, Seereepuram, Palakondah, Wooratlah, Anakapilly, Vamoodoopoody, Nuckapilly, Kinpally, and Coorpaum were also weaving centres of considerable importance. Though they were

44 M. Somesekhara Sarma (ed.), *Bobbili Yuddha Katha* (Telugu), (Madras: Government Oriental Manuscript Library, 1950). This ballad ended with a note on the assistance rendered by the Dubashi Lakshmanna, the Telugu interpreter to the French and Hyderjung to put down Rangarao, the Rajah of Vizianagaram. The contemporary literary works quite often spoke of the role played by these Dubashis in the politics of the region. For instance, mention was made to Kondregula Jogeepantulu in Gogulapati Kurma Nadudu's *Simhadri Narasimha Satakamu*, c 1750, a dvipada kavya narrating the atrocities committed in the region, especially in Bimha Singhi, Jamy, and Chodavaram areas; For their role in the weaving world, see chapter 6; For a recent discussion on this see, P. Sudhir, "Colonialism and the Vocabularies of Dominance: The Conquest of Telugu, c1600–c 1850", in Tejasvini Niranjana et al (ed.), *Interrogating Modernity: Culture and Colonialism in India* (Calcutta: Seagull, 1993), 334–47.

45 K. N. Chaudhuri in his *The Trading World of Asia and the English East India Company 1660–1760* (Cambridge: Cambridge University Press, 1978), 240–53, describes the manner in which the location and changes in the geographical distribution of the textile industry were determined by these four factors.

scattered over the entire district, the most important clusters of weaving villages were located in the settled agrarian areas.[46]

The weaving centres of Godavari district were mainly in the three ancient zamindaries: Peddapuram, Pitahpuram, and Cotah Ramachandrapuram. Falling within the fertile area of the major river basin zones and comprising the richest parts of the district, these three zamindaries occupied a very conspicuous position in the political economy of the region. They contributed not only to the agrarian prosperity of the district, they also produced popular fabrics such as long cloth of different assortments, *salempore*s (staple cotton fabric, used for block printing in England), *muslin*s (the finest cotton), *izzari*s (plain white fabric), and many other textiles meant for regional as well as local markets. Another cluster of weaving villages was located in the Mogulturu zamindari area, where long cloth of coarser kind was produced, besides considerable quantities of other varieties.[47]

On a lesser scale, different cloth varieties were produced in other zamindaries also. There were hardly any weaving centres in the upland areas or near the hill tracts. For instance, the few weaving centres around the Gutala and Polavaram zamindari areas produced cloth only for local consumption.[48]

In Masulipatnam district too, weaving centres were concentrated in the hereditary zamindaries, from where chay goods (name derived from the chay root used to make the red dye characteristic of these fabrics) of different varieties travelled a long way to the distant markets of Europe and Africa.[49] There were concentrations of weaving villages in the zamindaris of Repalli, Rauchur, Chilakalurpadu, and Sattenapalli. Here, various types of cloth were produced for export as well as internal consumption.[50]

In the haveli tracts of the Company, the weaving centres were in Eluru, Peddana, Gundoor, and Nizampatnam. The haveli lands of Toomedi and Peddana were situated in the neighbourhood of

46 Meng Dick, Visakhapatnam, to BOR, 28 March 1793, *Visakhapatnam District Records* (*VDR*) 2798, 525.

47 Orams, *Report on Zamindari Lands of Masulipatnam*, 15 February 1785, *MDR* 3009, 95–130.

48 Ibid.

49 See Table 1.9 in Appendix on the textile varieties produced in the northern Coromandel.

50 John Wrangham, Collector, Masulipatnam, to BOR, 9 January 1796, *PBR* 143, 194–96.

Masulipatnam; *punjum* cloth (same as long cloth) of different sorts, *gingham*s (fabric with multiple-stranded warp and weft) and *combali* (coarse woolen blanket material) were the main varieties produced in this locality. Groups of weaving villages in the vicinity of Nizampatnam specialised in producing coloured goods, as the raw materials were available locally.[51]

Textiles from the northern Coromandel were categorised into three distinct varieties—plain white cloth, chay goods comprising both dyed cotton and cloth patterned in the looms, and the painted and printed fabrics called chintz goods. The plain white varieties included long cloths, salempores, izzaries, muslins, *bettelle*s (fine and flowered fabric), *percaule*s (high grade plain cotton), *dungaree*s (coarse cotton fabric), and others mostly meant for export. By the latter half of the eighteenth century, the East India Company's indent lists from the Visakhapatnam, Ingeram, and Maddepollam factories included mainly two types: salempores and long cloth.[52]

Long cloth was a plain white cotton cloth, esteemed in Europe on account of its length—usually about 36 yards or 72 cubits. It varied in quality and price depending on the number of punjums (120 threads per punjum) that each piece contained. The Company's musters fluctuated between the ordinary 12½ punjum and the 50 punjum superfine variety. By the 1820s, only ordinary long cloth varieties were in demand for export.[53]

Salempore (locally called *salembari gudda*) was a staple cotton cloth variety produced in the Godavari and Visakhapatnam districts. The usual dimensions were 16 yards by 1 yard and the quality varied between an ordinary 12½ punjum and a superfine 36 punjum. It was exported to England where it was used, along with other calico varieties such as *mooree*s (white base cloth for printing) and percaules, for chintzes.[54]

By the second half of the eighteenth century, the dyed cotton varieties from the Masulipatnam factory area were *allegar*s (dyed cotton cloth),

51 Orams, *Report on the Farms and Haveli Lands Dependent on Masulipatnam*, 18 December 1786, *MDR* 3009, 48–92.

52 For a detailed description of textiles to be provided in the Madras Presidency under the jurisdiction of the various factories between 1782–1830, see *Commercial Department: Despatches from England* (hereafter *CDDE*) 1–40.

53 R. Fullerton to James Taylor, *GDR* 831, 44; Bird to BOR, 20 January 1844, *PBR* 1950, 1148; For definition of the textile terms, see Irwin and Schwartz, *Indo-European Textile History*.

54 Sir G. Birdwood, *Industrial Arts of India* (London: Chapman and Hall, 1880), 5.

callowpores (a cheap striped or checked fabric), and a wide variety of Masulipatnam *romals* (linen fabric used as handkerchiefs or neck-cloths).[55] The chay goods, especially allegars, callowpores and *sastracundis* (fabric patterned on the loom with the tie-and-dye technique), were meant for African markets, while the red-coloured romals of different assortments found their way into France, Germany, Holland, and other European countries.[56] The Court of Directors' indent lists for various textile varieties from the Coromandel coast provide an illustrative account of the textiles that were ordered by the English for requirement in Europe as well as in the West Indies.[57]

Allegars were generally striped, either red and white or blue and white, though checked allegars were also mentioned. They were not made in the Coromandel before 1670, whence they were shipped to Europe as handkerchiefs. The allegar was one of the main re-exported textile varieties meant for the African market, during this period, but the demand for this ceased by 1814, owing to the closure of the Masulipatnam factory.[58]

Callowpores were cheap, striped, or checked cloths, patterned in the loom, and apparently bought for the slave trade. The other cloth varieties patterned in the loom that were in great demand were red and blue ginghams and sastracundis. Ginghams, locally called *gin-temu*, were striped cottons woven with double-threaded warps and wefts.[59] The demand, mainly for red and blue varieties of 22 punjum cloth, declined by 1810. Sastracundis of 20 punjum cloth, the warp and weft of which were dyed in the thread before weaving, were re-exported from London to the African markets.[60]

Romals—Masulipatnam linen used as handkerchiefs or neckcloths—of both large and small sizes, ranging from 36 punjum to 11 punjum, found their way into the European markets, mainly in France, Germany, and Holland. Most of these romals were patterned on the loom with pre-dyed yarn.[61]

55 Letter from Court of Directors, 23 June 1793, *CDDE* 33–40.

56 Ibid.

57 For details on these aspects, see *CDDE* 1–40.

58 Irwin and Schwartz.

59 Letter from Court of Directors to BOT, 18 March 1807, *CDDE* 14.

60 Ibid.

61 Masulipatnam romals included varieties that were made with the use of pre-dyed yarn, namely, muslin, *doreas*, blue handkerchiefs, blue-dotted and checks. Anthony Sadleir, Chief and Council, Masulipatnam to Cotton Bowerbank Dent, BOT, 25 April 1791, *MDR* 2841, 56–58.

Thus, by the end of the eighteenth century, European indents for the textiles of the northern Coromandel were mostly for medium and coarser varieties. The requirement for the finer varieties appeared to have declined, as the punjum specification for romals did not go beyond 36, occasionally 40. Even the demand for superfine long cloth and salempore varieties declined by 1800.[62]

There was a distinct correlation between the production of these special varieties and geographical location. Even though most weaving centres could produce all categories of textiles, there was a high concentration of weavers producing white piece-goods of different denominations in the Visakhapatnam and Godavari districts.[63] Further, within each district the weavers arrogated to themselves spaces for providing different cloth varieties meant either for local or external markets.[64]

A new category of producers began to emerge within the spatial distribution of the weaving communities in the late eighteenth century. These were the "Company weavers", who produced cloth solely for the East India Company.[65]

Some existing literature on the geographical location of weaving centres producing white piece-goods indicate that

> there was a shift in the location pattern of these villages during the seventeenth century. For instance, John Irwin has suggested that in the first half of the 17th century, all these types of plain woven cloth came chiefly from Golconda, especially the coastal belt stretching from Masulipatnam in the South to Vizagapatnam in the North. By the end of the century, however, production was centered mainly along the coast of Madras proper.[66]

However, other documentation on the weaving centres of the northern Coromandel shows that there was continuity in the geographical patterns

62 Ibid.

63 The Company was dependent for piece-goods, long cloth, and salempores mainly from these two districts. For details on these, see Chapters 5 and 9.

64 For Masulipatnam, see Letter 31 January 1799, *MDR* 751, 96–99.

65 When the Company decided to reduce its demand for chay goods by 1800 itself, it attempted to keep the weavers under its control by making them provide piece-goods and allocated some amount towards this purchase. But, soon the idea had to be given up because of very poor quality.

66 John Irwin, "Indian Textile Trade in the Seventeenth Century: South India", in Irwin and Schwartz, *Indo-European Textile History*, 18–23.

of production centres well into the first half of the nineteenth century. And these weaving centres were able to sustain their production process owing to the large-scale availability of cotton from external areas.[67]

It is evident that while the centres located to the south of the Kistna specialised exclusively in chay goods, those to the north manufactured, in addition, a great deal of punjum and country cloths, both for home use and export.[68]

The special geographical features of the area contributed to the location of the chay goods manufacturers. The coastal sandy soils found in the Bandar and Bapatlah taluks of Kistna district were favourable for cultivating the best kind of chay root (*Oldenlandia umbellata*), used for the red dye in chay goods. The availability of this raw material in the district led to the concentration of centres producing red-coloured handkerchiefs, *loongi*s (a man's lower garment, usually patterned), *soosi*s (striped or checked fabric of silk or mixed cotton and silk), and other fabric in places such as Perala, Vetapalam, Mangalagiri, Rajahpeta, and Battiprole.[69] Moreover, deep and medium black soils along the banks of the Pranahita, Godavari, and Kistna rivers extensively supported cotton cultivation.[70] Besides, there was a community of weavers belonging to the Togata and Rangiraju castes in the Masulipatnam and Guntur districts. K. N. Chaudhuri has suggested that the availability of raw materials coupled with a concentration of hereditary craft skills cumulatively led to locations of specialised production.[71]

Similar factors were at work in determining the site of centres producing the painted and printed multi-hued chintz fabrics, locally known as *kalamkari*. Chintz production was concentrated in places like Masulipatnam, Palakollu, and Jagannathapuram because of two reasons.[72]

67 The weaving industry of the northern Coromandel region primarily depended on a number of production centres for its raw cotton requirements. For details, see Chapter 4.

68 Tables 1.1, 1.2, 1.3, and 1.4 in Appendix clearly show the demand for these varieties from 1787 to 1830.

69 A. F. Bruce, Collector, Guntur, to Chief Secretary, Fort St. George, 30 July 1836, Guntur District Records [hereafter *gudr*] 5392, 51–55.

70 S. Manzoor Alam and B. P. R. Vittal et al (ed.), *Planning Atlas of Andhra Pradesh* (Hyderabad: Government of India and Government of Andhra Pradesh, 1974).

71 Chaudhuri, *Trading World of Asia*, 241.

72 Report *on Zamindari Lands*, 95–130; Report on *Farms and Haveli Lands*.

One was the presence of running water, which is a prime requisite, for the printed materials required to be washed in gently flowing water to remove excess gum before being dyed. The second was the availability of water (whether from rivers, tanks, or wells) of a specific chemical composition—particularly substances such as calcium and alum—the presence of which helped in the dyeing process. The abundance of broken and rotten shells, an important source of calcium, in the sandy soil also contributed to the development of printing.[73]

While proximity to raw materials was no doubt an important factor in determining the position of a particular branch of the weaving industry, it was not however an absolute one. The most striking aspect of the location of weaving centres in the Visakhapatnam and Godavari districts was that they depended to a considerable extent on the inter-regional movement of raw cotton from places such as central Deccan and Nagpur. This was made possible by itinerant traders and merchant groups.[74]

These weaving villages were located close to towns that were the social spaces for the congregation of local artisans, producers, and traders. These towns were 'retain centres' and 'bulking points' for the immediate hinterland of the region, where a hierarchy of traders was observed in the exchange of important commodities such as spices, fine grain, textiles, and salt.

A high-level business in textiles was transacted at larger towns, which were generally transit *chowkis* (customs houses) for the long-distance and high-value trade. In the early nineteenth-century northern Coromandel, most of the towns were inhabited by weavers and traders, who primarily dealt with textiles, exporting to various regional centres.[75]

Such a concentration and specialisation of weaving centres was sustained throughout the period under study, owing to certain well-marked channels of transport and communication that linked the

73 Mulk Raj Anand, "Homage to Kalamkari (with reference to the painted cloths of India)", in *Homage to Kalamkari* (Bombay: Marg Publications, 1979), 1–19.

74 The various levels of the exchange economy of northern India in the early colonial period are discussed in detail in C. A. Bayly, *Rulers, Townsmen and Bazaars: Northern Indian Society in the Age of British Expansion, 1770–1870* (Cambridge: Cambridge University Press, 1983), chapter 3.

75 For instance, the Company's textiles were being sent from the weaving villages to the various factories through river channels, and dhonis were used for this purpose. The charges for these shipments was fixed by the Board of Trade, Fort St. George, while initiating the procedures for the investments of the Company each year. See *CDC* 1–50 for details.

hinterland of the weaving world to markets and port towns. Although there was a large volume of land-based traffic, where goods were being transported on pack oxen, the river systems, dominated by the Kistna and the Godavari and their tributaries and branches, played an equally important role.[76] While river and land traffic linked the hinterland to the coast, it was the ports that became the pivotal elements in linking the region to the world at large.

Visakhapatnam was the northernmost port town. It lay on a river which was barred at the entrance, but with eight to ten feet depth at the shallowest point, capable of admitting small boats and ships. Visakhapatnam was the headquarters of the Company's northern factories and was managed by a Chief and Council.

Coringa Bay, south of Visakhapatnam, was extremely important on the Coromandel coast. A number of ports—Coringa, Cocanada, Ingeram, Bandarlanka, Nursapur, Masulipatnam and Petaboli (or Nizampatnam)—lay on the bay and figured prominently in the region's long-distance trade.

Five miles southwards of Coringa were Nelapalli and Ingeram. The Company's factory at the latter place remained significant till the English retreated from the textile trade of the country in the 1830s. Ingeram, in fact, enjoyed great qualifications as a factory: it was situated near one of the principal mouths of the Godavari and its hinterland was mostly in the hands of important zamindars.

Nursapur in Rajahmundry was also a major port during this period. It adjoined Maddepollam and had the advantage of being on a large and deep arm of the Godavari, which flowed into the sea. It became an important supply centre for textiles in the eighteenth century. About 8 miles north-west of Nursapur was Veeravasaram, a small town known for its textiles.

At the height of the north-east monsoon, from October to mid-December, the port of Masulipatnam was virtually closed because of a heavy ground swell. Sand banks and shoals were common at the mouth of one of the branches of the Kistna river that entered the ocean here, and ships had to navigate cautiously. The town was about a mile up the river and the mouth had a bar with just one foot of water in the dry season. Ships were loaded and unloaded by *masoola* boats (wide-bottomed boats with timber tied together with coir) that sailed through

76 *Report on Zamindari Lands; Report on Farms and Haveli Lands.* Also see Arasaratnam, *Merchants, Companies and Commerce*, chapter 1.

the bar into the river. The river itself, though shallow, was reasonably free of silting, and boats had an easy passage upstream.

The foregoing general description of the agrarian structure of the northern Coromandel region, its economy, the location of weaving centres, its ports, and its ecological context, delineates the political, economic, and geographical contours of the world in which the weaver was situated. As important as the parameters of this world were the factors that shaped the social world of the weaver. It was, after all, a community of weavers that produced the textiles that the world sought, and its social structure merits examination.

THREE

The Social World of The Weaver

The social structure of the weaving world of the northern Coromandel during the period under study discloses the presence of a number of communities in the region engaged in, or otherwise related to, the weaving profession, though a few dominant communities virtually monopolised the work.

There was significant correlation between the caste of the weaver and the production of specific varieties of cloth. Sales—Padma Sales and Pattu Sales—were a notable weaving community. While Padma Sales specialised in coarse weaving, Pattu Sales, as their name indicates, confined their activities to weaving silk and superfine cloth.[1] Devanga weavers mostly produced pure cotton material.[2] Togatas wove the coarsest kind of cotton fabric, catering to the needs of the lower classes.[3] Traditionally, this group specialised in the production of red cloth.[4] Jandra caste weavers were skilled in weaving long cloth.[5] Evidence from the Guntur and Masulipatnam districts shows that non-traditional weavers produced ordinary cloth meant for local consumption.[6] Popular expressions and proverbs indicate that cloth was woven by Pariah (also called Mala) weavers.[7] Generally speaking, the finer varieties of cloth were made by castes higher in the social hierarchy.

According to the 1813 Population Statement in the Visakhapatnam district, the various weaving communities living there included

1 Edgar Thurston, *Castes and Tribes of Southern India* 6 (Madras: Government Press, 1909; reprint, New Delhi: Cosmo Publications, 1975) 265–78.

2 Thurston, *Castes and Tribes* 2, 154–66.

3 Ibid. 6, 170–72.

4 Potukuchi Subrahmanya Sastri, *Achha Telugu Kosamu* 2 (Tenali, 1979), 170–72.

5 Ibid.

6 G. A. Ram, Collector, Guntur to BOR, 13 January 1796, *PBR* 143, 473.

7 If cloth was not woven perfectly, a common saying was "Sagamu Sale neta, sagam Mala neta", meaning: "Half the weaving was done by Sales, the other half by Malas", P. Narasimha Reddy, *Telugu Sametalu, Jana Jeevanamu* (Tirupati: Sreenivasa Murali Publications, 1983), 137. The adage appears to represent the opportunities provided by SriVaishnavism for the participation of both Sales and Malas in the weaving world of the region.

Devangas, Padma Sales, Pattu Sales, Kaikolas (low-caste weavers) and Singamas (beggar castes).[8] The major part of the weaving activity was in the hands of two dominant communities—Sales and Devangas—while a few Kaikolas were located in the Vizianagaram, Kintavalli, and Jayapuram zamindaries.[9] In Godavari district, the bulk of the weavers belonged to the Devanga community, followed by the Padma Sale. However, in certain weaving centres, Pattu Sales and Padma Sales controlled the production process.[10] Other weaving castes, such as Karnabattus, Perikas, Bogamvallu, and Singamas were also found here.[11] In contrast, in the Masulipatnam and Guntur districts, although there were Sale caste weavers (primarily Padma Sales), non-traditional Pariah weavers emerged as a dominant group in certain areas. Jandras and Togatas were other important castes in these districts.[12] Perikas, mainly weaving tape cloths, Coorapa people, who produced blankets or combalis, Jangamas weaving *jidda* (coarse fabric) cloth, and others making gunny bags also worked in this area.[13]

The geographical distribution of weaving centres in accordance to the caste of the weavers was an essential factor that supported the social structure of their world. For instance, the Devanga community was concentrated in the Godavari district, primarily in major textile centres like Pitahpuram, Uppada, Rajahmundry, Ramachandrapuram, Samulcotah, Jaggempeta, Sivakodu, Peddapuram, and Bandarlanka. Pattu Sales were mainly settled in places such as Kottapalli, Mulapeta, Uppada, and Peddapuram. The Padma Sale community was located in Tuni, Samulcotah, and Peddapuram.[14] Likewise, in Guntur district, the looms of Pariah weavers were concentrated in Chintapalli, Marlauz Gunduroo, Venkatapathi Gunduroo, and Colloor. In Repalli, Rauchur, Chilakalurpadu, and Sattenapalli taluks, it was the presence of Sales that determined the production process.[15]

8 Smith, Collector, Visakhapatnam, to BOR, 20 September 1813, *PBR* 656, 12293–308.

9 Guntur District Collector to BOR, 24 May 1855, *gudr* 5409, 233–54.

10 D. F. Carmichael, *A Manual of the District of Visakhapatnam in the Presidency of Madras* (*VDM*) (Madras: Government Press, 1869), 65.

11 Hemingway, *GGD*, 102–04.

12 Ram to BOR.

13 Thurston 7, 191–94; Hemingway, *GGD*, 102–04; Guntur Collector to BOR, *gudr* 5409, 233–37.

14 Hemingway, *GGD*.

15 Ram to BOR.

One of the most important weaving castes of the region was the Sale community. The ancient traditions and customs of the community demonstrated three well-marked points of difference between Pattu Sales and Padma Sales. First, Pattu Sales wore the sacred thread, whereas Padma Sales did not. Second, Pattu Sales would accept food or water only at the hands of Brahmins, whereas Padma Sales could eat in Kapu, Golla, Telaga, and Gavara houses. Third, Pattu Sales wove superfine cloth and, in some places, worked in silk, whereas Padma Sales wove only coarse cloth. Both spoke Telugu and could be Vaishnavites or Saivites. These religious distinctions were no bar to intermarriage and interdining.[16] In the early nineteenth century, the geographical location of this community comprised only a few villages in the Visakhapatnam and Godavari districts.[17]

Togata weavers manufactured coarser fabrics, especially a variety of thick white cotton cloth with red borders, and handkerchiefs and romals, which were mostly consumed by the poor.[18] They claimed descent from Chaudeswari, and followed the Vaishnavite tradition. They also worshipped minor goddesses such as Polleramma, Ellamma, and Kotamma. The other weaving castes did not participate in the rituals of the Togatas.[19]

Various groups were attached to all the major weaving communities in the region as dependent castes. These subservient social classes—Sadhana surulu, Samayavaru, Padega rajulu (also called Koonapillavallu), Inakamukkubhatrazus, Veeramushtis and Jangamas—were supported by the main weaving castes through alms. Such a dependent status was continually underscored by a variety of rituals that emphasised their inferiority, with traditions being invented to legitimise and justify this link.[20]

Groups such as Sadhana surulu, Samayavaru, Padega rajulu or Koonapillavallu, and Inakamukkubhatrazus were various marginalised itinerant bands attached to the Sale caste. The mythological origin of the Sadhana surulu traces their name to an abbreviated form of *Renuka*

16 Thurston 6, 265.

17 Carmichael, *VDM*, 64–5; for Godavari district see Hemingway, *GGD*, 104–5.

18 Francis Buchanan, *A Journey from Madras Through the Countries of Mysore, Canara and Malabar 1* (London: East India Company, 1807), 217–28.

19 Thurston 7, 170–72.

20 Louis Dumont in *Homo Hierarchicus* (Chicago: Chicago University Press, 1970), 97–108 applies this concept. But he uses this as signifying the *jajmani* relationship between dominant castes and others. We are using this term in a different sense, as referring to those castes that are entirely dependent for their livelihood on charity.

Sakthini Sadhinchinavaru, i.e., those who have conquered Renuka Sakthi. According to tradition, Renuka was the mother of Parasurama, one of the *avatar*s (incarnations) of Vishnu, and is identified with the goddess Yellamma, who the Padma Sales revered. Sadhana surulu prayed to her on behalf of Padma Sales and, in turn, the latter paid them an annual contribution of four annas and helped to perform their marriages.[21]

Samayavaru maintained that they went back to Bhavana Rishi, the patron saint of the Sale caste. According to their traditions, in recognition of their help during a battle with *rakshasa*s (demons), Bhavana Rishi made Sales provide for the Samayavaru. They wandered from place to place in a cohesive family group. Whenever they decided to halt, they dressed up in ritually prescribed clothes and visited the house of the *pedda senapati* (headman), who fed them for the day. He then gave them a note showing the amount spent by him, perhaps to indicate that the Sale community of the locality had discharged its responsibility to the Samayavaru. On their visit to Sale houses, Samayavaru praised Bhavana Rishi. They married in the presence of, and with the aid of, Sales.[22] Like Samayavaru, Padega rajulu were also associated with Sales and, like them, were connected in their myths to Bhavana Rishi.[23]

These origin myths, while reinforcing the interdependent relationships between the patron caste and the marginal client groups, also suggest that the latter shared, however nebulously, common caste origins. It can be conjectured, therefore, that these dependent groups may have, over a period of time, become marginalised or impoverished and that the invention of a mythology of dependence enabled their survival and also, at the same time, reinforced the bonds of caste identity.

While the Sale community thus had as their dependents members of their own caste, the case of the Devangas was different. They had a sub-caste attached to them as *kulabhikshuvu* or mendicants. These were the Singamas, who were paid a small sum annually by each Devanga village for various services rendered, such as carrying fire before a Devanga corpse to the burial ground, acting as messengers, and for cleaning the weaving instruments.[24] Oral tradition indicates that the Singamas were given a very low status, even to the extent of stipulating that their hands

21 For a discussion on Sadhana surulu, see Thurston 6, 261; also see Bhadriraju Krishnamurti and Poranki Dakshinamurti (ed.), *Mandaleeka Vrithi Padakosamu 2, Handloom* (Hyderabad: Andhra Sahitya Parishat, 1971), 371.

22 Thurston 6, 290–91.

23 Thurston 6, 265–78.

24 Thurston 6, 389.

could serve as spittoons for Devangas.[25] This custom was an important public means of expressing power relations within the caste. The association of these groups with funerary practices also perhaps confirmed their inferior status by increasing their sense of impurity.[26]

Virtually all these groups had an etymological connection to valour or courage or a martial role in their names. There can be two explanations for this. One is that, traditionally, weaving communities had connections to war—the term senapati stood for a head weaver, for instance. The other is that the caste names euphemistically compensated for the extremely low status they actually occupied.

This peculiar linguistic twist can be seen in the name of another dependent caste linked to Devangas—Veeramushtivallu, literally the warrior beggars.[27] This group, mostly resident in the Godavari district area, received alms from Devangas as well as from Komatis. It can be conjectured that they too, like the other marginal groups described so far, were integrated into the caste through the rituals of mendicancy.

The most distinctive of the mendicant communities were Jangamas. Traditionally priests to the religious sect of Lingayats, Jangamas were disciples of Basava, the founder of Virasaivism, and were regarded as incarnations of Siva.[28] The association of Jangamas with Virasaivism and their activities in the society became part of the proverbial lore of the region. One such proverb illustrated the great anxiety they caused to the villages they were dependent on: "If children are born to a Jangama, they are only an annoyance to the village"—because they added to the number of beggars.[29] Devangas, who were essentially Saivites, sustained the Jangamas through giving of alms. This is illustrated in an eighteenth-century verse that speaks of the Jangamas' right to the wealth of Devangas.[30]

These mendicant groups were provided with land grants, especially for their sustenance. For instance, at Agiripalli village in the Kistna

25 Thurston 2, 154–66.

26 Thurston 6, 389.

27 For an interesting discussion on the mythological sanctions that led to the creation of such a custom, see Thurston 7, 406–11.

28 For a discussion of the Jangamas as a Saivite sect, see Narasimha Reddy, *Telugu Sametalu*, 233–34; also Thurston 2, 450–51; and Collector, Guntur, to BOR, 237.

29 M.W. Carr, *Andhra Lokakti Chandrika: A Collection of Telugu Proverbs* (1868; reprint, Delhi: Asian Educational Services, 1987), no. 943.

30 Adidamu Surakavi, "Ramalingeswara Satakamu", a dvipada kavya c.1600–1750. In Suravaram Pratapareddy, *Andhrula Sangheeka Charitra* (1949; reprint, Hyderabad: Andhra Sahitya Parishat, 1982), 346.

district, a piece of land was allotted as *Veeramushtivallu Vritti*, which included other social groups such as Chakalis, Mangalis, and Vettis.[31] That this was a long-standing tradition is indicated by a Nellore inscription that records the land grant made to the Jangamas.[32]

The foregoing account suggests neatly demarcated caste groups each with its own dependent caste, the only exception being Jangamas and Veeramushtivallu who were ritual dependants for more than one group. That the reality of the caste networks was not so simple is strikingly indicated by the custom by which a Devanga could be transformed into a dependant of the Padma Sales, even though by tradition they were polarised into opposed sects either by the Vaishnavite-Saivite divide or the left hand-right hand division. (The left-right classification, literally *idankai-valankai* respectively in Tamil, marked a vertical division of south Indian society from the eleventh to the nineteenth centuries into two ritually opposed social categories.) A Devanga of advanced age could receive alms from the Padma Sale community and on death was buried by Sales rather than his own community.[33]

There were several other important communities, not strictly weavers, who were, nevertheless, associated with the weaving world. One such caste was the Rangari, called Rangiraju locally. They were located in almost all the four districts of the northern Coromandel region. They dealt with the painting or dyeing of fabric with red colour extracted from the *coosamboo* flower. They worshipped the goddess Ambabhavani.[34] Neeligaru, a class of indigo dyers, was another group crucial for the survival of the weaving world.[35] Their specialisation was strictly protected under the caste rules.[36]

It would seem that the formal regulations and the entire ideology of the caste system, particularly as manifested in the left-hand and right-

31 "Agiripalli Kaifiyat", June 1815, Mackenzie Collections, *Grama Kaifiyatlu: Kistna Zillah* 1 (Hyderabad: Andhra Pradesh State Archives, 1990), 1–12.

32 Nellore Inscriptions, Ongole, no. 85, A.D. 1350 in Kanduri Iswara Dutt, *Sasana Subdha Kosamu Andhra Pradesama (Inscriptional Glossary of Andhra Pradesh)* (Hyderabad: Andhra Pradesh Sahitya Akademi, 1968), 11240.

33 A brief discussion on this practice is found in Thurston 2, 154–66.

34 Thurston 6, 242–43.

35 Thurston 4, see entry under Niligaru.

36 The Letters of Father Coeardoux, 1742 and 1747, Appendix A, in Irwin and Schwartz, *Indo-European Textile History*, 108; "Report on the Mode of Coromandel Yarn Practised on the Coast of Coromandel", Benjamin Heyne, Acting Botanist, to Hobart, President-in-Council, Fort. St George, 18 January 1795, *Public Department Sundries* [hereafter *PDS*] 60, 1–65

hand division, helped to maintain order in the society. This division, originating in or legitimised by ideology, was also reinforced by or even derived from economic rivalries that must have existed between the weaving communities. These rules and codes of behaviour prevented latent tensions from surfacing and destroying the social fabric.[37] During the late eighteenth and early nineteenth centuries, many disputes arose at Madras from conflicts between idankai (left) and valankai (right) castes.[38]

Devangas belonged to the left-hand schism and Padma Sales to the right-hand one.[39] The predominant weaving communities maintained their social identity very strictly within a village. For instance, Devangas and Padma Sales never lived in the same street and did not draw water from the same well. Like other left-hand castes, Devangas had their own *nautch* (dancing) girls called *jathi biddalu* (children of the caste), whose male offspring engaged in *acchhupani* (printing on cloth) and occasionally went about begging from Devangas.[40]

The groups associated with the left-hand division were slightly lower down in the social hierarchy, and they always strove to achieve a higher position through sanskritisation and the adoption of certain right-hand privileges. One such right asserted by the weavers of the region was the custom by which some Devangas joined the Padma Sale group. Says Thurston: "Once in twelve years, a Devanga leaves his home, and joins the Padma Sales. He begs from them, saying that he is the son of their caste, and, as such, has to be supported by them. If alms are not forthcoming, he enters the house and carries off whatever he may be able to pick up. Sometimes, if he can get nothing else, he has been known to seize even the lighted cigar in the mouth of a Sale and run off with it." The origin of this custom is not certain, but it has been suggested

37 For the origins and nature of the right-left divisions, see Arjun Appadurai, "Right and Left Hand Castes in South India", *IESHR* 11, no. 2, 1974, 216–59; also, Ramaswamy.

38 Appadurai, "Right Hand Left Hand Castes"; Brenda E. K. Beck, "The Right-Left Division of South Indian Society". In *Journal of Asian Studies* 29, 1970,779–98; Buchanan, *A Journey from Madras* 1, 77–80 provides details on the origins of idankai and valankai division of society; Recently, Mattison Mines, *The Warrior Merchants: Textiles Trade and Territory in South India* (Cambridge: Cambridge University Press, 1984), chapter 3, traces the position of the Kaikolas in the idankai-valankai schisms.

39 Buchanan 1, 77–80 provides a list of castes associated with the right-left divisions.

40 Thurston 2, 154–66.

that Devangas and Sales were originally one caste, and that they split when the former became Lingayats.[41]

This traditional division of the weaving communities into left-hand and right-hand castes was itself a source of serious conflict, because in reinforcing community identity, the prescriptive codes also paradoxically heightened the rivalry between Sales and Devangas. These antagonisms did not die down with the coming of the new economy. On the other hand, they may have been precipitated.

For example, George Maidman, Deputy Commercial Resident of Ingeram, was alarmed about an incident in which the refusal of the Sale weavers to honour the custom of giving alms to Veeramushtis led to a violent conflict between Sales on one side and Devangas, Karineelu, and Kaikolas on the other, the latter groups taking it upon themselves to champion the mendicant community. Veeramushtis, encouraged and supported by the other weaving communities, harassed the Sales and disrupted their work by unsettling the thread markets, destroying looms, and otherwise creating tension by assembling in large, menacing numbers. The Deputy Commercial Resident of Ingeram, worried about the effect of this conflict on textile production, instructed the Collector to arrange for the suppression of the disturbance.[42] The Company was caught in a dilemma, for perceiving the clash to be essentially a religious one, it was reluctant to interfere, but, at the same time, was compelled to restore peace as quickly as possible.[43]

There were clear grounds for believing that the strife was primarily religious. Veeramushtivallu, being Saivites, were necessarily supported by Devangas and others who were also Saivite weaver communities, while Sales were predominantly Vaishnavite. Besides, the conflict was also rooted in the deep ideological rift represented by the left hand-right hand division.

The Company's legal and jurisdictional structures, created to maintain the production process and to tighten control over the weavers, were not extended to cover those issues that fell under the sphere of religious and social customs. It was this limitation of the Company's authority that may have ultimately kept intact the rigidity of the Hindu

41 Ibid.

42 George Maidman, Deputy Commercial Resident, Ingeram, to Collector, 1st Division, Masulipatnam, 26 March 1803, *GDR* 946 B, 617–19.

43 R. Fullerton, Commercial Resident, Ingeram, to Collector, 1st Division, Masulipatnam, 2 April 1803, *GDR* 946 B, 635–37.

caste structures during this period. In 1802, the Collector of Rajahmundry district reported to the Board of Revenue that

> with reference to the religious issues, there followed different methods altogether. In all cases relating to religion, of the rights, privileges, and immunities of the respective caste, the higher orders of each one are either consulted, or the most learned Brahmins whose wisdom and piety may have raised them to public estimation of confidence are resorted to, who are supposed to possess a thorough knowledge of their divine institutes and to decide accordingly.[44]

The emerging colonial order, with its changes in production relations and structural arrangements, did not immediately produce a stable economic and political system. Towards the end of the eighteenth century, as the Company was consolidating its control, there were various upheavals in the economic system of the northern Coromandel region. In 1798, the Mahanauttee group disrupted the markets at Nelapalli and Yanam in Godavari district and sent orders to different villages asking the people not to pay revenue to the Company.[45] These Mahanauttees were obviously very powerful because their orders were obeyed, thus adversely affecting the Company's textile investment in the region.[46] Company officials suspected that some "designing persons" were behind these disturbances. The zamindar of Cotah and Ramachandrapuram, in fact, suggested that the merchants, dubashis, and other rich men of the region were supplying the Mahanauttees with money.[47]

Even though traditional antagonisms surfaced from time to time, there were instances of co-operation among these caste groups in opposition to other elements in the society. Indeed, the same weavers of the Godavari and Visakhapatnam districts expressed their solidarity in organising a revolt in 1796 against the tightening of control over the

44 G. Balmaid, Collector, Rajahmundry, to BOR, 21 December 1802, *GDR* 936 A, 73–86, especially 79.

45 John Snow, Commercial Resident, Ingeram to Benjamin Branfil, Collector, Rajahmundry, 9 May 1798, *GDR* 917, 102–03.

46 Benjamin Branfil to BOR, 13 May 1798, *GDR* 917, 105–07; John B. Travers, Deputy Secretary, BOR, to Benjamin Branfil, 24 May 1798, *GDR* 919, 138–40.

47 Branfil to BOR. The Company tried to put down these disturbances sternly by using force. See, for details, Benjamin Branfil to Heater Lean, Commanding Officer, Samulcotah, 29 May 1798, *GDR* 917, 141–42; Benjamin Branfil to Alexander Denton, Superintendent of the Cocanada farm, 29 May 1798, *GDR* 917, 142; Benjamin Branfil to John Snow, 29 May 1798, *GDR* 917, 144.

production processes in their economy. Company officials had to negotiate with the heads of the four major castes of the weaving community in order to find some solution to their problems. Weavers also got together in other instances against the Company or the zamindar or the *copdar* (contractor)—as part of the broader contradictions within the society.

Producers from the Periphery: The Pariah Weaver

The Report of the Fact-Finding Committee (Handloom and Mills), set up by the Ministry of Commerce, Government of India, in 1942, held that the entrance of low-class, non-weaving castes into the handloom industry was a nineteenth-century phenomenon. It has also been suggested that "as demand for export quality textiles increased, caste weavers ceased to produce coarser domestic fabrics for export, opening opportunities at the bottom of the weaving industry for non-weaver castes."[48]

In the later half of the eighteenth century, the weavers of Guntur district were categorised into three groups: weavers weaving for the company, weavers weaving for the natives, and Pariah weavers weaving for the natives.[49] Pariah weavers, called Mala Muggalavallu (Malas) in the district records, were one of the major weaving communities in the village economy of Guntur district. They contributed considerable revenue towards moturpha taxes in villages such as Amrithaluru and Modukuru.[50] It was specially mentioned that they were not employed by the Company.

This view, that weavers from the peripheral castes appeared only in the nineteenth century, is open to challenge. The participation of Pariahs in the weaving industry of south India was a very long-standing one. An eleventh-century inscription of the Tamil Chola king Raja Raja, for instance, refers to the Paraiyan caste and its two sub-divisions—*nesavu*

48 Brennig, "Textile Producers and Production", 347; G. N. Rao, "Stagnation and Decay of the Agricultural Economy of Coastal Andhra", in *Arthavijnana* 20, no. 3, 1978, 232–33.

49 Ram to BOR.

50 For details see John Read, Collector, Masulipatnam, to William Patrie, BOR, 10 November 1800, *MDR* 2998, 5–101 and Read to Patrie, 11 November 1800, *MDR* 2998, 98–142.

or weavers, and *ulavu* or ploughmen.[51] Evidence related to the presence of Pariah weavers in Andhra is available in the inscriptional and literary sources pertaining to the sixteenth century. In 1522, in the village of Addankiseema in Dharmavaram taluk, there were four important communitios associated with the weaving industry, namely, Sales, Jandras, Malas, and those who specialised in weaving borders or making designs on cloth. An exclusive *pettah* (division of the town) called Akala Sabhanapuram was constructed, where separate spaces were allotted to these on the basis of land grants.[52]

The presence of Mala weavers in the social structure of the weaving world can perhaps be attributed to the socio-economic changes brought about by the new religious movements of the twelfth and the thirteenth centuries—the Bhakti movements like Virasaivism and SriVaishnavism. The Virasaiva movement originated in the twelfth century at Kalyani in the Kanarese country under the leadership of Basava as a protest against Brahminism. The social base of this egalitarian movement comprised trading groups, shoemakers, tanners, tailors, weavers, and even a few untouchables. In course of time, it compromised with the brahmanical creed and perfected the caste system.[53] Although the spread of Virasaivism was limited in Andhra, it left a deep impression on society.

Within SriVaishnavism, the Tengalai (southern sub-sect) movement was responsble for bringing into its fold many of the low Sudra castes. Though SriVaishnavism developed concurrently with Virasaivism in Andhra, it was limited to the Palanadu area of Guntur district and was given state patronage under dynasties such as the Velama Cholas of Vengi and Haihayar of Palanadu. Brahmanaidu of Palanadu, a SriVaishnavite of the Velama caste, introduced certain social reforms such as the practice of inter-dining among people belonging to different castes (*chapakudu* or commensalism).[54]

Most of the Devangas came under the influence of Saivism or Virasaivism, while Tengalai Vaishnavism had a large following among

51 Thurston 5, 77–139, In the entry under Paraiyan, 82–3, mention is made to the Census Report of 1901 in which this inscription of the Chola king dated about the eleventh century is referred to.

52 "South Indian Inscriptions", X 753, A.D. 1522. In Dutt, *Inscriptional Glossary* 2.

53 For a discussion on the origins of Virasaivism and SriVaishnavism and their influence on the socio-economic world of weavers in south India, see Ramaswamy 59; 60–63; 107.

54 For a brief discussion on reform trends that arose in Andhra along with the rise of the Bhakti movements, see V. Ramakrishna, *Social Reform Movement in Andhra (1848-1919)* (Delhi: Vikas Publishing House, 1983), 39–42.

the Padma Sale community. Devanga and Padma Sale groups attempted to give a tangible form to their mythological origins in popular language. About 1532, the Devangas requested Bhadra Lingakavi to write their *kulapurana* (history of a caste or community). He accordingly composed the *Devanga Purana* in Telugu through the medium of native prosody (*desimatra*) in *dvipada* (couplets). Bhadra Lingakavi was also the author of another *dvipada kavya* (literary work), pertaining to the Devangas, called *Sananda Charitra*.[55] Not to be outdone, the Padma Sales asked Ellara Narasimha Kavi to translate their kulapurana, *Markandeya Purana,* into Telugu in the dvipada poetic form, as it was difficult for them to read this in Sanskrit.[56]

These religious and social forces gradually led to geographical and spatial distinctions in the region. While Saivism was most popular among the weavers of Godavari district, Vaishnavism had a large following in Visakhapatnam and Kistna districts. The Lingayat movement was almost entirely concentrated among weavers of the Kistna district.[57] The entry of non-traditional groups into the weaving world of Guntur and Masulipatnam, where, for instance, Malas and Madigas were considered essential workers in the textile industry, was due to Vaishnavism as well as state sanction. The absence or limited presence of these groups in the Visakhapatnam and Godavari districts could be related to the strict adherence of the weavers here to Saivite philosophy which was more rigid, less egalitarian, and less open than Vaishnavism.

In the fifteenth century, under the patronage of the Vijayanagara rulers, the emergent egalitarian ideology of SriVaishnavism spread over a large area and incorporated into its fold many new artisan groups.[58] In the seventeenth and eighteenth centuries, in the Palanadu and Rayalaseema region, individuals such as Vemana and Pothulur Veerabrahmam, with their personal philosophies, attacked the social institution of caste and uncivilised practices like untouchability and pollution.[59]

55 Arudra, *Araveetee Rajula Yugamu,* volume 9 of *Samgrah Andhra Sahityamu*, (Madras: M. Seshachalam and Co., 1966), 229.

56 Ibid., 230.

57 This inference has been made on the basis of the religious composition of castes in Madras Presidency in *Report on the Census of the Madras Presidency, 1871*, 207–10; 217–19; 240–41; and 242–43.

58 It appeared that a large-scale incorporation of Sudra professionals into the Vaishnavite cult took place during the time of the Vijayanagara ruler, Saluva Narasimha. See Ramaswamy, 113–14.

59 See, for details, Ramakrishna, *Social Reform*, 39–42.

It was not that religion alone had caused the entry of Malas into the weaving world. The economic dispensation that was arising was an important factor in their integration into the weaving society of the Kistna and Guntur districts. The creation of new demands by the arrival of the European companies led to the large-scale participation of low-caste weavers, a feature substantially illustrated from the evidence of eighteenth-century records. Pariahs or Malas were placed along with four major communities—Sales, Jandras, Komatis, and Gollavallu—within the tax-collection structure of the society. They paid an amount equal to that paid by the traditional weaving and Bania caste groups.[60] Besides the loom tax that all the weavers paid, additional taxes were levied on Pariah weavers because of their social position. One such was the *boota parashee*, referred to as *pallaputtada* in the southern districts. This tax was paid by the various low-caste groups of the village, including Pariah weavers.[61] The groups included in this tax had to pay a certain amount per house to the government.[62] Further, it was also the custom to fine people found guilty of working contrary to the custom of the caste.

The presence of Mala weavers in the weaving world of the region was not, therefore, only a nineteenth-century circumstance. The place accorded to them along with traditional weavers and other social groups in the taxation structures of the society and the maintenance of their group identity as a left-hand caste recognised in the levy of boota parashee clearly indicate that Malas were part of the weaving world much before the arrival of the European powers. Besides the English records, their presence was supported by the evidence available in the Mackenzie Collections of Cuddapah district. Mutasiddi Narayana Rao submitted a report in 1813 to Colonel Mackenzie titled *Gandikota Durgam Kaifiyat*, which contained a detailed description of the textiles produced in various villages, with their prices. Here, a mention is made of the coarser variety of cloth produced by Malas and Madigas along with Sales and Mangalivallu (barbers).[63]

60 Ram to BOR, 27 March 1796, *PBR* 151, 3345–46.

61 Ram to BOR, 13 January 1796, *PBR* 143, 469–74.

62 Collector, Guntur, to BOR, 25 November 1796, *gudr* 978 B, 482.

63 "Gandikota Durgam Kaifiyat", 30 April 1813, Mackenzie Collections in N. Venkataramanayya (ed.) *Cuddapah Silasasasanamulu* (Madras: Tamil Nadu Government Oriental Manuscripts, 1974), 139.

New Influences

The arrival of the European traders opened the way for Christian missionaries and their work in the northern Coromandel region. The London Missionary Society began its activities around the turn of the century when two of its branches were set up—at Visakhapatnam in 1805 and at Cuddapah in 1807. The activities of this society were essentially related to teaching and spreading the new doctrines in these districts. The influence of the novel ideologies was more dominant after 1813, when the entry of missionaries into India was eased under the Charter Act of 1813. A number of schools came up subsequently, the enrolment in these being opened to all castes. The response of the weaving community was illustrated by the fact that they also sent their children to these schools. By 1829, there were eleven Mission Schools in Visakhapatnam district. The children of Brahmins, artificers, weavers, shepherds, oil-makers, farmers, common labourers, Mohammedans, country-born Portuguese, merchants, and painters attended these schools. The caste-wise enrolment of students were Brahmins: 34, Mohammedans: 37, Weavers: 16, and General: 14.[64] Two schools were meant exclusively for girls—one in the fort and one at Allapoorem.

The attitude of the indigenous communities towards this new education was clearly demonstrated in the following letter of James Dawson:

> The inhabitants from this village are weavers and labourers in the fields, in general very poor, but industrious. They are not greatly prejudicial against Christianity but see no necessity of attending to a religion which their fore-fathers knew nothing of. They are disposed to converse on certain subjects, such as the works of gods and the providence of god in regard to the seasons, particularly the falling of rains at the times in the year when most required. They approve of schools for their sons (and most of the village received KS Instruction in the Mission School which was long been established there) but they could not easily be persuaded to send their daughters to be taught to read and write.[65]

64 James Dawson to Director, London Missionary Society (LMS), Visakhapatnam Station. Council for World Mission Archives South India: Telugu [hereafter *MASIT*], microfiche, Nehru Memorial Museum and Library, New Delhi. Box no.1, nos. 962, 963, 965, 967; Census Statement of Eleven Native Schools at Visakhapatnam, 9 December 1829, *MASIT* Box No.1, no.961, 4th Lane, 5th Slide; for a brief description of missionary activities in early nineteenth century Andhra, see Ramakrishna, 50–53; also see Guzzarlamudi Krupachary, *Telugu Sahityanika Kristavula Seva* (Guntur, 1988), 26–67.

65 Dawson to Director, LMS, 29 July 1828, *MASIT* Box.1, no.960, 5.

However, the poor economic conditions of the various communities constrained the educational activities of the London Missionary Society. The Census Statement of 1829 clearly illustrated this:

> Most of the scholars who have left the schools during the years was in consequence of the extreme poverty of their parents not being able to support them longer and were obliged to earn their daily substance but few have left in consequence of their parents objecting to our mode of instruction.[66]

To carry forward their proselytisation campaign along with the educational activities, a number of societies sprang up. By the 1840s, these were: The American Baptist Missionary Union in Nellore (1840); the Andhra Evangelical Lutheran Church with its branches at Guntur (1842), Rajahmundry (1842), and Eluru (1846); and the Church Missionary Society at Masulipatnam (1842) and Eluru (1854).

Though open to new ideas, the weavers remained largely outside the proselytising influence of these missionary societies. By 1871, as indicated in the Census report, the percentage of weavers converted to Christianity was quite low, ranging from 0.002 percent in Visakhapatnam district to 0.9 percent in Kistna district.[67] The powerful devotional tradition associated with Saivism might have opposed the entrenchment of Christianity in the Godavari district, where Devangas were dominant. Moreover, the higher percentage of conversions in Kistna district could be due to the presence here of the non-traditional weavers, mainly Pariahs. It has been seen that the lower castes responded better to Christianity because of the transformation of their social status.[68]

The contrasted impact of Christianity on the weavers of the northern Coromandel serves to underline the complexity of their social world. The varied social and cultural mechanisms in the region helped to maintain communal cohesion and social order, although, on occasion, as in the conflict over Veeramushtivallu, these did break down. The anomalous entry of Mala weavers into the textile economy indicated, too, that the seemingly impermeable, inflexible social structures were not so watertight after all. Tolerant religious views such as those of

66 Census Statement, *MASIT*.

67 *Census, Madras Presidency,* provides early details on the religious composition of various castes. For details on Visakhapatnam district, see 217–19; for Godavari district, 240–41; and for Kistna district, 242–43.

68 For a discussion on low-caste conversions to Christianity, see Duncan Forrester, *Caste and Christianity* (London: Curzon Press, 1980), especially 72–92.

Sri Vaishnavism helped the weaving community cope with the accelerated pace of changes that came with the linking of the region to new world markets. There was, of course, more than culture to sustain the weavers through the travails of change. There was the entire system of production, developing through centuries, which lay at the base of the textile economy.

FOUR

The Production of Textiles

One of the most crucial factors that determined the nature of the textile economy was the availability of cotton in its raw form as well as in its partially metamorphosed form of thread. The weavers of the northern Coromandel region depended on internal production as well as external sources for their cotton requirements during the period under discussion. By the second half of the eighteenth century, raw cotton supplies were contingent upon both agrarian and trading elements in the economy.

The two main cotton varieties produced in the region were white cotton or *tella pattee* and brown cotton or *yerra pattee*. White cotton was part of mixed-crop cultivation. In Godavari district, it was sown with *cundooloo* (red gram, *Cajanus cajan*) and *valadahpadi* (black paddy), and with cundooloo and *aurgooloo* (a sort of coarse grain, *Paspalum frumentaceum*). The seeds were broadcast on plots where water did not stagnate. Its cultivation provided collateral security to the farmer, as cotton could be produced in abundance during periods of scanty moisture whereas the other crops required more water.[1]

Brown or red cotton was a separate crop, never practised as mixed cultivation.[2] No other crop could be obtained from the land for the year nor could it produce good harvests of brown cotton for two consecutive years. The method of cultivation of brown cotton was as follows:

> The husbandry of this division allots to the black soil which crumbles and cracks in the dry and becomes clammy and adhesive in the wet season an annual alteration of crops and brown cotton is succeeded by jonaloo (cholum, Sorghum vulgare), sanagaloo (Cicer arietinum, Bengal grass), annoomoloo (Dolichos cultratus) and oil seeds. In contradiction to white cotton, instead of being thrown broadcast, it is sown in drills and the seed covered by drawing bushes across, and the preparation of the land before the seed is committed to it is extremely open while when

1 Thomas Snodgrass, Collector, 3rd Division, to Edward Saunders, BOR, 28 August 1795, *GDR* 4630, 3–6; see also, Benjamin Branfil, Collector, 3rd Division, to Edward Saunders, BOR, 17 January 1798, *GDR* 847, 157–63.

2 Branfil to Saunders.

> the plant has shot up it required weeding, raking and ploughing between the drills, and with sedulous and laborious attention.[3]

Brown cotton was more expensive to grow, as it required more animal draft power and other costly inputs. As white cotton was grown in tandem with another crop, there was greater certainty of reaping some harvest.[4]

The areas falling under the jurisdiction of the Peddapuram and Pitahpuram zamindaries were responsible for almost the entire cotton production of Godavari district. A very limited quantity of cotton was produced in Visakhapatnam district.[5] In Masulipatnam district, the cultivation of cotton was confined to a few areas such as Vassireddi Venkata Naidu's zamindari, Nundigamah, Wuyur, and Chintalapudi. Cotton was a mixed crop in the Vassireddi zamindari area, where it was usually sown with *jonna* (sorghum) and other grains. Generally it was sown in August and harvested in March. Land suitable for cotton cultivation was rented out at a rate ranging from 16 to 32 pagodas per *cutchel* (approximately 25 acres), from which a cultivator could obtain 8 to 16 *candis* of cotton (one candi was equal to 500 lbs or 20 *maunds*). Costs for this cultivation were 16 pagodas per cutchel, and the cultivator usually depended on advances. The price of cotton produced in these territories was 4 pagodas per candi.[6]

The areas of Devaracotah, Wuyur, Madoor, Bezoara, and Nunasthalam were suited for the cultivation of cotton as they were situated on the banks of the Kistna river; cotton was part of a mixed crop cultivation in the first three parganas. The farmers usually preferred to cultivate cotton after the harvest of the principal crop, or when there was apprehension of adverse weather affecting the principal crop.[7] In

3 Ibid.

4 Snodgrass to Saunders.

5 Extract of a letter from the Commercial Resident at Visakhapatnam dated 8 March 1796, noted in the extract of a letter from the Government dated 16 April 1796, *GDR* 926, 243–51.

6 Extract of a letter from Rajah Vasireddy Venkatadri Naidu, Zamindar, in E. Russell, Collector, Masulipatnam, to Commercial Resident at Masulipatnam, 7 December 1812, *GDR* 832, pp.454–55. For a brief note on the cultivation of cotton in Masulipatnam district in the late eighteenth century, see John Wrangham, Collector, 4th Division, to Edward Saunders, BOR, 16 July 1795, *PBR* 133 A, 5557–63.

7 Letter of Madally Padmarauze, Darogah of the Town Duty of Nunasthalam, 7 October, 1812, *GDR* 832, 456.

Nunasthalam, almost the entire land was taken up for cotton as it could be expected to yield 1000 candis annually.[8]

The availability of limited quantities of cotton in Masulipatnam induced the ryots to import it from Guntur and Palanadu districts. The price of cotton in Palanadu in 1826 was only 16 rupees per candi (approximately 4 rupees were equal to one pagoda), while in Masulipatnam the selling price was 20 rupees. Cultivators turned the cotton into yarn for the weavers.[9]

Extensive cultivation of cotton was undertaken in the Palanadu area. Cotton was not sown in the monsoon months as the shoots perished from excess moisture. April and May, the hot season, were not suitable either. The seeds were sown at the end of August or the beginning of September, and the bolls would come to maturity in February. They were harvested by the end of March. In 1812, nearly 3642 candis of cotton were produced, 2582 candis of which were exported to the Nizam's dominions. The price of cotton varied from 12 to 15 Madras pagodas per candi. The rent from the cultivated land depended essentially on soil conditions—a cutchel of the best soil would pay an amount of 24 Madras pagodas annually to the state, that of the worst would fetch only 5 Madras pagodas.[9]

Cotton cultivated in both wet and dry lands was required to be watered during the height of the hot season and in the period when strong winds blew. The ground, however, had to be allowed to dry well between watering for the berries would rot if the ground was still moist.[10] A report pertaining to Guntur district disclosed that

> very heavy dews have a very unfavourable effect on the cotton crops. The young pods and leaves fall off, and the stems of the plants change from a green to a dark brown colour. The stems afterwards are attacked by an insect called *penoobunka* which proves exceedingly destructive..."[11]

The sowing of seeds was an expensive business. Generally, five seeds were sown in each hole, and when they put out shoots, only two or three were allowed to remain and the rest were plucked off. [12]

8 Vempaty Ramiah, Darogah of the Town Duty of Nundigamah and Wuyoor, 25 September 1812, in Russell to Commercial Resident, *GDR* 832, 455.

9 C. Robert, Collector, Masulipatnam, to BOR, 18 November 1826, *MDR* 4061, 241–44.

10 Sarada Raju, 96–101.

11 *Boards Miscellaneous Records (General)*, Vol 14, 10, Tamil Nadu State Archives.

12 *GDR* 926, 243–51.

Apart from the costs of cultivation and soil and weather conditions, there were other disincentives that prevented more extensive cultivation of cotton in the second half of the eighteenth century. In Visakhapatnam district, there was no motivation to extend cultivation because the cultivator was denied the profit from the increased tillage under the short-term lease structure.[13] Brown cotton cultivation in Godavari district was meagre, owing to the heavy taxation principles there.[14] Further, in the Peddapuram and Pitahpuram zamindaries, the land revenue estimate was based on the visabadi system which included the *malaverty* (increased tax) assessment by which the zamindars could levy an additional tax in cases of increase in production.[15]

Thus, with the quantity of cotton produced locally being inadequate, the shortfall had to be met by imports. For instance, in 1785, for 2481 looms employed in producing punjum cloth for the Company, the quantity of cotton required in Godavari district was 1897 *pooti*s, of which 1500 pootis of good-quality cotton was produced in the district. The difference of 317 pootis had, therefore, to be imported.[16] As this was only for the coarser 14 punjum cloth, the finer varieties would, *ipso facto*, have needed greater imports.

The non-availability, locally, of specific varieties of cotton for particular kinds of textiles was yet another reason for imports. For instance, the weavers of Guntur district preferred to use the imported kind as the native cotton was reddish in colour.[17]

Itinerant Traders: The Banjaras

During the latter half of the eighteenth century, the weavers of the region sourced their cotton requirements from the Mahratta country and from the Nagpur and Berar zones of central Deccan.[18] A crucial role in transportation of cotton was played by the ubiquitous itinerant traders, the Banjaras.[19] These traders constituted an important link in the

13 Snodgrass to Saunders.

14 Ibid.

15 Branfil to Saunders.

16 Collector to Edward Saunders, BOR, 8 March 1797, *gudr* 979 B, 663–68.

17 Ibid.

18 Extract of a letter from Court of Directors dated 23 May 1798, *VDR* 3712, 218–19.

19 For a detailed discussion on the nature of Banjara trading operations in Godavari district see Branfil to Saunders; for details on Banjara trade in Visakhapatnam district, see *VDR* 3712

commercial networks of the time, bartering various commodities from place to place. The Banjaras brought cotton to the northern Coromandel from places such as Nagpur and Sadah, and exchanged it for salt. In 1795, the Banjaras imported 505¼ of the 864¼ *putties* of cotton brought into Godavari district.[20]

The annual journeying of the Banjara traders between the Deccan and the coast was a significant contribution to the rhythm of the commercial and social life of the regions through which they passed. The growth of northern Coromandel exports, especially textiles, opened up the Banjara trade.[21] Though cotton constituted a major item, these itinerant traders also dealt in other articles such as wheat, tamarind, jaggery, and so on. During the second half of the eighteenth century, the nature of their trading activity was speculative and risky. They would usually ascertain market conditions before bringing their products into the region, as maximising profits from their caravan activities was their main interest.[22]

In 1796, the profit on cotton imported from Sadah was calculated as follows:

> | | |
> |---|---|
> | Price of cotton at Sadah | 9 pagodas per pooti |
> | Road customs | 7 ½ pagodas per pooti |
> | Expense on gunnies | ½ pagoda |
> | Total expense | 17 pagodas |
>
> If they hired bullocks at the rate of ½ pagoda per bullock, the Banjaras could get nothing out of it. Since most of them owned cattle, they could afford to sell their produce at 18 pagodas per pooti.[23]

The increasing demand for the region's textiles motivated the Banjaras to continually supply cotton from central Deccan to the weavers of the northern Coromandel. Though they did not make much on the raw cotton trade, the Banjaras undertook it because of the greater profits the finished textiles would fetch them at home.[24] They exchanged commodities only for salt, because it was abundantly available at low cost, with the local method of measuring salt—the heaped *kunchum*—

20 Branfil to Saunders.

21 J. Brennig, "Textile Producers", 333–56.

22 Branfil to Saunders.

23 Ibid.

24 F.A. Savage, Commercial Resident, Ingeram, to Board of Trade, Fort St. George, 19 June 1823, *CDC* 34, 870–71, provides the reasons for raw cotton imports into the region by the Banjaras.

being advantageous.[25] The Banjaras were involved in transporting cotton within the region too, procuring it from centres such as Daravadah, Nallakonda, Devarakonda (Palanadu), for selling at markets such as Visakhapatnam, Kottapalem, and Poduru.[26]

Elsewhere, by the end of the eighteenth century, the Banjaras were being pushed into peripheral economic roles.[27] Here, in the northern Coromandel, their continued commercial presence helped sustain textile production. For example, the manufacture of cloth in Visakhapatnam district, which produced about 600 bales between 1770 and 1790, was made possible only by the Banjara trader.[28] This contrasts markedly with the system that operated in Bengal. There, the procurement and distribution of cotton were in the hands of big merchants and agency houses.[29]

In the northern Coromandel too, there were some merchant groups, mainly belonging to the Balija community, who were involved primarily with trade in cotton produced within the region.[30] In 1795, for instance, cotton was imported into Godavari district by merchants residing at Yerrannagudem and Anantapalli. The profit made in the cotton trade by an ordinary merchant was much less than that made by the Banjaras. Cotton imports were usually exchanged for different varieties of coconuts—green coconuts, whole kernels sold in bulk, and empty shells with holes bored in them to clear out the kernels.[31] In places such as Guntur, some of these merchants also used salt as a medium of exchange, like the Banjaras, especially when trading with places such as Nizampatnam and Kottapalem, but sold the cotton for cash when marketing it in other areas.[32]

Gradually, however, the increase in demand for cotton in the wake of the growing investment in textile production overcame the inhibitions that may have been caused by the low profits and high risks. Many new

25 John Smith, Collector, Rajahmundry district, to BOR, 8 October 1823, *PBR* 966, 9082–85. For instance, at the turn of the eighteenth century, the price of salt was 10 rupees for a Coringa *garce* of 600 kunchum, of 3¼ *seers* volume per kunchum. This was equivalent to 25 rupees per sicca or Madras garce.

26 Collector, Guntur, to Saunders, *gudr* 979 B, 663–68.

27 See Bayly, *Rulers, Townsmen and Bazaars*, 211–12.

28 *VDR* 3712.

29 For a recent discussion on cotton trade in Bengal during this period, see Hameeda Hossain, *Company Weavers*, 24–27; also Bayly, 237.

30 Collector, Guntur, to Saunders.

31 Branfil to Saunders.

32 Collector, Guntur, to Saunders.

merchants were attracted to the cotton trade. The Collector of Godavari district reported that in the 1790s merchants started to invest their capital in the cotton trade. Earlier, they were trading in specie, copper and broad cloth, which they obtained from the Dutch and French territories at Jaggannathapuram and Yanam.[33] These merchants usually operated in specialised cotton markets, such as those at Dwarapudi, Jaggempeta, and Tuni.[34]

Since the cotton trade was crucial to its textile economy, the Company sought to ensure the maintenance of supplies of cotton and thread to the weavers. A major problem encountered initially was the disruption in cotton supplies brought about, ironically enough, by the Company's own administrative and political policies.[35] Its attempts to subdue and control the various rural magnates such as zamindars and hill chiefs, and the wars of succession among some zamindar families, created a situation of unrest which made it difficult for the Banjaras to operate, because they were forced to pay custom duties twice over.[36]

The Company took two major steps to facilitate the Banjara trade, without which the textile economy of the northern Coromandel would have virtually ground to a halt in the 1790s. One was to abolish all inland duties on the cotton that was imported from the Mahratta and other territories. Zamindars and hill chieftains were also asked to repeal all vexatious and oppressive duties levied upon the Banjaras.[37] The second was to send special contracts to the principal Banjaras in the production zones, especially in the cotton-rich Nagpur territory.[38]

The problem of cotton supply to the region was compounded by the development of trade with China. The Company procured cotton for export to China from Bombay, Bengal, and Madras.[39] The items from

33 Branfil to Saunders.

34 F. W. Robertson, Collector, Rajahmundry, to BOR, 13 September 1819, *GDR* 881, 238–40.

35 The Company's pacification programmes in the region caused discontent among the zamindars and other elites. The very fluid situation caused by the Company's rule also created tensions between the zamindars or among their successors, and thus led to the dislocation of the political economy of the region.

36 Branfil to Saunders.

37 BOR to M. N. Webb, Collector, 2nd Division of the Visakhapatnam district, 5 January 1799, *VDR* 3714/A, 56.

38 Letter addressed to Edward Saunders, BOR, 27 July 1796, *VDR* 3706, 338–40.

39 This business was developed by the British as a means of avoiding the emergence of an adverse balance of trade consequent to the increasing imports of Chinese tea into Britain; for a discussion on Bengal's trade with China, see Bayly, 237.

Madras were cotton and sandalwood. The Ceded Districts of the Andhra region and the Tinnevally district were the principal areas in the Madras Presidency supplying cotton to China in the early nineteenth century. The best sort of sandalwood was procured from Mysore.[40]

Although, initially, the Madras supplies of cotton came only from the Ceded Districts and Tinnevally, the Ingeram area was also seen as a source by 1814. The Company intended to procure 500 candis of cotton, or more than 15 per cent of the prospective total supply from Madras.[41] Nevertheless, only 298 candis could actually be procured from the entire northern Coromandel region, and that too only from the Ingeram and Maddepollam areas.[42] Despite cotton being produced in considerable quantities in the Palanadu region of Guntur district, nothing could be exported from here because of internal requirements.[43] By 1819, however, no cotton at all was available for export.[44] Of the two explanations for this, one was the slight but significant increase in the Company's investment in textile production.[45] The other, perhaps more important reason, was a shortfall in the cotton imports into the region.[46] This deficit, among other outcomes, was caused by the acquisition of monopoly over salt by the Company in 1809.[47]

By establishing control over salt, the Company, in fact, further attenuated the power of the landed elites. The effect of such a policy was felt drastically by the itinerant traders whose profits were reduced heavily. Consequently, cotton supply to the weavers declined, thus leading to a further rise in price. The situation was such that the Company on one occasion had to dispatch Tinnevally cotton to Ingeram, in order to relieve the acute shortage.[48]

40 General Report from Board of Trade up to 11 February 1815, *CDC* 1, 385.

41 For details, see statement of funds required for the provision of cotton, saltpetre, and sandalwood in 1814, in General Report from the Board of Trade to Hugh Elliot, Governor-in-Council, Fort St. George, February 1815, *CDC* 4, 427–29.

42 General Report of Board of Trade up to 15 February 1815 addressed to Hugh Elliot, Governor-in-Council, Fort St. George, 30 May 1814, *CDC* 2, 475–89.

43 Ibid.

44 Robertson to BOR, *GDR* 881, 238–40.

45 For data on Company's indent and the actual bales provided at the Visakhapatnam, Ingeram and Maddepollam factories between 1809 and 1829, see I. Gwatkin, Commercial Superintendent, to the Chief Secretary to Government, 3 December 1827, *CDC* 48, 953–58.

46 J. Daniel, Secretary, BOT, to the Chief Secretary to Government, 4 August 1823, *CDC* 34, 869–70.

47 Smith to BOR, *PBR* 966, 9082–85.

48 *CDC* 20, 1608.

According to an official report, the sole reason for the setback to the Company's investment was its monopoly over salt, for

> ....it would appear, that the trifling importation of Maharatta cotton into the Circars for the last several years, which deter the Lambadies and merchants from speculating in that articles as formerly. The Commercial Resident at the same time adverts to the deficiency in measurement as another cause of complaint on the part of these people.[49]

The Commercial Resident, Ingeram, had stated that 35 rupees per garce for salt was too high for those who had benefited by the earlier liberal rate of 10½ rupees per garce set by the zamindars.

Not just the rise in the price of salt, but even the mode of measurement under the new system was reason for complaint. The Company replaced the existing heaped kunchum by the *parah* measure in 1809. Under the former, the traders used to get for one garce twice what the parah measure yielded.[50]

Because of the establishment of monopoly over salt, cotton imports into the various districts declined drastically. For instance, between 1819 and 1823, Godavari district received hardly 50 candis of cotton.[51]

Between 1817 and 1821, Ganjam district received 2797 candis of cotton through the Banjaras, who took salt in exchange. In the same period, they traded 4163 candis of cotton for salt and other commodities such as cloth, tobacco, and fish in the Visakhapatnam district. The average selling price here at that time for cotton not separated from the seed was 20 rupees per candi, while the cleaned, deseeded cotton was priced at 75 rupees per candi.[52]

In the eighteenth century, the Company had tried to shore up traditional networks of production and trade of cotton by supporting the activities of the Banjara traders. By the beginning of the nineteenth century, however, it was looking for ways of more directly controlling the production and distribution of cotton. Consequently, the role of the Banjaras in the textile economy became more or less peripheral.

49 Daniel to Chief Secretary, *CDC* 34, 869–70.

50 For a description of the mode of measurement and price of salt during this period, see Savage to BOT, *CDC* 34, 870–71; also see Smith to BOR.

51 Smith to BOR.

52 John Smith, Collector, Visakhapatnam, to BOR, 6 June 1823, *PBR* 951, 4831–32.

Cotton for Export

The Company, in order to protect its investment, attempted to ensure continued supply of cotton to the weaver through political means. In 1823, it was suggested that it would be expedient

> ....to offer large price for cotton or engage to exchange the commodity for a given quantity of salt, commensurate to the intended rise in price. [it was] suggested that if these methods appeared to be possible rather than entering into a contract for an annual supply of Maharatta cotton with a merchant at Chanda, the best method a proclamation of the intentions of government through the Maharatta states, by means of residents of Hyderabad and Nagapore.[*sic*] [53]

With the ceding of Palanadu to the Company in 1801, the jurisdictional embarrassments that might have earlier restricted the free movement of cotton in the region were completely erased. Since this area was a principal cotton-supply zone, even the requirement of the weavers of Visakhapatnam and Godavari districts came to be met by Palanadu during the first half of the nineteenth century.[54] Where the Company did succeed, although indirectly, in facilitating the growth of cotton in the region was in the adoption of revenue policies. For example, when in 1802, the Company adopted the Permanent Settlement, it abolished prior practices such as the malaverty assessment that taxed increased production.[55] Thus, there was incentive to expand cultivation. Besides, there was some inducement for taking up cotton cultivation in districts like Godavari, where the rate of assessment was not dependent on the nature of the crop. The land tax was the same whether the fields were cultivated with cotton or grain. It was left entirely to the cultivator to sow whatever he pleased.[56]

53 Smith to BOR.

54 I. C. Wish, Collector, Guntur district, to BOR, 6 December 1823, *PBR* 970, 10152–53; I. Goldingham, Collector, Guntur district to BOR, 14 December 1841, *gudr* 5399, 204–22.

55 The sole purpose of preventing enhancement of rents and assessment in the Permanent Settlement of 1802 centred round the fundamental principle that the rate of rent and tenure should be fixed in perpetuity. See Rao Sahib P. K. Gunasundara Mudaliyar, *A Note on the Permanent Settlement in Madras* (Madras: Government Press, 1940).

56 Robertson to BOR.

Regular export of cotton from India started in 1793, but the quantity remained small until the beginning of the nineteenth century. British industrial capitalists pressed the East India Company to discourage the export of cotton to China and to divert it to England. British merchants, however, preferred to export cotton to China as it was more profitable.[57] Finally, the millowners prevailed, as they were powerful enough to determine government policy. After 1813, private British shippers were free to load Indian cotton from Bombay under the overall supervision of the Company.[58]

Efforts to increase exports of cotton to Britain included the encouragement of cotton cultivation. From the beginning of the nineteenth century, Collectors of the various districts of the northern Coromandel were continually requested to try the new varieties of cotton—Bourbon, Tinnevally, and American.[59] However, soil conditions coupled with revenue assessment patterns foiled every attempt of the Company to begin cultivation of the new varieties. As early as 1810, attempts were made in Masulipatnam district to persuade cultivators in the cotton-growing areas of the Vassireddi zamindari, Nundigamah, Wuyur, and Chintalapudi to try new varieties such as Bourbon and Tinnevally, but to no avail.[60] Even in the Palanadu district, where cotton was grown in three-quarters of the land, the Bourbon variety was not taken up.[61] By 1826, the Masulipatnam cultivator was still reluctant to

57 For a brief discussion on this, see Amalendu Guha, "Raw Cotton Trade of Western India: Output, Transport and Marketing, 1750–1850". In *IESHR* 9, no. 1, 1972, 1–42.

58 For details on Bombay's trade with China during this period, see N. Benjamin "Bombay's 'Country Trade' with China, 1765–1865". In *IESHR* 1, no.2, 1974, 295–303.

59 Russell to Commercial Resident, *GDR* 832, 452–57; C. Roberts, Collector, Masulipatnam to BOR, 18 November 1826, *MDR* 4061, 241–44; T. A. Oakes, Collector, Guntur district, to BOR, 9 May 1813, *gudr* 982, 184–86. For replies from Collectors on the possibility of introduction and extension of American cotton in Guntur district, see P. Grant, Collector, Guntur, to Secretary to Government, Revenue Department, Madras, 10 November 1835, *gudr* 3991, 37–42; H. Stokes, Collector, Guntur, to BOR, 19 February 1846, *gudr* 5405, 303–05; "Memorandum on the subject of encouraging the culture of cotton in the Guntur Circar" dated 7 July 1795, *MDR* 3047 B, 555–58.

60 Russell to Commercial Resident.

61 T. A. Oakes to BOR, *gudr* 982, 184–86.

consider the promotion of the Bourbon and Tinnevally types. In fact, it may be said that the farmers were generally indifferent towards cotton cultivation itself. Apart from the fact that the soil of Masulipatnam district was only suitable to grow coarse staple cotton—used for the manufacture of a rougher variety of cloth—it was less profitable than other grains as a larger outlay of labour and capital was required.[62]

In the 1830s, the Court of Directors sent samples of American cotton seeds to try and extend this variety in the Guntur district. Though the attempt failed owing to an unfavourable season, the Collector continued to be hopeful, because of the benefits of American cotton. The fibre was superior in strength and fineness and whiteness, and the proportion of wool to seed was greater. The cultivator could perhaps be motivated to try this variety provided the rent for land was sufficiently reduced.[63] The response of Guntur district was negative even by 1847. There were no exports from Guntur district to Europe or other markets.[64] In 1848, H. Stokes, Collector of Guntur, disclosed that the cotton of his district was regarded as being of inferior quality to that of Tanjore, Tinnevally, Cuddapah, Bellary, and Coiambatore and, therefore, unsuited for export to the European market.[65]

Dyeing Materials: Indigo and Chay Root

Cotton is the most crucial raw material in any textile economy. Nonetheless, there are other raw materials, such as dyes, which are almost as critical. The most commonly used dyes in the region under study were those produced from indigo and chay root and, to a lesser extent, from cochineal.

Indigo was mostly grown in those villages which were under the jurisdiction of the Pitahpuram zamindar. Almost the whole quantity needed in the northern Coromandel was from these local sources, although the Hyderabad area also supplied a little. The crop was usually raised in the months of August and December. The seeding had to be preceded by three ploughings each time, and, provided the rains came on time, the crop could be harvested.[66]

62 Roberts to BOR, *MDR* 4061, 241–44.

63 Grant to Secretary, Revenue Department, *gudr* 3991, 37–42.

64 Stokes to BOR, *gudr* 5405, 59–81.

65 *CDC* 17, 289–90.

66 Samuel Stratham, Warehouse Keeper, Masulipatnam, to Chief and Council, Masulipatnam, 3 August 1790, *MDR* 2840, 90.

The average price of indigo produced in this district was about 10 Madras pagodas per maund. The much superior Hyderabad variety generally sold for twice as much, but was, nevertheless, in great demand.[67]

Chay root was mainly grown in a stretch of land from Peddaganjam to Nizampatnam, covering nearly 30 miles of the area of Guntur. The availability of this dyeing material in the vicinity of Masulipatnam was one of the causes for the chay goods manufacturing centres being located at Perala, Vetapalam, Mangalagiri, Rajahpeta, and Battiprole.[68]

There were three main varieties of chay root, locally named *neeratypalloo*, *enakapalloo*, and *yetampalloo*, the first two varieties being the most widely used.[69] Neeratypalloo, otherwise called jungle chay root, grew naturally in the jungles located in the sandy soils of the coastal region, nurtured by seasonal rains. It was considered the best for producing the dye. This root took about two to three years to mature, and its quality could be affected by rain at the time of gathering.[70] The enakapalloo variety, known as the *potti* or short chay root, was also produced in the sandy soils of the coast, particularly in the region around Masulipatnam and Nellore. Unlike the jungle variety, this required very painstaking cultivation. It was sown between August and October, watered carefully by large pots, and fertilised with goat and cow dung. The produce was dug up from April to June.[71]

The third variety of chay root—yetampalloo—was chiefly cultivated in Guntur district. It was sown in February, watered by *picotah* (traditional irrigation system), and the produce was extricated in August.[72]

Both the jungle chay root and potti chay root were dug out entire, that is, root and branch, tied up in small bunches and kept in the sun. After drying, they were made up into larger bundles of 1¾ maund each. Only the roots were used to prepare the dye, the upper parts being discarded.[73]

The total quantity of chay root produced in Guntur district was about 400 candis each of the jungle and potti types per year. The price of jungle

67 Ibid. See also T. Prendergast, Collector, Rajahmundry, to D. White, BOR, 11 December 1847, *GDR* 6771, 378–82, for a brief report on indigo cultivation in Godavari district in the 1840s.

68 Bruce to Chief Secretary, *gudr* 5392, 51–55.

69 Ibid.

70 Read to BOR; Bruce to Chief Secretary.

71 Bruce to Chief Secretary.

72 Read to BOR.

73 Ibid.

chay root was 1¾ to 2 rupees per maund, while potti chay root would fetch around half the amount depending on its quality.[74]

The production of jungle chay root was organised either by the farming-out method or the *aumany* system (land and weaving villages usually placed under the direct management of the Collector). Under the latter, the state paid a hire of 1 rupee per maund and sold the produce. The other method entailed the renters' digging out the root at their expense and keeping the proceeds of the sales. In the case of potti chay root, it would appear that the cultivators would pay the state *kist* (fixed payment) on it, and sell the article themselves.[75]

Chay root was, therefore, a crucial element in the production of textiles. Indeed, it was so important that it acquired an extraordinary economic value, even being frequently stolen.[76]

Apart from local producers, the Nizam's territory was a major source of chay root to the weavers of the northern Coromandel. A large quantity was being imported into Masulipatnam district from this area by the 1830s, which continued even into the second half of the nineteenth century.[77]

Turning Cotton into Thread

Cotton, the primary raw material, had to be turned into thread before the weaver could spin it into cloth. The spinning of thread was an established process in textile manufacture. It was essentially a subsidiary occupation of many social groups, and one in which women participated in great numbers.

The weavers themselves could turn the cotton into thread and possessed the necessary tools such as the spinning wheel (called *ratanamu* in local terminology).[78] In fact, evidence is available to suggest that spinning was undertaken by all the members of the weavers' families, especially the women. However, since certain kinds of thread required

74 Bruce to Chief Secretary.

75 Ibid.

76 Read to BOR. For details on the chay root theft, see letter from the renter of jungle chay root to Collector, Masulipatnam, 20 January 1795, *MDR* 2900, 6–7; From the Subedar of Bapatlah on the same subject, *MDR* 2900, 7; Collector's orders to the renter of Ongole district, 22 February 1795, *MDR* 2900, 7–9; in *Guide to the Records of Masulipatnam District 1682–1833*, vol. 3, 1, 17 and 97.

77 Benjamin Branfil, Collector, 3rd Division to John B. Travers, BOR, 18 February 1801, *GDR* 937, 28–43.

78 *GDR* 926, 243–51.

highly specialised skills, it is quite likely that such thread was produced by specific groups.

In Guntur district, agriculturists who cultivated cotton used to spin thread, which they then supplied to the weavers to be woven into cloth for themselves. Interestingly, they paid a coolie or wage to the weaver for this service. Moreover, if any thread remained (in excess of the spinner's requirements for cloth), it was sold to the weavers and thread merchants.[79] Ordinarily, one may expect such transactions in a primitive rural economy to rest upon a simple and mutual exchange of commodities and services. Here, however, we have a spinner paying a "wage" to the weaver for turning thread into cloth, and "selling" the remainder of the thread.[80] While it is difficult to establish the origin of this practice, it was, at any rate, prevalent at the turn of the eighteenth century, reflecting the high degree of commercialisation in the rural economy of the region.

In another interesting transaction, the families of a group of ryots and Woodiyar Reddys marketed the thread they produced in their homes for the price of cotton and a coolie payment for their services.[81]

Pariah communities were highly skilled in turning raw cotton into extremely fine thread. The thread spun by Malas and Chucklers (another low-caste group belonging to the Madiga community) was of much better quality than the coarse variety produced by the cultivators, and was, therefore, in great demand by the merchants and weavers.[82]

The payment for both the coarse and the fine types of thread was the same—5 *fanams*. This was discriminatory as the thread turned out by the Pariahs should have received a higher price for its superior quality. This was an example of the economic exploitation of the lower castes.

In Godavari district, it was the coarse thread that was more in demand because it was used for the Company's 14-punjum cloth and textiles catering to the needs of the lower and middle classes of society. The customary allowance for turning one maund of cotton into thread was 1 pagoda and 6 fanams. Out of this, the cotton beater got 12 fanams, while the spinner's allowance was 42 fanams. Spinning finer thread was better paid, but as it took more time, the difference in remuneration did not have much impact on the spinners' earnings. For instance, turning one maund of cotton into coarse thread usually took two months, while

79 Collector, Guntur, to BOR.

80 Ibid.

81 Ibid.

82 Ibid.

spinning the finer variety could take nearly 1½ to 2 years. Moreover, the loss of cotton while preparing coarse thread was only one-sixteenth of a maund while twice that was wasted for the finer sort.[83]

In Visakhapatnam district, the spinning was done by people of various castes—except Brahmins—and chiefly by women and children and disabled people who could not find other employment. The cotton was cleaned, de-seeded, beaten out, and by means of a simple wheel and spindle device, spun into thread. The remuneration to a single person for this was half a fanam a day. The thread was then brought into the market, and sold from 3 to 5 seers to the rupee; it has also been known to fetch 7 or 8 seers to the rupee.[84]

It was not only the supply of cotton that determined the availability and price of thread, but agricultural operations mattered too. The price of thread was very high during cultivation and harvest because most of the rural population was employed in the farming sector.[85] As the popular Telugu proverb put it: "The spinning wheel is come, out of the way with your cart."[86]

Natural calamities disastrously affected the availability of thread. Continued drought about 1792 created acute scarcity in the Ingeram and Maddepollam factories because of high mortality among the spinners, especially Pariahs. Only 7 *viss* of thread (as against the earlier 11) and 5 kunchums of paddy (previously 20) could be got for a pagoda. And even at that rate, paddy was not easily available in some villages.[87]

The quantity of investment at Visakhapatnam primarily depended on the price of cotton and thread rather than on the competence of the Commercial Residents. For instance, a piece-good of 14 punjums used 25 to 26 seers of thread, and the payment to the weaver was 7½ rupees. In 1796, when thread was bought at 3¼ seers per rupee, the weaver had to buy nearly 8 rupees worth of thread. As his pay was 7½ rupees, he had to save at least 1½ rupees to make ends meet. The consequence was that the weaver reduced the quantity of thread to 20 or 21 seers, and the quality of the fabric was compromised.[88]

83 Branfil to Saunders.

84 *GDR* 926, 243–51.

85 Ibid.

86 Carr, *Andhra Lokakti Chandrika*, No.1862; *GDR* 926, 243–51.

87 John Rowley, Resident, Maddepollam, to E. William Fallofield, Board of Trade, 18 December 1792, *GDR* 830, 218.

88 BOR to Webb.

There was also a decline in the Company's investment owing to the scarcity and dearness of thread following the famine of 1792 that overwhelmed the entire Godavari district. The Company sought to ensure the maintenance of supplies to the weavers by protecting the thread trade through administrative policies.[89] In the case of chay goods, the system of procurement through middlemen was reinforced. Guntur district, known for its chay root and thread, was under the control of the Nizam till 1788. Any attempt by the Company to deal directly in ensuring proper supply of thread, chay root, etc., would have led to political embarrassment. It had, therefore, to continue the practice of using middlemen.[90]

In almost all the districts of the northern Coromandel, the weavers could purchase thread directly either from retail shops or from thread markets operating in specific places. In Godavari district, Company weavers bought thread from the markets at Relangi, Kunalah, Kanur Agraharam, Nidadavole, Jallepudi, Nedamarru, Akeeved, and Pentapad. With rising demand and the consequent rise in prices, it would appear that those involved in marketing the thread became more difficult to work with. Thus, in 1796, we find weavers protesting that the Balijas (perhaps the Dudi Balijas, who specialised in cotton) were monopolising the sale of thread.[91]

There was a variety of specialised shops, both retail and wholesale, trading in all the articles needed in the textile economy. The moturpha revenue collections of the districts clearly specify the structure of such shops in each district of the northern Coromandel. In Guntur district, most of them were in the hands of Banias or Komatis, the traditional mercantile community, who seemed to have possessed several shops of different descriptions.[92] There were 45 shops for blue and red thread, 204 cotton shops, 838 cotton cleaners, 18 dyers, 31 dyers of blue thread and 1 *sunkoomdiara* (one who smoothed or glazed cloth).[93] Masulipatnam could lay claim to 151 shops selling cotton, 49 cloth

89 Letter to Saunders, *VDR* 3706, 338–40.

90 BOR to Webb.

91 The Chief's Minute on the Question of Balances Due by the Company's Merchants, nd. [1787], *MDR* 2900 A, 137–42.

92 Richard Dillon, Commercial Resident, Maddepollam, to Branfil, Collector, 3rd Division, Masulipatnam, 8 April 1796, *GDR* 926, 699.

93 Stokes to BOR, 1845, *PBR* 1975, 9241.

shops, 74 sellers of red thread, 87 Rangiraju dyers, an equal number working on chintz and painted cloth, and 15 cotton spinners.[94]

Weaving Tools

The weavers of the northern Coromandel followed different techniques in their production processes, from simple weaving to the creation of complex patterns on the looms, and also printing, painting, and dyeing of fabric. Very little evidence on their weaving technology is available in the official records of this period. Telugu literary works, however, provide a great deal of information on the process of turning cotton into thread and thread into cloth and the instruments used in these processes.

Before turning cotton into thread, however, there was an extensive sequence that brought the cotton to the spinner: selection of cotton, combing, ginning, cleaning, carding, and silvering. For separating the seed from cotton or ginning, an instrument called *ratnam* or handmill was used. In 1835, the Guntur Collector described this as a device "which contains two wooden contrarily revolving rollers which are set in motion. These rollers draw the cotton inwards and as they revolve very closely towards each other the seed which is too large to be admitted with the cotton falls down forwards on the ground. The above is the only mode which obtains in this district of separating the seed from cotton."[95]

References to *pinjamanu* and *ḳamanadasta* in a contemporary dictionary clearly show that these two instruments were also used in cleaning the cotton. The pinjamanu, also called *dudiḳavillu*, was used to extract the seeds from the cotton, while the kamanadasta was a large bow for cleaning the cotton.[96] An instrument called *wallagu*, made from the upper jaw of a freshwater shark, was used to card or disentangle fibres from the cotton.[97]

94 R. T. Porter, Collector, Masulipatnam, to BOR, 28 November 1845, *PBR* 2001, 16808–09.

95 Grant to Secretary, Revenue Department, *gudr* 3991, 40.

96 C. P. Brown, *Dictionary Telugu–English: Explaining the Telugu Idioms and Phrases with the Pronounciation of Telugu Words* (Madras: Society for Promoting Christian Knowledge, 1903; reprint, New Delhi: Asian Educational Services, 1986), 755 and 747.

97 E. B. Havell, Superintendent, School of Arts, to the Director of Revenue Settlement and Agriculture, 28 May 1886. In. Havell, E. B. "The Industries of Madras", *Journal of Indian Art and Industry* 3, no. 27, 1889, 25–26.

The *Suka Saptati*, a late seventeenth-century text by Palakaveri Kadiripati, describes not only the process of turning cotton into thread but also the various stages involved while preparing thread of different dimensions.[98] Most of the village women had taken up spinning as an important occupation and were closely associated with all the processes involved in the arrangement of warp threads. They used the *kaduru*, a spindle, for turning the cotton into fine thread. Often, the ratanamu, the spinning wheel, was employed for large-scale work, although the thread produced by it was much coarser.[99] In fact, the ratanamu was one among many devices which a weaver possessed during this period.[100] According to the *Suka Saptati*, the women prepared *enika*, a yarn of 3 or 4 intertwined threads and punjums of thirty skeins of thread.[101] The *pante* was a weaver's whirl (not a distaff), shaped like a pyramid, on which the thread was wound. Further, the women prepared the *padugu*, the woof or threads that ran the whole length of the warp, and the thread was woven as a piecework called *kulipadugulu*. *Kande* was a ball or roll of thread on a straw, which was put into the shuttle.[102]

Dyeing Techniques

The thread did not always go directly from the spinner to the weaver. As the region was famous for its colourful weaves, often the thread had to be dyed and only then given to the weaver. Turning the ordinary thread into a coloured one with use of dyes was a very complex and elaborate process, which was monopolised by distinct social groups such as the Rangirajus and Neeligarus.

Benjamin Heyne, Acting Company Botanist located at Samulcotah, outlined the various stages involved in the mode of dyeing red cotton yarn on the Coromandel coast in 1795.

98 Palakaveri Kadiripati, *Suka Saptati* (c 1750). B. Ramaraju (ed.) (Hyderabad: Andhra Pradesh Sahitya Academy, 1979) 2, 416–21.

99 Havell, *Reports on the Arts and Industries*, 25–26; Also see P. Sankaranarayana, *English–Telugu Dictionary* (Hyderabad: Asian Educational Services, 1978), entry under Spindle; and Ayyalaraju Narayana Kavi, *Hamsavimsati* (c 1770–1775), C. V. Subbanna Satavadhani (ed.) (Hyderabad: Andhra Pradesh Sahitya Academy, 1977).

100 Kaduru is a spindle and Ratanamu is a spinning wheel, Brown, *Dictionary*, 239, 1080.

101 Brown, 767, called *pundazam* in Telugu.

102 Ibid., 691.

First, the yarn was washed and arranged, as this was particularly necessary to prevent it from becoming entangled and to make all portions of it sufficiently penetrable and accessible to the colouring particles.

After being separated, the yarn was divided into little bundles of 30 to 40 threads. A cotton binding was drawn through each of these, in the middle and at the extreme; the yarn was then spread out to expose every single thread to the sun.

The yarn prepared thus was ready to receive the dye. This stage consisted of two parts. The first was the prolonged and repeated soaking of the yarn in cold water interspersed with pressing and beating. After the texture of the thread was loosened, a mordant was applied to the yarn. Now it would receive the actual substances that would turn it into a coloured thread.

Cassah (*Memecylon capitittalum*) leaves were generally used along with chay root to dye the yarn red. The cassah leaves would add a degree of astringency and brighten the yarn and also provide the red colour from the chay root a gloss. The yarn was generally put into a paste of pounded coarse cassah leaves, and by several manipulations, it would receive uniform contact with the liquor.

A day later, when the yarn was removed from the paste and spread out on a bamboo to be sunned, it would receive a fine orange colour. At this stage, fresh cassah leaves were mixed with an equal proportion of chay root, and a couple of hours later, the yarn was kept in this mixture. The repetition of the process on the third day changes the yarn into a reddish yellow and on the fourth day into a light red colour. In the evening of the fifth day, the yarn, after being washed and dried in the sun, was put into a dry paste made up of cassah leaves and *gingili* (sesame) oil, and, after a couple of hours, a handful of chay root was applied to this. Next morning, the process was repeated, but at night, the yarn was put into liquor made entirely with chay root. On the seventh day, the treatment was repeated, but the yarn was placed in a mixture of cassah leaves and chay root. In this way, the process of infusing, soaking, steeping, drying, etc., would take nearly a month to complete. The yarn was then boiled, to provide firmness to the colouring that it had received while being soaked. During boiling, proper care was taken to effect an equal degree of heat through the whole. When the yarn turned cold, it was washed and beaten as before and exposed to the sun. In this manner, white yarn was turned into a red yarn in the Northern Circars. A slight variation was observed when an inferior colour was to be obtained. After being washed repeatedly, the dyed yarn usually received a fine lustre. However, it was the fineness of the yarn and the quality and quantity of dyeing materials that determined the distinct colour. Benjamin Heyne further observed that, most of the time, the weaver himself would undertake the process of colouring the thread, sufficient to his needs.[103]

For obtaining blue-coloured yarn, the process that was followed in the region involved mixing of powdered *chunam* (limewash) and extract of chakondah (*Cassitoralin*). This was then placed in an earthen vessel partly buried in the ground, and the yarn was steeped in it for eight days. Then different shades of blue would appear. When the yarn was soaked in a light preparation of the same mixture thrice a day, the colour that was produced was a sky-blue.

If white yarn was soaked in a paste made of cadokye powder (*Termilia chebula*, *Chebalic myrobolam*) and green vitriol (*Anna bharies*) and again steeped in a bath of tank mud, then, depending on the intensity of dye, different shades of black would be obtained.[104]

The indigo for dyeing was supplied by farmers who controlled the use of indigo pots and vats. Such indigo farmers could be found all over the region. As the Company extended its domain, it came into conflict with these farmers who claimed that indigo was traditionally under their monopoly. Company weavers and contractors, however, insisted that they should have the right to dye the Company's cloth in their own indigo pots.[105] This conflict appears to have been resolved by arranging for the dyeing to take place within the factory.[106]

The vivid fabrics of the Coromandel needed other colours too. Green-dyed yarn could be obtained, for example, by soaking the bleached yarn in indigo and then steeping it in a solution of turmeric (country

103 For a detailed account on the process of dyeing red cotton yarn, see Heyne to Hobart, *PDS* 60, 1–69.

104 Maclean, 3: Glossary, entry under *Shayam tsaya*, 816; Buchanan 1, 209–12, for details on the silk-dyeing process practised by the Pattugars.

105 Representation of the Company's *careedar*s or weavers residing in Paddavah village to Vincentio Corbrett, Commercial Resident, Masulipatnam, 10 August 1799, *MDR* 3075, 284–85; Representation of careedars residing in Chennapuram village to Vincentio Corbrett, Commercial Resident, Masulipatnam, 19 August 1799, *MDR* 3075, 287–88; V. Corbrett, Commercial Resident to John Read, Collector, Masulipatnam, 20 August 1799, *MDR* 3075, 282–83; Representation of Vencanah Naik and Velloore Vencatareddy Naik, contractors, to Edward Cox, Commercial Resident, Masulipatnam, 31 July 1812, *MDR* 3079, 119–20.

106 Edward Cox, Commercial Resident, to Collector, Masulipatnam, 3 August 1812, *MDR* 3079, 177.

saffron) powder and water for 48 hours, and finally washing the yarn in a mixture of lime juice and water.

Another popular colour was orange. The following is an account of the process used: "Tie a quantity of *arnatto* seeds in a piece of cloth, soak it in water for 12 hours, squeeze the coloring matter in a basin of fresh water and coconut water, lime and alum (*Padicauram*) powder, steep the yarn in the mixture for four hours and then boil it for an hour, squeeze and let it dry."[107]

Some of the Coromandel textiles could be placed under the category of tie-dyed fabrics, which could be produced only by resist-dyeing techniques. Masulipatnam romals of different assortments, such as muslin doreas, blue handkerchiefs, blue spotted and checked varieties, were important textiles of this kind.[108] These romals were mostly dyed cloth patterned on the loom with pre-dyed yarn, catering to a specific design. For instance, in 1791, the weavers were asked to reduce the breadth of the borders of the romals, which they found difficult to take up immediately as they had to employ the dyed thread in a different manner.

> ... It is to be observed that by reducing the breadth of the borders, and increasing the middle part of the handkherchiefs, the thread employed in manufacturing them must be dyed in a different manner, as the intervals of white left in dyeing the thread must be shortened, and the tied red part of the thread lengthened. For this reason, no part of the quantity of thread already dyed for manufacturing Romals of the Company's usual assortments can be made use of in the present investment, but other thread must be dyed particularly for the purpose, which the contractors inform us will require a considerable time, and that the price will like wise be increased, by reasons of the greater quantity of red dye which the new patterns will require....[109]

A contemporary French report of 1783 stated that "Masulipatnam was famous for the handkerchiefs with red grounds and checks, made at Vetapalam and Sasserganti villages situated in the Province of Condavidu. The cotton threads were dyed/steeped (+ steeped and dyed) before being woven, in a slightly purplish red. Even when the cloth was heavily used, the colour kept all its brilliance. This was due to the excellence of the water of the Condavidu country and also to the use that was made throughout India of the root of the 'Chay', which gave a

107 Maclean 3: Glossary, 816.

108 The indent lists of chay goods to be produced at the Masulipatnam factory have detailed specifications of each variety for different markets. See *CDDE*.

109 Sadleir to Dent, *MDR* 2841, 58–66.

brilliancy to the colours that one could not imitate in Europe."[110]

From the Company's indents it would seem that sastracundis occupied a significant position in the textile trade in the vicinity of Masulipatnam. This was a type of cotton fabric, the warp and wefts of which were tie-dyed before weaving.[111]

How were these tie-dyed threads prepared? In the case of simple motifs like dots, the yarn threads were bunched up and tied or knotted irregularly at different points. For more complex designs, bands of thread were arranged in narrow patterns. Yet more complicated designs were produced by spreading the yarn out in a frame and making the design in individual clusters called sets (*ikat*). Traditional representations were mostly simple geometrical forms that involved two or three colours on each piece. After dyeing, the patterned yarn was transposed to the loom to be finally woven.[112]

During the period under study, such weaving was carried out in Perala, Vetapalem, Mangalagiri, Rajahpeta, Battiprole and other nearby places.

Looms

Ayyalaraju Narayana Kavi's *Hamsavimsati*, a Telugu literary work dating to the second or third quarter of the eighteenth century, provides a comprehensive description of a weaving loom. Among the parts of the loom listed were *kunchu* (*kande*): a brush, a whisk, a carding instrument or teazle for wood; *paggamu*: a tether cord or a rope used by the weaver to stretch the warp; pante: a weaver's whirl or a trundle; *palaka*: the small bars of the loom; *atchoo*: a weaver's reel, a comblike frame in a loom through which the warp threads were passed and by which the weft threads were pressed or battened together; *chidu*: a skein or bundle of seven punjums or a hundred threads; *chidudabba*: an instrument used by weavers for winding the thread; *vuduta*: a staff used as a prop by a

110 For recent writing on the resist-dyeing fabrics of Chirala, telia rumal, see Alfred Buhler, Ebenhard Fischer, Marie-Louise Nabhol, "Indian Tie-Dyed Fabrics" in *Historical Fabrics of India* IV (Ahmedabad: Calico Museum, 1980), Introduction and Chapter 2; Pupul Jayakar, "A Neglected Group of Indian Ikat fabrics", *Journal of the Indian Textile History*, 1955, 35–39; Irwin "Indian Textile Trade in the Seventeenth Century, South India" in Irwin and Schwartz, *Indo-European Textile History*, 28–43.

111 See Table 1.1 in Appendix.

112 "Glossary of Textile Terms" in Buhler et al, 149–50.

weaver for his warp; *nade*: a weaver's shuttle; *lakalu*: small sticks; *lakakattu*: the unfinished warp of a cloth with pieces of wood still stuck in it; *koti pullalu*: specific sticks fixed in a loom; *gutambu*: the roller of a loom; *maggapugunta*: a pit loom; *doney*: a wooden revolving bar round which the woven cloth is wound; and *made cumboo*: the warp beam.[113]

Other sources of information about the materials and utensils required while undertaking the process of turning yarn into thread mention *conjee*: the starch used by weavers in preparing thread for the looms; *kunde*: an earthen pot; *kota chuvakathi* (*sura kathi*): a small knife used for separating the woven cloth from the doney; *gante* (*garite*): a spoon; *golenu*: a kettle or boiler; *neelikadava*: a large water pot or earthen vessel used for manufacturing indigo; and *kulayi* (*kullaya*): a large vessel for manufacturing indigo.[114] From all this it can be gathered that the weavers generally used throw-shuttle pit looms for simple weaving as well as for patterned and pre-dyed fabric.

It appears that salempores and long cloths of different denominations were produced in the Godavari and Visakhapatnam districts only. It is not certain whether this was due to the loom technology available in these districts or to other factors. The usual dimension of salempores was 16 yards by 1, while punjum cloth was 37 yards in length. Further, according to the French report of 1783, "one judges the fineness of this cloth by the number of "Conjons" or the number of times that 120 threads of warp are contained in the width which is generally of 1 aune and an eight (the aune is equal to 1 metre 18 centimetres).... These guineas of yanaon were made of 'roui' cotton which has very long threads."[115] Punjum cloth of the Coromandel was esteemed in Europe even after 1830, as the new looms set up in England after the Industrial Revolution could not produce this length.

Masulipatnam Chintz

Kalamkari cloth, the printed and painted fabric of Masulipatnam district, was produced by hand painting or resist dyeing fabrics. It is not

113 Narayana Kavi, *Hamsavimsati*, Part 2, 122, stanza 11.

114 This information has been culled from the following sources: Brown; Maclean; Krishnamurti and Dakshinamurti; Subrahmanya Sastri, section on Sudravargamu, 719–48.

115 *Le Commerce Des Tissue De Coton A Pońdicherry Aux 17c Et 18C Siecles*, 1783. English translation provided by Dr. Deborah Swallow, Victoria and Albert Museum, London.

clear how old this technique is. Irfan Habib agrees with John Irwin that calico printing was not known in India before the seventeenth century.[116] Vijaya Ramaswamy, on the other hand, has cited literary and lexical evidence to argue that printing techniques had been mastered as early as at least the twelfth century.[117]

A broad distinction can be made between fine and common varieties of kalamkari fabrics. The first kind usually had the mordants and resists painted freehand on the material, using the equivalent of a *kalam* (pen) or brush. The more common kind was the printed cloth where the mordants were thickened with gum and applied by a print block.[118] The printed fabric suffered in quality because the gum mixed into the mordant reduced its efficiency as a chemical agent.[119]

Kalamkari fabrics manufactured in Masulipatnam in the early nineteenth century ranged from furnishing items like tent canopies, hangings, floor spreads, coverlets, and prayer mats, to those meant for common consumption among the local people.[120] The chintz fabrics exported from Masulipatnam by Armenian and Persian merchants included about 77 varieties of the painted and printed types, as is evident from the special attention drawn to the painted ones.

Elaborate techniques and designs signified and distinguished the Masulipatnam kalamkari of this period. For instance, *amberchas* had black, red, and green *butahs* (dots or small flowers) on a white background.

116 Irwin; Habib, "Indian Textile Industry".

117 Vijaya Ramaswamy, "Notes on Textile Technology in Medieval South India with Special Reference to the South", *IESHR* 17, no. 2, 1980, 237.

118 The term 'kalamkari' used for the painted and printed fabrics of Masulipatnam does not appear in contemporary records, and the only reference we have in an early nineteenth-century source is "Bandar Kaifiyat" in *Grama Kaifiyatlu: Kistna Zillah* of the Mackenzie Collections (Hyderabad: Andhra Pradesh State Archives Publications, 1990), 13–29. Sometimes the word *zulum haree* was used to describe these fabrics.

119 For a discussion on various aspects relating to kalamkari techniques, see *Homage to Kalamkari* (Bombay: Marg Publications, 1979). N. H. Sethna's *Living Traditions of India: Kalamkari Painted and Printed Fabrics from Andhra Pradesh* (New York: Mapin International, 1985), is a recent work on Masulipatnam kalamkari. A detailed description of the kalamkari-manufacturing process prevalent in the early medieval period is given in William Hadaway, *Cotton Painting and Printing in the Madras Presidency* (Madras: Government Press, 1870) and C. P. Baker, *Calico Painting and Printing in the East in the XVII and XVIII Centuries* (London: Edward Arnold, 1921).

120 John Irwin and Margaret Hall, *Indian Painted and Printed Fabrics* (Ahmedabad: Calico Museum, 1971), 127.

Khanabaddi, perhaps cummerbunds, were worked with designs similar to those of the amberchas, again on a fine white background. *Mutarphy*, called *maharatu*, was a kalamkari cloth of strap work in black, red, and green, with the middle portion having white butahs. Big and small butahs were printed on a white background for a *kasaloo* (sari) type of cloth. Red, black, white, and green spotted designs occupied the middle section of a *lachauk* (a type of kalamkari), while *palampores* were generally made with small and large white butahs.[121]

The most popular colours used in Masulipatnam kalamkari work were red, black, and green. Colours such as pink, blue, yellow, and brown were also in vogue. Ten main stages were involved in chintz work, irrespective of the size of the piece, employing colours such as black, red, pink, blue, green, and yellow.[122]

The dry season, the sandy flats of river beds, dotted here and there with pools of water and running streams, offered favourable conditions for the dyer and printer. The fabrics were bleached or dyed customarily in the months of April and May, and printed goods were dried after washing.[123]

By the first decade of the nineteenth century, Masulipatnam chintz had to face competition from the printed cottons of England. These were mostly used as furnishing fabrics in wealthy merchants' houses and there was a craze among the Portuguese for wearing a fine printed cotton jacket. For common use, however, Masulipatnam chintz was cheap and was consumed in large quantities in parts of India as in Bombay and in the Persian markets too.[124]

What is remarkable is that the transformation of cotton into thread, the dyeing of thread, and, finally, the production of cloth, was all accomplished through the use of the simplest technology.[125] This homespun craftsmanship does not seem to have changed much over the

121 "Bandar Kaifiyat" (p.26) has a description of kalamkari cloth being manufactured at Bandar Masulipatnam.

122 The Letters of Father Coeardoux in Irwin and Schwartz, *Indo-European Textile History*, 104–19, contain information of a technical nature on the methods adopted in India for painting or printing of cloth. Also see Baker, *Calico Painting and Printing*, Chapter 2, "Indian Methods of Printing".

123 Irwin and Hall, *Painted and Printed Fabrics*, Chapter 2, "Early Coromandel Group, Seventeenth Century."

124 Lotika Varadarajan, "Towards a Definition of Kalamkari", in *Homage to Kalamkari*, 19–22.

125 Habib, "Indian Textile Industry", 181–99; Ramaswamy, "Notes on Textile Technology", 227–43.

centuries. Even the increased requirement created by the European companies did not spur any major technological innovations, obviously because the abundance of skilled labour could meet the rise in demand.[126]

It would seem that the Company did not adapt technology to increase production or lower costs. In its calculations, technical change was perhaps not a prerequisite. What it found, on the contrary, to be very essential was the restructuring of the production process. And this it set out to do in a systematic manner.

126 T. Ray Chaudhuri, "The Mid Eighteenth Century Background", in *Cambridge Economic History of India* (*CEHI*) 2, 18.

FIVE

Structural Changes in the Weaving World

The attempts of the East India Company to consolidate its newly acquired power were manifested in changes to the structural arrangements of the weaving villages. The Company intended to directly control the weavers by decreasing the power of the elites of the weaving world. The colonial authority's principal preoccupation was with the intermediate parties who actually facilitated commercial transactions. In the second half of the eighteenth century and well into the next, the Company conducted its business through several layers of such go-between groups, whose operations were limited to specific geographical pockets within the northern Coromandel.

These included head weavers, copdars, local merchants and careedars (agents). The head weaver was the prominent and most prosperous of a group of weavers who were bound by caste and kinship ties. He was their spokesman in various commercial and social undertakings. In some areas, the head weavers were called senapatis (literally, head of an army). While the term thus affirmed his superior status, it also evoked memories of an earlier time when there was a direct connection between soldiering and weaving.[1] The copdar was essentially a broker, mediating between the local merchant and the head weaver. Even the literal meaning of the name makes clear that the copdar was only a contractor for supplying long cloth.[2] He usually, but not always, belonged to the same caste as the weaver. These groups were limited to areas under the jurisdiction of the Visakhapatnam, Ingeram, and Maddepollam factories.[3] The merchant was also a mediator, often operating through the head weaver and the copdar. The careedar was yet another person

1 Ramaswamy, *Textile and Weavers*, 14–16. It appears from Krishnamurti and Dakshinamurti, 381, that the senapatis were mainly located in east Godavari, mostly in Korukonda, Peddapuram, and Uppada, and in a few villages of Visakhapatnam district, and may have belonged to the Padma Sale community.

2 Brown, *Dictionary*, 294 and 296.

3 This conclusion is drawn from detailed evidence available in the records of the period.

acting as a mediator, and was found only in the region of the Masulipatam factory.[4]

Structural Changes

When the Company's political control was established over the region, its investment in the textile economy at Visakhapatnam, Ingeram, and Maddepollam were being conducted by the principal merchants. Their power extended to nearly 358 villages spread over 100 miles in the Godavari and Visakhapatnam districts. At this time, the French and Dutch also possessed trading rights on par with the East India Company in all these villages.[5] Under these arrangements, the weaver worked for the merchant to whom he was linked by traditional patron-client ties, with the merchant often providing aid to the weaver in times of distress.[6]

Soon after the inception of colonial rule, commercial officials of the Company wished to bring the weavers under their firm control in order to improve the quality and quantity of the Company's investment. In addition, they hoped to curtail the activities of the French and the Dutch. An early attempt in this direction was made by Anthony Sadleir, the Resident at Ingeram, who tried, in 1774, to re-group weaving villages into administrative units. The villages in the Visakhapatnam and Godavari districts were divided into 30 divisions or *mootahs*.[7] These administrative units were placed under the charge of head weavers, gumastahs, kanakapillais, and peons, who superintended the common weavers and managed their accounts.[8] Moreover, all advances of cash and the accounts of cloth produced were under their management.[9]

4 V. Corbrett, Commercial Resident, Masulipatnam, to Board of Trade, 14 October 1803, *GDR* 832, 412–40.

5 Inquiry Committee to Lord Pigot, President and Governor-in-Council, Fort St. George, 26 December 1775, *PDC* 115 A, 1–7.

6 Ibid.

7 Proceedings Relative to Enquiry into Conduct of Sadleir While Resident at Ingeram, 1775–76, 28 November 1775 to 30 March 1776, *PDS* 24A, 70. These mootahs were Mandapeta, Doolah, Pasalapoody, Pundalapauka, Colavarocondah, Venkatapallam, Bandarlanka, Amalapuram, Peddapoody, Peddapatnam, Dungaroo, Rustumbadah, Tanuku, Chintaparty, Uppada, Hassanalibadah, Rajahmundry, Angarah, Arrivatum, Coprepollam, Dharmavaram, Relangi, Duvva, Tuni, Bheemavaram, Penumadam, Marteroo, and three others.

8 Ibid.

9 Committee to Pigot, 1–7.

Sadlier also issued orders that curtailed the freedom of the weavers as well as the traders. First, weavers were ordered not to manufacture cloth for any foreign or native merchants other than the English Company. They were threatened by the newly appointed officials if the order was not obeyed.[10] Second, those weavers who were manufacturers of finer assortments were forced to weave coarser varieties.[11] The third measure related to the categorisation of cloth. Earlier, a 14-punjum fabric was categorised into two kinds: that which sold at Madras pagodas 32½ per *corjee* (20 pieces) and rejected cloth of a coarser variety sold at 31¼ pagodas per corjee. But, after the change in the mode of investment, 14-punjum cloth was assorted into four types—the first two were meant for the Company's investment, the third on Sadleir's account, and the rejected cloth was returned to the weaver at a low price.[12]

Sadleir's interpretation of his jurisdiction, however, clashed with that determined by the Company's officials at Visakhapatnam who believed that Tuni, closer as it was to Visakhapatnam, naturally fell under their control. Particularly since they believed that the weavers were deceitful and took "advances from two or three for the same piece of cloth", they felt that the new territorial arrangements proposed by Anthony Sadleir, apart from causing confusion, facilitated such deception. Pointing out that Visakhapatnam merchants had so far purchased cloth only in Tuni, they asked Sadleir to withdraw his gumastahs from Tuni.[13] He, however, disagreed with the contentions of the Visakhapatnam Council, claiming that the political transformation in the region had rendered the territorial delimitation appropriate to an earlier time no longer suitable to the new situation.[14] Weavers, merchants, and the European traders all felt that the new structural and intermediary

10 Testimony given by the head weavers of Peddapatnam, Amalapuram, Hassanalibadah, Arrivatum, Dungaroo, and Rustumbadah. In Proceedings Relative to Sadleir, 112–15.

11 Inquiry Committee Report, 10 February 1776 to 31 March 1776, *PDS* 25, 21–26

12 For details on the issue of low prices paid by Sadleir on rejected cloth, see the questions put by Hamilton and Yeates to all gumastahs, head weavers, and common weavers of all mootahs, in Proceedings Relative to Sadleir, 111–15.

13 George Stratham, Chief and Council, Visakhapatnam, to Anthony Sadleir, Ingeram, 8 January 1775, *PDC* 113A, 111–12.

14 Anthony Sadleir to Stratham and Others, 11 January 1775, *PDC* 113 A, 115–16 and also 165–68.

arrangements were oppressive and curtailed their freedom and vehemently resisted the continuance of such measures.[15]

The next person to introduce new systems of production management was the Company's contractor, Basil Cochrane, in 1786. The price of cloth was fixed after taking the consent of the zamindars and head weavers; contracts were entered into with weavers for a certain number of pieces of cloth, but an advance was given for only two pieces. As per the agreement, the Company had to be provided a piece of cloth every month, for which the weaver received a fixed price. Measuring and sorting of cloth was done at a central place in each mootah and differences in sorting were settled by mutual agreement. The Company's *chop* (seal or stamp) was affixed on the cloth immediately. A table of rates was fixed for inspection in every mootah and a register of the Company weavers' names was kept open for general inspection. These attempts were aimed at providing a link with the weavers, besides appeasing the local zamindars and head weavers, whose interference had caused interruption to the Company's production on earlier occasions.

By February 1788, Basil Cochrane recognised the influence the native merchants wielded over the weavers, and apprehended a continual debasement of the Company's investment if the weavers continued to provide cloth for other foreigners or individual traders. He, therefore, proposed a plan by which native merchants could re-enter the Company's investment arena, provided they fulfilled certain conditions such as paying fixed prices to weavers and replacing the existing combs of looms at their own expense. He also stipulated that merchants' agreements with the weavers should contain particulars such as the time schedule for delivery of goods and that these contracts should be given to the Resident, and a public register of the Company's weavers maintained.[16]

15 Jogee Rauze to George Stratham, 26 December 1774, *PDC* 113 A, 120–21. For names of merchants trading at Tuni, see translation of a gentoo paper sent by Anthony Sadleir to George Stratham, Chief and Council, Visakhapatnam, 11 January 1775, *PDC* 113A, 169–71; also Proceedings Relative to Sadleir, 111–15.

16 Memorandum of a Proposition made by Basil Cochrane to Mungo Dick, Resident, Maddepollam, 13 February 1788, *MDR* 2839, 17–18.

Copdars

Native merchants were perceived by the Company as the sole intermediaries between itself and the weaver.[17] But, in course of time, it was evident that these merchants were actually utilising the services of the copdar, a very powerful element in the weaving world of the northern Coromandel.[18] The copdars were paid a commission that ranged between 3 and 5 per cent for their assistance.[19]

The merchants closely controlled the copdars, not allowing them to supply more than 25 bales of cloth. Consequently, the copdars did not have much scope for manipulating the production process. The nature of their business operations varied, as they either purchased the cloth from the weavers or advanced loans on their looms. The copdars could easily facilitate their contracts. Since most of them resided in the same localities, they could exercise considerable influence over the weavers. They extended all possible help to the weavers in times of distress, and also provided grains at an advantageous rate.[20] The patron-client relationship thus established helped the copdars exert subtle extra-economic pressures on the weavers. In certain places, such as Ingeram and Maddapollem, the copdar also belonged to the weaving community. The bonds of community thus provided a more cohesive structure for the organisation of production.

In Visakhapatnam district, the Company followed the *aumany* system at the initial stages. Under this, Company officials dealt directly with the copdars and head weavers, that is, without the mediation of the merchant.[21] The Company preferred the system because of its many advantages such as securing a standard quality of goods and curbing the inflationary tendency of prices. This meant, however, that the copdars and head weavers became more powerful. Soon, they began to take advantage of the Company's contracts and used the Company's services and peons for their own private trading.[22]

17 R. Fullerton, Deputy Resident, Ingeram, to James Taylor, Acting Secretary to the Committee of Reforms, 14 March 1799, *GDR* 831, 41–42.

18 Ibid., 45.

19 Ibid., 45.

20 Ibid., 45.

21 General Letter to England, Commercial Department, 14 April 1800, *CDDTE* 3, 239–61.

22 Fullerton to Taylor, 41–42; Council, Sadleir to Stratham, 23 July 1774, *PDC* 113A, 33–34.

The Company, therefore, tried all possible ways to totally extinguish private trading activity. Two alternative methods were considered: first, the introduction of the mootah system by which an entire district was to be divided into many mootahs or units, each under a merchant whose jurisdiction was limited to his mootah. The primary responsibility of the merchant was to give advances; the second was to regulate and streamline the existing system of copdars.[23] There was also perhaps the expectation that these new administrative units would enable the Company to reduce the importance of intermediaries and deal directly with weavers. It was particularly keen to eliminate the middlemen merchants, who were thought to be misappropriating the investment of the Company.[24]

Under the copdari system of 1802 introduced at the Ingeram and Maddepollam factories, the changes initiated were mainly at two levels—at the level of primary weavers and at the level of intermediary groups, the copdars.

The clauses of the Regulations relating to the primary weavers read:

> That the weavers from the Godavari district were invited to enter into engagements with the Company for providing one piece of Company's assortments 14-16-18-20 & 22 punjums per month, on a voluntary basis; those who entered into engagements with the Company were exempted from every kind of tax and were given protection. Those who were unwilling to enter into such engagements had to pay every kind of tax. After fulfilling the contract of providing one piece of cloth to the Company every month, the Company's weaver was allowed to manufacture the cloth for private trade or any other cloth.[25]

The copdari system rested on four principles that were essential for its operation:

> The copdar must necessarily belong to weavers; the copdar must be a resident of those villages where the Company's looms were located; the copdars must be those chosen by weavers who might agree to work under them; and each copdar, in return for his services, was allowed to take 5 per cent on all the Company's advances. He was responsible for sending the cloth to the factory, the transaction of which he had to pay for, and in case of any balance due from the weavers under his management, the copdar was ultimately responsible.[26]

23 *PDC* 113 A, 46.

24 Ibid., 43–49.

25 Bayly, 6.

26 R. Fullerton, Acting Commercial Resident, Ingeram, to Benjamin Branfil, Collector, 3rd Division of the Masulipatnam District, 17 February 1802, *GDR* 940 B, 239–46.

The copdar had to obtain written engagements, called *woppandums*, from the weavers, specifying the details of their contracts. He had to maintain an exact account of the advances given, indicating also the reasons for extra advances. The copdar was required to include all the particulars in the weavers' *woogettas* (register of transactions), and advance all the money intended for the investment except 5 per cent that he could keep for his service. In case of non-fulfilment of these conditions, he could be removed from his position and a new copdar appointed in his place.[27]

The Company facilitated the operation of the copdari method through the creation of new administrative units for the weavers, called *mocaums* or *muggam*. Literally, a muggam is a loom. It is not clear whether this was a traditional administrative unit or the concept was entirely new. Nor is there evidence to enable us to trace the etymology of the word. Each unit or mocaum encompassed a certain number of looms and these units were superimposed over the existing spatial distribution of the weaving communities. Thus, a given mocaum could, and in many instances did, embrace weaving villages falling in different zamindaries and/or proprietary estates.[28]

The Company attempted to limit the influence of the copdar to a specific locality where the looms of his mocaum were located, and he was forbidden to interact with weavers of other mocaums or copdaris. The intention in enacting such a measure was, perhaps, to restrain the local elites of the weaving world from using the extended territorial solidarity in times of disturbances. The structural arrangements of the process of production limiting the influence of the copdar to a territory initiated a new administrative cohesiveness to, and realignment of, the textile economy. These structures operated without any conflict with those of the revenue systems.[29]

Rules for the proper sorting of the cloth and rejecting those pieces that were not up to the standard of the Company's assortments were also set out. On each piece of cloth supplied, the name of the weaver

27 Fullerton to Branfil, *GDR* 940 B, 239–46.

28 See enclosure to letter from J. Smith, Collector, Visakhapatnam, to Board of Revenue, 22 March 1819, *VDR* 3757, 130–33.

29 Fullerton to Branfil, *GDR* 940 B, 239–46.

and the copdar, the name of the village where it was produced, the number of punjums, were all to be marked in the presence of the weaver concerned. Later, it was the copdar's responsibility to shift the cloth to the concerned factory.[30]

The copdari arrangement was extended to the weaving villages of Visakhapatnam district by 1803. The principles were very similar to those implemented at the Ingeram and Maddepollam factories.[31] The political economy of the region and different taxation structures under specific land revenue systems had caused difficulties in the execution of the copdari arrangement.[32] The pacification programmes and the new revenue policy of the Company, however, enabled its success. Company weavers worked over a large territory falling under the jurisdiction of the different zamindaries and other landed estates. The Company, therefore, had to woo the zamindars in order to protect its commercial interests. In Godavari district, the Company weavers were conveniently clustered around the three zamindari areas of Peddapuram, Pitahpuram, and Cotah and Ramachandrapuram. In 1802, there were 2265 looms in the Peddapuram zamindari working for the Ingeram factory's investment. Under the copdari method they came to be administered under 18 mootahs or mocaums.[33] However, the number of looms in these mootahs decreased, mainly because of the reduction in the Company's investment. After 1811, there was a substantial reorganisation and many mocaums were merged. By 1819, this process left only 5 mocaums.

The situation was different in Visakhapatnam district. The weaving community here was widely spread, encompassing almost the entire area. The textile economy of the district was under the influence of various groups who, in fact, manipulated the situation to their advantage

30 Ibid.

31 For particulars on the principles of the copdari system introduced in the Visakhapatnam factory area, see a letter circa 1810 from Masulipatnam to Fort St. George found in an unclassified volume, number 22759, serial number 225, rack 7, Pre-Mutiny Records section, Tamil Nadu State Archives, 61–68. Each sheet has four sides: a, b, c and d.

32 Revenue Statement of Collection and Charges of Several Districts, *PBOR (Miscellaneous)* 246, 39–43, shows the gross revenue collections from the Company's territories in 1786–87 and provides a complete list of zamindari and haveli lands in the four districts of the northern Coromandel.

33 M. Lewin, Collector, Rajahmundry, to Board of Revenue, 24 September 1835, *GDR* 4648, 190–94.

for controlling the production process also. A varied taxation structure added to the problem. In the first half of the nineteenth century there were, in Visakhapatnam district, long-established zamindaris, minor zamindaris, and aumany estates.[34] About 1793, the looms that registered for the Company's investment at the Visakhapatnam factory were divided into 29 copdaris.[35] Of these 10,829 looms, 6647 that fell under the jurisdiction of the Vizianagaram zamindari area were placed under 18 mocaums. Similarly, 845 looms of the Bobbili zamindari were under 4 mocaums.[36] The new units, by cutting across the existing territorial and revenue arrangements, further diminished the already attenuated powers of the zamindars. The copdar was placed in charge of the complete administration of these units and as the sole intermediary between the Company and the weaver.[37]

The immediate effect of the copdari system on the weaving world of the region was that it kept out the economically less powerful elements as well as socially dominant groups such as the head weavers from holding any official position. For instance, in 1796 there were 248 copdars and head weavers in Visakhapatnam district.[38] In 1803, only 29 copdars were recognised as having definite control over the management of the weaving villages.[39]

The copdari system worked in those villages that produced ordinary and middle varieties of textiles. As the investment on the superfine variety was large, the Company provided additional safeguards to maintain it. Thus, simultaneously, the collection of 36-punjum cloth was placed under the direct management of the Commercial Resident, and this gave no scope for the entry of any other element, including the copdar. Moreover, as the advances distributed were large, the Company made it the collective as well as individual responsibility of the weavers of each village for the sum owed by any one of them.[40]

34 For a brief note on land revenue systems of 1803 in Visakhpatnam district, see D. F. Carmichael, *VDM*.

35 Minute of Fullerton dated 20 February 1818, *CDC* 13, 586–609.

36 John Smith, Collector, Visakhapatnam, to BOR, 22 March 1819, *VDR* 3757, 122–33.

37 Smith to BOR, *VDR* 3757, 130–33.

38 Extract of Letter from the Commercial Resident at Visakhapatnam, 22 March 1793, *PBR* 2798, 525.

39 Fullerton, Minute, *CDC* 13, 586–609.

40 Letter in Pre-mutiny Records. For a description on the arrangement of superfine cloth, see especially 66d to 68a, paragraphs 475–84.

Entering into a review of the principles on which the commercial concerns of the Company were to have been conducted at the factories of the northern Coromandel, a Minute of Lord Clive dated 9 February 1814 specified the objective of introducing the copdari system in the region.[41]

The proper implementation of the copdari scheme in accordance with its essential features was achieved only in the Ingeram factory. A Report of 1818 pointed out that all copdars who were selected and put in charge of these mocaums belonged only to the weaver caste. The officials hardly faced any problems even while placing the looms under different mocaums and the Ingeram factory was noted for its correct management in the early nineteenth century.[42]

The implementation of the copdari arrangements at the factory in Maddepollam was not total because of the constraints in the social organisation of the production process. The new administrative units of the weaving villages covering the looms were set up correctly, in accordance with the principles. But, by 1810, the copdars who were put in control of these mootahs (all except two) did not belong to the weaver caste, rather they were Banias.[43]

How did Banias penetrate this profession? It was, earlier, when the Company had organised its textile investments through merchants or contractors that Banias had entered this system. Under the new copdari dispensation, the Company's merchant had stayed on as the copdar. Other than this simple replacement of name, no changes had been brought in by Company officials in those villages coming under the jurisdiction of the Maddepollam factory.

Banias were preferred, as the Company always thought that they would have better means and thereby place its investment on a sound basis. Moreover, the commercial officials were also of the opinion that weavers did not possess adequate knowledge about accounts. But, in reality, the copdari system of maintenance did not require much accounting to be maintained—only a consideration of the money advanced to each weaver and that of cloth delivered by him.[44] At the same time, the commercial officials were also apprehensive that the Banias might use their facility with accounting to cheat the Resident and impose extra sums on the weavers too. Gumastahs were appointed in the mootahs to examine and compare the accounts between weavers

41 Fullerton, Minute, 586–609.

42 Ibid., 595–98.

43 Ibid.

44 Ibid.

and copdars, and to make sure that they corresponded with those at the factories.

While there were no complaints from the weavers registered at the Maddepollam factory against Bania copdars, the experience of the Company at Visakhapatnam was different. The replacement of the traditional copdars by Banias here was legitimised on the pretext that the former had not fulfilled their contracts in time.[45] For instance, by 1814, many weaver caste copdars owed large sums to the Company.[46] Although these copdars were given some time to clear their outstanding balances and were keen to re-enter the Company's service, they were ultimately dislodged from holding any supervisory position.

The total failure of the Company's investment in Visakhapatnam district came to be charged to the negligence of the principles of the copdari agency. Four divisions out of seven came to be controlled by Bania copdars in 1816. These four divisions had under their jurisdiction 12 copdaris out of 26.[47] The evidence from the records suggests that the influence of these copdars extended to all branches of production. Primary weavers suffered under the oppressive and unjust power structure and were continually deprived of their earnings.[48]

Bania copdars were often responsible for the debasement of the Company's assortments, using all sorts of business tricks. Motumarry Paupadoo, Grandy Vencataramoodoo, and Maumedy Sooriah, among others, usually purchased readymade cloth from the advances which they received at the time of the contract. They placed charcoal endorsements on these pieces and passed them off as the original manufacture of the Company's registered weavers.[49] These copdars began to keep rejected fabric instead of returning it to the weavers, buying it at a lower price than that fixed by the Company. They then sold this at Visakhaptanam to private traders who were in collusion with Chinnum Jaggapah, a powerful copdar there. So enterprising had the Bania copdars become that they extended their dubious business practices even to the *aummen* mocaums, which were supposedly under the more direct control of the Company.[50] All these activities ultimately affected the profits of the Company.

45 Ibid., 586–609.

46 Letter in Pre-Mutiny Records, 64a to 66d.

47 Fullerton, Minute, 598–601.

48 For details, see W. A. Fraser, Deputy Commercial Resident, Ingeram, to Hugh Elliot, Governor-in-Council, Fort St. George, 17 July 1818, *CDC* 13, 291–331, especially 295–99.

49 Fraser to Eliot, 297 and 374–95.

50 Ibid. Testimony given by six weavers of Goorampallam mocaum, 374–95.

Bania copdars schemed with Company officials, head servants, land magnates, and other rural officials to further their business interests. With the help of these power groups, the copdars evolved a kind of triangular trade to their own ultimate benefit. From the yearly advances that they received from the Company, they used to loan large amounts to zamindars and others, who desperately needed the sums for paying off their land revenue dues to the Company. It was a general phenomenon in the region that land revenue or kists were realised in those months, whatever might be the season of the year, when advances were released from the respective factories. Such revenue collections were made possible, because the credits of the Company, instead of reaching the weaver directly and immediately, often went to the zamindars and renters, who used the amount for paying off their kists.[51] Besides paying exorbitant interest rates, the zamindars also exchanged the produce of their lands such as grain, cotton, tobacco, and so on for cash advances. These articles were forced on the weavers by the copdars at very high prices. Weavers were also made to pay cesses on marriage occasions and other ceremonies.[52] The Bania copdars used such trade tactics to keep the circulation of money within the district and thus accumulated great profits from every single transaction.

Chinnum Jaggapah Chetty was a powerful Bania copdar at the Visakhapatnam factory. He entered service in the Resident's office for a paltry sum of 14 rupees a month.[53] In course of time, he won the confidence of the Commercial Residents of the Visakhapatnam factory, and became dubashi and head servant by 1810. Under Henry Taylor, the Commercial Resident who took over in 1811, Chinnum Jaggapah used his newly acquired influence to depose the weaver caste copdars and place all their mocaums under the supervision of Bania copdars. These comprised his own relatives like his brother-in-law and the father-in-law of his brother. Even other caste copdars including Devangas came to be employed on his recommendation.[54] In six years, from 1811 to 1816, Chinnum Jaggapah acquired various possessions ranging from landed estates and big houses to maintenance of large boats, which he

51 I. T. Lane, In-charge Secretary of the Visakhapatnam factory, to Board of Trade, Fort St. George, 11 September 1818, *CDC* 15, 1732–66, especially 1735–37.

52 Fraser to Elliot, 291–331, especially 297–98.

53 Petition of weavers addressed to George Strachy, Chief Secretary to Government, 19 March 1817, *CDC* 10, 1249–56.

54 Fullerton, Minute, 586–609.

used for private trade.[55] The position of the weavers become so low under these Bania copdars that they were reduced to using wooden *mangalsutras* (token of marriage) instead of the usual gold ones in their marriage ceremonies.[56]

Apprehending the danger of continued oppression by copdars like Chinnum Jaggapah, weavers assembled at Simhachallem, a pilgrim centre near Visakhapatnam, and brought their problems to the notice of the Company. In the 50-odd years from 1765 to 1815, the power and influence of the copdars seemed stronger than the strategies that the Company devised to keep them in check. Company officials evolved a new, multi-pronged plan to clip the wings of the copdars and to protect weavers from their oppressive practices. This scheme took into account the problems of the textile economy and formulated administrative changes in the weaving villages.

One of the principal problems for the Company's investment during this period was private trade. The involvement of copdars, sometimes weavers too, in this activity led to the debasement and failure of the Company's textile investment at the Visakhapatnam factory.[57] The Acting Commercial Resident suggested that rejected cloth be withheld at the godown and purchased on the Company's account. It could be useful in other factories. If the quantity was large, it could be sold at a moderate price.[58] The Board of Trade, realising favourable market conditions for coarser cloth in Europe, considered the possibility of reclassifying the rejected cloth, giving it an inferior number, and exporting it, after proper washing and bleaching, to the English markets. To satisfy the copdar and weaver, the Board suggested that credit should be given for the amount sold but without commission to the former, and this would reduce the general·balance.[59] The Commercial Residents were empowered with discretionary authority to purchase rejected cloth and either take it into the stores or put it up for public auction. In all

55 Petition of the weavers' agents to the Company's Punjum Cloth Weavers' Division of Visakhapatnam district addressed to the Board of Trade, Fort St. George, 11 March 1817, *CDC* 10, 1277–85.

56 Weavers' Petition to Strachy, *CDC* 10, 1249–56.

57 Petition of the weavers' agents to Robert Fullerton, Board of Trade, Fort St. George, 29 November 1816, *CDC* 10, 1257–64, especially 1259.

58 Lane to BOT, 1732–66.

59 Ibid., 1736–40.

this, the speedy settlement of outstanding balances was the primary object.[60]

Regarding the adjustment of outstanding balances, the Acting Commercial Resident suggested the revoking of the earlier practice. Generally, the copdar would take "on himself the liquidation or collection of the outstanding balances of his predecessor or, in other words, to purchase his appointment on the speculation of being able to recover part of the amount from the weavers, deduct it from the future advances or to allow it to run on from year to year. At all events, whatever balances are collected in a mocaum for a former year after fresh advances are made will be to the prejudice of the current years investment if in money..."[61] In the new policy, the idea was that the copdar should receive his appointment clear of all former accounts. The first advances were to be given in the presence of the Resident to those weavers who had cleared all their balances. They were to be made to understand that if they failed to deliver the cloth for the money advanced, no fresh credits would be granted. Except in case of genuine sickness or other unavoidable misfortune, this clause was to be followed, and the weaver had to provide the agreed amount of cloth before taking on any fresh agreement. For all outstanding balances, however, the copdar was to be held responsible at the end of the year. The copdar had to submit a list of those weavers who had failed to provide the contracted cloth; they could not participate in the investment till their accounts were cleared.[62]

Ultimately it was the Commercial Resident's responsibility to see that all the accounts between the copdar and the weaver were adjusted, before any fresh advances were made. It was "an established rule and an article in the written agreement of a copdar that when the *woppandum sunned* (agreement) is taken from and fresh advance made to a weaver at the commencement of an investment, all accounts of former years are considered as fully adjusted and that on pain of dismissal he is not to demand from the weaver a single piece on any pretence whatever since and except on account of the woppandum sunned then delivered in."[63] The Board of Trade, being only too keen on maintaining clear accounts without any outstanding balances, accepted these proposals. It further asked the Commercial Resident "to give public notice in the different

60 Extract from the Proceedings of the Board of Trade, 18 September 1818, *CDC* 15, 1753–66, especially 1759.

61 Lane to BOT, especially 1740–41.

62 Ibid., 1744.

63 Ibid., 1745.

mocaums that no advance will be made in any mootah until the balances of that mocaum are all adjusted and that advances in future will be confined to those who have settled their accounts."[64]

In placing the entire investment on a firm base through changes in the structural arrangements of the Visakhapatnam·district, the real intention was perhaps to pare the power of the copdars. None of the former or existing copdars were to control any of the mootahs or mocaums they had been in charge of earlier; copdars were to be transferred once in two years so that strong alliances could be prevented; members of other castes were to be appointed as copdars along with those of the weaver caste, as they would act as a check upon one another; the authority of copdars was to be limited to 350 looms only; copdars had to provide an annual security of Rs.5000; and the Resident was to check all his accounts every year.[65]

The Board of Trade was, however, not sure that all these measures to control the copdars could be implemented successfully. For instance, moving of copdars to new mootahs or mocaums would disturb the long-standing relationship that existed between them and the weavers. Nevertheless, the Board stated that all copdars should be explicitly told that they were liable to such transfers.[66]

The Board objected to the suggestion of taking security from copdars, as it would tend to turn them into mere contractors. Instead, the entire responsibility for protecting the investment and curbing the power of the copdars was placed in the hands of the Commercial Residents, whose duty was constant and active supervision. The Residents were authorised to cut down the 350 looms a copdar could supervise if they thought that he was not able to manage his looms effectively.[67]

There was also disagreement on the idea of employing other caste groups as copdars. It was argued that "...there are circumstances inherent in the case which must give the weaver caste a decided preference. The duty is entirely professional if attended with profit, and it seems but justice to the manufacturing class that the industrious respectable among them should have that office to look up to, besides which, the trade of the weaver's caste is confined to his own profession. That of a banian [sic] is general and as there is always a greater risk of advances being misappropriated by the latter."[68]

64 Proceedings of BOT, *CDC* 15, 1754 and 1760.
65 Lane to BOT, especially 1745–47.
66 Proceedings of BOT, 1761.
67 Ibid, 1761.
68 Ibid., 1763–64.

A simultaneous redesigning of the existing administrative structures for the weaving villages was also undertaken around 1820. For a couple of years from 1818 onwards, the Company followed interim measures to continue its investment operations. For instance, the copdars in charge of aumany mocaums were asked to take over other mocaums as acting copdars; they were also made responsible for those mocaums that had earlier been under Bania copdars.[69]

The geographical location of some of the weaving villages near hilly tracts as well as the ineffectiveness of the Company to exercise complete control over the political economy of the district added to the existing problems and caused a setback to the Company's investment. The long-standing disputes between Boyana Apparayadoo, a hill *dorah* (local chieftain or ruler), and Gotamookala Ramachandrauze led to frequent robberies and murders in the district. Boyana Apparayadoo was dorah at Boosiahoolsah in Poram pargana, while Gotamookala Ramachandrauze was a renter of a village in the same district.[70] The actual cause of the conflict between them was not known. Nevertheless, from the available evidence it appears that Boyana Apparayadoo frequently visited the villages with his men and indulged in dacoities and murders. Four to five hundred men owed allegiance to him and 2 or 3 groups were stationed at Poram, Aukoolcallah, Paryan, and Lovahs.[71] The nature of their atrocities in the district, including those at the town of Visakhapatnam, affected activities in various mocaums such as Bobbili, Guzzepatinagaram, Mardam, and Cuncharam. Many inhabitants, including weavers, ran away from their villages. Those weavers who braved the situation suffered as they did not receive advances from their copdars in time.[72]

There were more incidents of robbery and plunder in Visakhapatnam district. Mookiwars and Mannigars from the hills descended on the weaving villages in hordes.[73] In 1820, nearly 400 such bandits caused depredations in many of the villages. Denkapoolee, a hill dorah, came with 200 men carrying country guns, spears, and picks to Tekkali (where

69 This statement has been based on details in translations of copies of 12 *arzee*s sent by the Commercial Resident at Visakhapatnam to I. Smith, Magistrate, Visakhapatnam district, *CDC* 20, 1899–1911.

70 Robey Sail, Acting Copdar of Guzzepatinagram, arzee No.1 dated 23 August 1819, to Commercial Resident, Visakhapatnam, *CDC* 20, 1899–1900.

71 Ibid., 1900.

72 For details, see translations of arzees, *CDC* 20, 1899–1911.

73 T. Daniel, Secretary, Board of Trade, to the Chief Secretary to Government, 24 November 1820, *CDC* 26, 203.

ten of the Company's weavers of the Narlamurlah mocaum resided) at dead of night and plundered the entire village. Denkapoolee "untied the cloths of the women and carried the cloths away, burnt their houses and others', and many cattle were lost." Many of the weavers' houses were burnt. Raperty Tunmiah, a weaver captured by the miscreants, was not released, and the weavers of the village lodged a complaint with the gumastah. The godown, where many pieces of the Company's cloth were stored, was guarded by the gumastah with the assistance of peons.[74] The weaving villages in the vicinity of Simhachallem were also in a state of alarm due to raids by the Mookiwars and Mannigars.

As these robberies caused great disturbances among the weaving villages, the Commercial Resident reported the situation to the Commanding Officer of the troops in Visakhapatnam. He was asked to send some forces for protection and thereby unstil confidence among the weavers working for the Company.[75] The Collector of Visakhapatnam was asked to increase the vigilance of his police and *sibbandy* (irregular troops/soldiery), and the Commanding Officer at Chicacole was requested to furnish the guard to accompany the Collector to the mocaums at Tuni and Payakarraopeta.[76]

The Company had thus to constantly struggle to protect its investment. By the 1820s, the suggestions of the Commercial Residents to reinforce the power structure came to be implemented. The first step the East India Company took in this direction was to reorganise the mocaums by reducing variations in the number of looms assigned to a particular mocaum, removing existing anomalies, and introducing uniformity into the new administrative structure. Under the revised system, there were 250 looms to a mocaum in Visakhapatnam district and a total of 8,000 looms in 32 mocaums.[77] With the outstanding balances of the copdars increasing at an alarming rate, the Resident further divided the whole district into 28 mocaums and placed these under the charge of 14 copdars, each looking after 2 mocaums.[78]

74 W. Brown, Resident, Visakhapatnam, to T. Daniel, Secretary, Board of Trade, 7 November 1820, *CDC* 26, 207–09; Coputty Seetiah, gumastah of Narlamurlah, to William Brown, Commercial Resident, 3 November 1820, *CDC* 26, 202–04.

75 W. Brown, Resident, Visakhaptnam, to the Commanding Officer of the Troops in the Visakhapatnam district, 9 October 1820, *CDC* 26, 209.

76 Brown to Collector, Visakhapatnam, *CDC* 26, 7 November 1820, 207–08.

77 Brown to BOT, 25 June 1820, *GDR* 832, 203–32, in *Guide to District Records, Godavari District* 1, 33.

78 Brown to BOT, 6 July 1820, *GDR* 832, 156–60, in *Guide to District Records, Godavari* District 1, 32.

More importantly, the Company created a new unit consisting of two mocaums, that is, 500 looms, over which a gumastah was appointed to supervise the delivery of cloth. In addition, the Company recognised the traditionally important senapati again and put him in charge of the supply of thread to each mocaum. The Company itself undertook to give advances directly to the weavers, limited to 1½ pieces per loom.[79]

By fragmenting the matrix of power relationships within the weaving community and by reinforcing, in particular, the positions of the gumastah and the senapati, the Company effectively reduced the power of the copdar. He was transformed into a mere collector of cloth. Further, the Company merged the existing copdaris, placing them under the effective management of a few copdars.[80]

In assigning a new status to the traditional leaders of the weavers—the senapatis—the Company was not only creating a new locus of power, it was also trying to secure a more stable operating environment for itself. It was the senapatis who had led the weavers' agitation in 1816, and by giving them a specific, officially recognised role, the Company was not only acknowledging their position as leaders of influence but was perhaps buying insurance against future disruptions of the textile economy.

Despite opposition from higher commercial officials, Company men at Visakhapatnam also sought to protect themselves against malfeasance by the copdars by introducing a system by which a leading individual of the locality stood surety for the investment advanced to the copdar.[81] For instance, in 1820, the Commercial Resident, W. Brown, stated that the balance for that year was only 10,000 rupees compared to the very large sum of 1,50,000 rupees in 1819. This was the result of the security system that had been introduced.[82]

Interestingly, two kinds of security arrangements for the Company's investment were followed in Visakhapatnam district. When a copdar was placed solely in charge of a mocaum, he had to get a leading member of the community to provide security. Sometimes, the same person guaranteed two copdars. But, when two copdars were in joint charge of

79 Brown to BOT, 25 June 1820, *GDR* 830, 203–32, in *Guide to District Records, Godavari District*, 1, 33.

80 Ibid.

81 Brown to BOT, 6 July 1820, *GDR* 832, 156–60, in *Guide to District Records, Godavari District* 1, 33.

82 Brown to BOT, 25 June 1820, *GDR* 832, 203–32, in *Guide to District Records, Godavari District* 1, 34.

one or two mocaums, then they did not need to provide any security. However, at the Ingeram factory there were no joint copdars. Instead, a mootah was placed under two or three copdars who had to be indemnified by a prominent member of the society. In most cases, it was a Bania or Komati who was the guarantor in Godavari district.

By 1828, the Company seems to have gone ahead with the transfer of copdars in an attempt to prevent them from becoming too entrenched in the locality.[83] Other methods to curtail the rapacity of the copdars and to reduce the opportunities they may have for misappropriation of the Company's investment were to specify the number of pieces per loom that each weaver could contract for and to secure *muchalika*s (written agreements) from the copdars to the effect that they would not demand anything but cloth from the weavers.[84]

The efforts of the Company to create a seemingly effective structure of control over the weaving world of the northern Coromandel—particularly over the copdars—appeared to have continued into the late 1820s, a time when the direction of the textile trade itself was irrevocably reversed.

What was the effect of the Company's retreat from the textile economy on intermediary structures, especially copdars? Despite the copdari system being implemented comprehensively in weaving villages under the Ingeram factory, it lost its hold in the textile industry with the closing down of the factory in 1830. As the Company's investment in punjum cloth started declining, it began to recover the balances from copdars.[85] In 1832, 14 copdars from the villages of Marteroo, Amalapuram, Nelapalli, Palakollu, Duvva, Penumadum, Bandarlanka, Maumedala, and Cottapalli owed large sums to the Company's factories at Ingeram and Maddepollam. These loans dated back to the 1815 investment. Almost all the copdars at Maddepollam were Banias who owned *pucca*

83 H. Taylor, Commercial Resident, Visakhapatnam to Commercial Superintendent, Madras, 29 April 1828, *CDC* 51, 497–513.

84 Brown to BOT, 30 September 1820, *GDR* 830, 22–38, in *Guide to District Records, Godavari District* 1, 35.

85 A. Crawley, Collector, Rajahmundry, to Deputy Warehouse Keeper, Madras, 23 Feburary 1832, *CDC* 61, 113–15; Arthur Maclean, Secretary, Marine Boards Office, Madras, to Chief Secretary to Government, Fort St. George, August 1836, *CDC* 61, 118 A, 118 B.; for further correspondence on this, see T. Daniel, Secretary, BOT, to Chief Secretary to Government, 14 July 1821, *CDC* 28; I. Gwatkin, Commercial Superintendent, Madras, to Chief Secretary to Government, 23 May 1825, *CDC* 40, 397–402; Taylor to Commercial Superintendent, *CDC* 51, 497–513.

tiled houses and traded in commodities like cloth and paddy. After the total abolition of its investment, the Company's insisted that the copdars needed to clear the balances and held the various guarantors also responsible for the repayments.

In spite of financial problems caused by famine and other conditions, the copdars agreed to pay off their balances in cloth at reduced prices and the monies through instalments. The Collector of Rajahmundry district consented to the proposal, but pointed out that then it would not be possible to go ahead with the suits that had been instituted in the *adawlut* court of the district.[86] The copdars did not deny the justice of his assertion, but they expressed their inability to pay for the expenses involved in court procedures.[87] In the end, however, it was the use of colonial legal procedures and the auctioning of the copdars' possessions that had to be resorted to.[88]

While the Company restructured the production process in the weaving villages of the Visakhapatnam and Godavari districts, the weaver in Masulipatnam appeared to have been less affected by these changes. Here, careedars and gumastahs were the key figures in the smooth transaction of business with the weavers.

Careedars and Gumastahs

The careedar was one of the major elements in mediating between the Company and the ordinary weaver for getting the required supply of chay goods from Masulipatnam district. There were three distinct classes among these careedars, depending on the economic and social status they occupied in the local economy. There were the weavers of substance who received full payment from the contractors of the Company and then supplied cloth. Many a time, economically less well-off weavers were dependent on these careedars for their maintenance, especially when they were unemployed. Being weavers, these substantial mediators sometimes provided or manufactured cloth in their houses. They also at times employed 'outdoor weavers', who were probably paid a wage and who in turn paid a 'fee' to the careedar.[89] There were careedars of

86 A. Crawley, Collector, Rajahmundry to Commercial Resident, Madras, 12 July 1831, *GDR* 4644, 119–21.

87 Ibid; see the mode of arrangement proposed by some of the copdars of the former Ingeram factory for the liquidation of the Company's credits.

88 Crawley to Commercial Resident, 119–21.

89 Vincentio Corbrett, Commercial Resident, Masulipatnam, to BOR, 14 October 1803, *GDR* 832, 412–26.

other castes such as the Brahmin careedars at Battiprole, who usually received the full price from the contractors. In turn, they employed weavers and deducted a specified fee from the amount that they had to pay them for their work. Then, there were the wealthy and important elements of the weaving community, who would take up the responsibility of supplying chay goods on their own account and enjoy the entire benefit from such operations.

In 1800, the Commercial Resident at Masulipatnam maintained that the success of the Company's activity in the district was essentially due to the services rendered by these careedars. Indeed, they stood guarantee between the weaver and the public contractor or the Company and they would supervise the work in the villages.[90]

The other intermediary in Masulipatnam district was the contractor-gumastah. From the time of inception of the Company's investment at the Masulipatnam factory, these contractor-gumastahs used to receive a fee from the amount of advances that was provided to weavers and washermen, and it varied from place to place and sometimes within a village.[91]

The fact that there was little re-arrangement in the organisation of production in the Masulipatnam region could be attributed to several factors. One was the virtual absence of powerful elements within the weaving communities of the region, whose authority needed to be curbed. The clustering of the weaving villages also facilitated the transaction of the Company without any changes in jurisdictional arrangements. Then again, the Company did not see the need for changes perhaps because the production process was not seemingly affected by the oppression and exploitation of weavers by dominant groups like zamindars and merchants. These issues need further study.

The Company's search for the ultimate mechanism for controlling the production of cloth in its territory necessarily went beyond the copdars, careedars, and gumastahs and sought to embrace other elements involved in the textile economy such as washermen.

WASHERMEN

The fabric produced by weavers had to pass through a number of additional processes such as washing, and beating before the cloth was

90 Ibid.
91 Ibid.

ready for final packing and shipment. Thus, in the northern Coromandel region, the washerman (called *chakali* in Telugu) was an essential factor in the weaving world.[92]

In the early period of its commercial operations in the region, the Company tried to give intermediary merchants the responsibility of getting fabric washed by compelling them to take on the expenses and co-ordination for the job. Thus, in the 1787 investment proposals, a clause to pay for the washing and embaling of the Company's cloth was also included. Most of the merchants or contractors who came forward to undertake the work consented to pay for the washing and embaling.[93]

The requirement of washing the finished fabric and the recognition of this by the washermen created a situation of conflict and tension between them and the Company. Attempts to regulate their functioning precipitated a precarious situation because washermen were disinclined to give up their economic independence. The Company sought to counteract this reluctance by various means. One method was to ensure that the washing was done under supervision within the factories. Vast areas were, therefore, allocated inside their premises for this purpose. These special areas, provided with wells and tanks and free of buildings, were known as washing greens. Payments to the washermen were fixed, and the washing was closely supervised.[94]

The system of supervision required a hierarchy of agents, mostly from the washermen community itself, to be part of the administrative structure of the factory termed the 'native establishment'. In the Visakhapatnam factory, for instance, the overseeing was entrusted to three persons, namely, the head washing kanakapillai and two assistant kanakapillais, who were employed at the two washing greens—Pettah Green and Waltair Green—with fixed monthly salaries.[95]

92 The Telugu for washerman is chakali (also written as *kakali*) or *rajakulu*. In Visakhapatnam district there were two groups of washermen—*Chapu Kakali* and *Vadde Kakali*. The latter were usually palanquin bearers.

93 Mathew Yeates, Resident, Ingeram, to BOT, 7 April 1788, *MDR* 2839, 178–80, with enclosures.

94 Advertisement notices for selling by public auction all property relating to the factories mention washing greens and washing stones, besides the estate. See the advertisements given by I. H. Bell, Head Assistant Collector in Charge, Rajahmundry, 5 April 1837, in Maclean to Chief Secretary, 12 April 1837, *CDC* 62, 36–46.

95 List of Servants Proposed to be Employed in the Commercial Department of Visakhapatnam for the year 1828–29, in Taylor to Commercial Superintendent, 19 February 1828, *CDC* 50, 315–20.

Washermen were not always willing to come to the factory. Many of them were also involved in agriculture and going to the factory meant a disruption of their agrarian activities and consequent inability to maintain the usual revenue payments. Some washermen resisted being employed at the factories. In some villages there were only one or two washermen, and this meant that they could not enter the Company's service, as they were required to work in their own villages and at times even in the adjoining villages.[96]

The Company used coercion as well as persuasion to procure the services of the washermen. Peons were sent to the nearby villages to fetch the required number of washermen to be employed at the factory. Or, sometimes, revenue officials were asked to persuade washermen under their jurisdiction to work for the Company. From time to time, factory headmen (called *maistris*) and peons went into the villages to forcibly bring the most experienced and hardworking washermen to the factories.[97]

The maistri, given a *dustack* (revenue order) to fetch washermen for the Company's service, proceeded to the villages not only as a representative of the Company's power but also as a caste head who could exercise his own authority. Such compulsion and social power having been used in the case of two washermen, Narsegah and Nagaishaga, of Rayapudi and Maddepollam villages, to bring them to the Maddepollam factory has been recorded in 1795.[98]

On the other hand, washermen responded to such tactics by absconding from their villages. They, like peasants and weavers, often resorted to this practice in situations of crisis or forcible action.[99]

Interestingly, C. A. Bayly describes a similar phenomenon at work in northern India:

> Europeans came up against a similar problem in procuring labour for personal service of public works.... If the Europeans tried to force a supply of labour through the good offices of the Headman or police, the whole system might collapse, with the labourer disappearing to

96 Letter to John Rowley, Resident of Ingeram and Maddepollam factories, 1 August 1795, *GDR* 841, 226–28; Letter to Edward Saunders, BOR, 23 November 1795, *GDR* 841, 383–414.

97 Letter to Mungo Dick, Ingeram, 27 July 1795, *GDR* 843, 218–19; Letter to Saunders, *GDR* 841, 383–414.

98 Letter to Rowley, *GDR* 841, 226–29.

99 Samuel Skinner, Collector, 2nd Division, to Acting Commercial Resident, Ingeram, 4 May 1802, *GDR* 848, 200–04.

another part of the city. The only way for the Europeans to ensure supplies of labour was to create their own patterns of clientage.[100]

The Company did try create methods of retention by the grant of remissions and prerogatives to the washermen. One early suggestion was to give them additional pay as they were an essential service group at the factory.[101] They were also granted the enjoyment of common privileges such as collecting the dried dung in the neighbouring villages.[102] In 1824, the Commercial Resident at Ingeram further requested an exemption in favour of the factory washermen from the tax that was to be levied on that class of labourers.[103] Other means of placating the washermen were also tried. For example, when, in 1794, unemployed washermen caused some trouble in Visakhapatnam, a huge quantity of cloth was moved into the district for washing purposes to pacify them.[104] An order was issued to the dissident washermen to return and to complete the business in which they were already employed in, "at the time their assistance was required for the English Company provided they have not deserted from their service."[105]

Payment to washermen was usually at piece rate, and this was decided by the Board of Trade in Madras. For the investment of 1828, the Board of Trade fixed the payment at the rate of 7 Madras rupees and 8 annas per bale in the case of the Ingeram and Maddepollam factories, and at 8 rupees 4 annas per bale at the Visakhapatnam factory.[106]

Throughout the period of its operations in the textile economy of the region, the Company, thus, had to contend with washermen, whose collaboration was so necessary for cloth to reach its destined markets.

100 Bayly, 256.

101 Letter to Saunders, 383-414.

102 Letter from Rowley to District Collector, 26 July 1795, *GDR* 841, 215–17; Letter to Rowley, 13 July 1795, *GDR* 841, 175–76; Letter to Mungo Dick, Ingeram, 27 July 1795, *GDR* 843, 218–19.

103 I. Gwatkin, Secretary, BOT, to Chief Secretary to Government, 29 November 1824, *CDC* 38, 1138–40.

104 Rowley to William Fallofield, Board of Trade, 8 July 1794, *GDR* 831, 146.

105 Rowley to Boucher, 8 July 1794, *GDR* 831, 145.

106 See for details, statement showing the difference between the indent sent by the Court of Directors and the estimate of the general factory at Ingeram of the coast investment of 1828–29, F. A. Savage, Commercial Resident, to BOT, 26 September 1827, *CDC* 50, 64 A and B, 318–19.

LEGAL MEASURES AND COMMERCIAL CONTROL

Colonial attempts to penetrate more deeply into the textile economy involved the construction of juridical structures and the setting up of legal provisions.

In the pre-colonial period, there were indigenous courts at Rajahmundry and Eluru, where *khazis* (judicial officers) administered justice according to Islamic law. *Foujdars* (military governors of a district) were responsible for dealing with cases relating to capital punishments and those involving considerable property. The *kotwal*, who was the Superintendent of Police, and the *nurkee*, who regulated the prices of various provisions, were other important officials in the judicial machinery. For a few decades following the acquisition of political hegemony over the region, no attempt was made to create a new judicial system; while simple and trifling disputes were settled by karnams and leading inhabitants, those of greater consequence were referred either to the renters or the Chief and Council at Masulipatnam.

The colonial government conceived the idea of providing some legal framework within which the fundamental status of the weavers, Commercial Residents, and other agents associated with the Company's investment could be clearly defined.[107] In 1795, the Court of Directors recommended the extension of the Bengal Regulations to its commercial concerns on the coast. These provisions essentially sought to provide arrangements for procurement, to define weavers' relations with other traders, to ensure proper implementation of agreed contracts, and to guard weavers from the prejudicial interests of Company officials and agents.[108]

The Regulations specified that the weavers enter into a strict obligatory relationship with the Company. Weavers, once having agreed

107 For the Board's views respecting the weavers, their situation, and the necessity of some regulations for them, see *Miscellaneous Records* 190 [Board's Proceedings on the Introduction of the Judicial and Revenue Systems of Bengal], Fort St. George, 2 September 1799, 316 (para 321)–17. For details on Proposed Coast Regulations where Courts of Justice were not established, see *Judicial Department Consultations* [*JDC*] 1, 46–91 and 93. For the Regulation of 1806 for the conduct of the Commercial Residents and Agents, and all persons employed or concerned in the provision of the Company's investment, see Minute of the President dated 14 January 1806, *JDC* 14, 129–64. For a recent discussion on legal provisions adopted for placing Bengal weavers under the Company's effective control, see Hossain, *Company Weavers*, 108–28.

108 Hossain, 108–28.

to work for the Company's investment, could not change their place of residence nor sign new agreements and receive advances from other private traders, until the completion of the contract. All the details of the contract—the quantity of cloth to be provided, price of cloth, advances received—were required to be recorded on paper, binding the Resident on the part of the Company, and the weaver had to reciprocate by submitting the muchalika to the Commercial Resident.[109] The status of weavers as Company employees was formalised under Article 9 of the Proposed Regulations, whereby they were registered at the factory. Lists of weavers on the payroll of the Company were to be posted in the cutsherry of the Collector and obligatorily updated weekly or monthly. Moreover, the Commercial Resident had to submit a copy once in three months to the judge of the district.[110] The intention was to enable merchants and revenue as well as judicial officials to distinguish between the Company's weavers and the rest.

The Regulations also laid down penalty clauses in the case of non-fulfilment of the agreed contract. Weavers were liable to be prosecuted in the adawlut court for offences committed in violation of Article 4 of the1806 Commercial Regulation. No prosecuted weaver could work for private or bazaar sales until he completed his engagement on account of the Company's investment.

If weavers who were lagging in their deliveries to the Company sold the cloth to individuals, they had to refund to the Company the full amount received from the sale of these goods at the bazaar value "which shall exceed the ordinary prime cost of thread in them, in addition to the cost of the suit." [Article 6 of the 1806 Regulation] Moreover, in case of delay in providing cloth at the stipulated periods, the Commercial Resident was empowered to place peons over the weaver. [Article 5 of the 1806 Regulation] Legal control over the weaving activities appeared to be absolute, as it left no ground for weavers to work for others. Of particular relevance was the case of weavers employing more than one workman and owning more than one loom. They had to pay a penalty of 35 per cent of the stipulated price of every piece of cloth to the Company,

109 For details relating to the conditions in which weavers were engaged for the Company's investment, see Articles 1 to 7 in Proposed Coast Regulations, *JDC* 1, 49, 55, 57; Commercial Regulations for Weavers passed on 14 January 1806, Section II, clauses 1 to 8, *JDC* 14, 129–32.

110 Article 9 of Proposed Regulations, *JDC* 1, 65 and Section III of 1806 Regulation, *JDC* 14, 132.

in addition to returning the advance they received, when they failed to provide cloth as per their agreement.[111]

The next step was to place restrictions on the relationships that existed between weavers and dominant groups of the locality like zamindars, local administrative personnel like *talukdar*s (revenue collectors), and other less powerful landed elites like farmers and ryots. Often weavers acted contrary and declined the Company's credit, because of the influence of these groups.[112] Section V of the 1806 Regulation sought to negate these local alliances by making it clear that by no means could any person prevent individuals being engaged in the Company's employ.[113]

Weavers who appeared to have landed possessions were placed on par with ryots, and were subjected to similar regulations. However, the Company had created space for a few exceptions that would in turn prevent unnecessary interruption to its investment. By Article 2, section VII of the 1806 Regulation, weavers or any other persons connected with the provision of the Company's investment "should not be summoned by any native like proprietor, farmer of land or any other body dealing with the collection of rents from lands." While the Company intended to place the weavers and their production under the grip of legal provisions, it also promised at the same time to provide regular judicial procedural formats through which weavers could obtain justice against any offensive practice like unjust exactions and *batta* charges (allowance for daily expenses).[114]

If a weaver had a complaint against native agents, he was at first required to approach the Commercial Resident. But if the complaint was against commercial officials, then the weaver was allowed to take the issue directly to the Collector. On his part, if the Collector found the Commercial Resident or contractor attempting to suppress the truth, or if the answers provided by them were not convincing enough, he was empowered to take the case up to the Governor-in-Council. The only occasion when the weaver could approach the Presidency Government was when he was not satisfied with the proceedings followed by the

111 Article 4 of Proposed Regulations, 49 and Section II, Clauses 6 to 8, in 1806 Regulation, 131–32.

112 The influence exercised by zamindars and local administrative officials on various facets of the weaving world are detailed in Chapter 8.

113 Section V of 1806 Regulation, 134.

114 For rules relating to those weavers who had land, see Sections VII and VIII of 1806 Regulation, 135–37.

Collector. For this, weavers could go in a delegation of not more than ten members.[115] Under the new judicial machinery, the weaver could seek legal help only when he failed to obtain redress from the Commercial Resident. In such a situation, he could get his grievances settled by special orders from the Board of Trade or the Governor-in-Council.[116]

Directing the activities of private traders through legal provisions was yet another important method through which the Company wanted to achieve total control over textile production and marketing. The various clauses of the Regulations, therefore, sought to specify that no weaver indebted to the Company or in the service of the Company was allowed to give away its cloth to other traders, whether European or native.[117] They could not take up new contracts nor weave bazaar cloth. In the case of illegal private trading, weavers were liable to be prosecuted in the adawlut court, and if the charge was proved, they had to totally forfeit the cloth sold, in addition to bearing all costs and penalties.[118] However, the same regulation allowed the conditional procurement of weavers' services by private traders, provided the weavers had fulfilled their agreed contracts with the Company. Those weavers not under the Company's service were free to work their looms for anyone. But soon, the commercial officials at Masulipatnam factory were afraid that, if the weaver was provided a choice, the presence of competitors in the market would be detrimental to maximising procurement. Weavers, instead of being limited to the Company's service, usually preferred to join in private trading activities, where the conditions of work were less rigid and formal. In an effort to secure the weavers' services entirely for the Company, the Commercial Resident proposed to invite all registered weavers from the villages, through the orders of the Commercial Resident and the Resident, to work for the merchant or the contractor authorised to produce cloth. And the remaining weavers were also required to fulfil the contract, whenever necessary. Moreover, to avoid any alliance with private traders, the joint responsibility of weavers in a village was also restricted.[119]

115 See Article 11 of Proposed Regulations, 65, 67, 69 for details on this.

116 Ibid., 67, 69, 71.

117 1806 Regulation, 163–64.

118 Article 78 of Proposed Regulations, 57, 59, 61.

119 Section X of 1806 Regulation, related to transactions between private traders and weavers, 149.

Section XII of the 1806 Regulation provided for the control of gumastahs and all native servants at the factories. Gumastahs were liable to be convicted in the adawlut court for misdemeanours such as giving away the Company's cloth to other traders, obtaining extra sums from weavers out of the advances granted to them, manipulating accounts by maintaining false balances, etcetera. If the charges were established, the gumastahs had to pay double the value of the cloth sold or the money embezzled, alienated or exacted, and the punishment also included imprisonment extending up to a year. Further, the Board of Trade could recommend to the Governor-in-Council that they be removed from service.[120]

Through the legal provisions, the colonial authority tried to define the relationship of Commercial Residents and their native officers with the weavers. Under Section XII of the 1806 Regulation, Commercial Residents became liable for prosecution in the adawlut court, if they had not paid a proper price to the weavers as contracted or failed to settle the accounts fairly or collected unjust taxes from the weavers, and so on. Residents and their officers had to defend suits instituted against them at their own risk, and, further, Residents could also take upon themselves the defence of suits set up against their officers. Various clauses of regulations provide details as to how the process issued against Residents had to be served.[121]

This detailed account of the rules and regulations devised at the beginning of the nineteenth century underlines the manner in which the Company's structural, organisational, and legal re-arrangements created a space within the wider administrative structures, which enabled it to control the production of textiles. These modifications were essentially confined to the northern districts of Visakhapatnam and Godavari. There were perhaps three major reasons for this. First, the weavers in the southern districts of Masulipatnam and Guntur were not as agitated and restive. Second, there were no strongly entrenched intermediaries in the southern districts who needed to be displaced. Third, the Company's investment began to be focussed more sharply in the northern districts, thus requiring greater control.

These various structural alterations proceeded, however, on one premise—that dividend would lie in strengthening the caste nexus.

120 Punishments for gumastahs acting contrary to those rules laid down in 1806 Regulation, see Section XII, 150–51.

121 For details on these judicial procedures, see 1806 Regulation, 153–64.

Whether in revising the copdari system or integrating washermen into the production process, the Company relied on the potent power of caste.

The Company's intervention with the Coromandel weaver that lasted for over half a century was thus responsible for many changes in the production transactions. But in the end, it would seem, the various traditional groups retained, although in a truncated form, many of their customary powers . There were, however, others who were not so resilient and who almost totally succumbed to the hegemonic power of the Company. Most notable among them were the textile merchants of the northern Coromandel region.

SIX

Textile Traders in the Northern Coromandel

Marketing the finished fabric was of utmost importance in the textile economy. The product was marketed at several levels. Apart from village fairs and *santas* (weekly markets), where the rural buyers procured their cloth, there were also retail outlets in the towns. However, the textile merchant played the most crucial role in the transaction.

In the Coromandel region, many traders traditionally acted as the financiers of the textile economy, giving advances to the weavers and arranging for the distribution and marketing of the finished fabric. The arrival of the European companies, and, later, the political conquest of the region by the East India Company began to alter the status of the indigenous trading groups. The stage was set for the rise of the merchant.

PIECE-GOODS MERCHANTS

The textile trade in the Godavari and Visakhapatnam districts, dealing with long cloth and salempores of different denominations meant for the English Company's investment as well as that of others like the French and the Dutch, was handled by local merchants.[1] The East India Company's merchants were among the prosperous and wealthy sections of the trading groups.[2] Prior to 1757, the local merchants extensively utilised free-trading opportunities, without being harassed by political powers in the region. The merchant-contractors, who ought to have been the intermediate agents between the weaver and the Company, in fact, fulfilled their contracts with the assistance of the copdars, who were more powerful and dominant.

After the Peace of Paris in 1763, the competition among the three major companies—the French, the Dutch, and the English—further intensified.[3] To secure a firm hold over textile production, the colonial

1 Committee to Pigot, *PDC* 115A, 1–7.

2 Fullerton to Taylor, *GDR* 831, 41–49.

3 Arasaratnam, *Maritime Commerce and English Power*, 130; Yeates to BOT, 7 April 1788, *MDR* 2839, 178–80, enclosure, 7–9.

authority attempted to establish a direct commercial link with the weaving villages by eliminating merchants.

Under the new structural arrangements initiated in 1774 by Anthony Sadleir, merchants were not allowed to purchase superfine cloth without permission from the Commercial Resident.[4] Earlier, they could buy any of the varieties on behalf of the European companies and for their own private trade too. Moreover, with the 1774 changes compelling weavers to work only for the Company's merchants, many of them became indebted to local merchants who traded with the French in the region.[5]

One of the factors that precipitated the weavers' revolt in 1775 was the displacement of merchants from the export trade. The Company now had to necessarily accept the importance of this trading link. It realised the fact that it could recover all outstanding balances from the weavers only by employing merchants who could take on the credit and make repayments in one or two years.[6] Severe shortage of money for advances to continue the textile trade was yet another reason that forced the Madras Government to permit its officials as well as other European companies and Indian and European individuals to undertake private trade.[7]

In 1776, Hamilton, the Resident at Ingeram, formalised contracts with the principal merchants under the Ingeram and Maddepollam factories. Pragada Venkataramoodoo, Pandi Madirem, Cottah Mullah, Luckaumchitty Mulloo, Mokameddey Paupiah, Pedda Mulloo, Doum Balliah, Domtaumchilty Veerapah at Ingeram, and Chinta Comikiah, Comma Chitty Baupiah, Manna Mulloo, Chinta Narasimloo at Maddepollam were the twelve merchants who signed joint and separate bonds agreeing to be accountable to the Company for liquidating debts

4 For details on the structural arrangements initiated by Anthony Sadleir, see Chapter 5.

5 Testimony given by Gumdady Ramiah, a merchant of Samulcotah and others, Proceedings Relative to Sadleir, *PDS* 24 A, 21; Inquiry Committee Report, *PDS* 25; Testimony given by Rustumbadah weavers, *PDS* 24 A, 106–10; *PDS* 25.

6 Committee to Pigot, 1–7; Board of Trade's Resolution, 11 August 1776, *PDC* 115B, 403–05.

7 Arasaratnam, *Maritime Commerce and English Power*, Chapter 3, 94–127.

8 Alex Davidson, Resident, Ingeram, to George Stratham, Chief and Council, Fort St. George, Madras, 11 September 1776, *PDC* 116A, 512–14; Agreement executed by the Principal Merchants, Ingeram, 5 September 1776, *PDC* 116A, 515–16; Letter from Court of Directors, 14 October 1786, *CDDE* 1, 51–57, provides details on the terms of the contract.

incurred by weavers.[8] The bonds the weavers had entered into were distributed among these merchants. By this agreement, these merchants consented to provide goods at Tuni and its adjacent villages, because of the favour and protection they would get from the Company. However, in due course of time, they found themselves in difficulties as they could not recover the credit amounting to 11,000 pagodas from the weavers, many of whom had became insolvent and had absconded.

The local merchant group could not retain its hold over the Ingeram and Maddepollam factories for long. Individuals in the Company's administration managed to get into the textile trade and influenced the decisions of the local commercial officers. For instance, Seetiah, a kanakapillai at Maddepollam, and Jogee Pauntulu, dubash and renter at Nelapalli, started to trade in the Company's cloth from January 1778.[9]

In Godavari district, the traditional Bania traders lost their command over the provision of the Company's investment, as they could not comply with the new proposals. Local merchants Mantripragada Venkataramudoo and Masulukunta Jogee Pantulu agreed to provide the whole of the Ingeram interests, but without any security, and they wanted a commission of 10 per cent above the usual prices.[10]

There were Europeans also in the textile trade of the district. Quite often, these were officials of the Company trading on their own personal account. One such private merchant was Darwall who agreed to provide the goods, but like the local merchants also, insisted on 10 per cent higher returns. Nor did he offer to provide any security for the money advanced. Basil Cochrane, on the other hand, proffered lower prices and, in addition, "gave unquestionable security for the money advanced him."[11] As Cochrane's proposals were far more advantageous to the Company, the entire investment concerning Ingeram and Maddepollam factories were placed under his management for the 1786–1787 investment.

> The involvement of Europeans in the trading arena affected the weaving villages dramatically compared to local merchant groups, whose responsibility was limited to its nominal intermediary role. Basil Cochrane's involvement at the production process was total, as he

9 *PDC* 116 A, 515–16.

10 A similar problem arose in the case of chay good merchants who were not prepared to give security for undertaking the Company's investment.

11 Yeates to BOT, 179–80, enclosure, 1–23.

> introduced a new system in order to fulfil his contract. First, he fixed the prices of cloth, after taking the consent of the zamindars and head weavers. Then he entered into contracts with the weavers for a certain number of pieces of cloth, but he advanced money to them only for two pieces of cloth, for which he got their engagements. Accordingly, the weaver had to deliver to Basil Cochrane one piece monthly for which they were to be paid. Further that the cloth was to be measured and sorted in the central place in each Mootah and in the presence of the weavers and if any difference arose in the sorting, it was to be settled by arbitrators mutually chosen on the spot. A chop was affixed in the presence of the weaver on the punjum cloth received.[12]

A table of rates was fixed for inspection in every mootah and the name of every weaver in Cochrane's employ was registered in a book kept for the purpose that was open to whosoever chose to look at it.

Despite all this, Cochrane was not able to provide a regular investment to the Company. His failure demonstrated the preponderant influence exercised by English free merchants and Company officials, who had been carrying out the Company's investment concerns in the district earlier. Cochrane had appointed Jogee Pantulu as one of the merchants for conducting the actual transactions in the district and had also advanced him a large sum of money. He soon discovered that Jogee Pantulu was the dubash of Mathew Yeates, who had been involved in the textile trade earlier. Jogee Pantulu received money from Yeates in January 1788 to provide cloth and sent a great quantity of piece-goods to him. Jogee Pantulu then returned the cash he had taken from Cochrane, saying that it was not in his power to provide the Company's assortment of cloth.[13]

The lucrative trade and competition in textiles caused tension and strain among the European officials. This was reflected in a conflict between Yeates and Cochrane in 1788. Yeates attributed Cochrane's success in conducting his business to the special privileges and justice accorded to him by higher officials.[14] The Chief and Council of Masulipatnam were convinced that Cochrane would spare neither industry nor efforts in fulfilling the agreed contract and would succeed in restoring the Company's interests to the previous quantity and quality. They accepted his system of establishing direct links with weavers.[15]

12 Ibid.
13 Ibid., enclosure, 8.
14 Ibid., enclosure, 7–10.
15 Ibid., enclosure, 9–14

Cochrane started working towards the completion of his contract by seeking the assistance of merchants. However, when he realised that these merchants were not helpful, he attempted to keep all the weavers under his direct control, for which he got special favours from the Council and Board of Trade. Subsequently, in July 1787, the Company issued orders to all the principal zamindars, requesting them to extend all possible help to him. The zamindars obliged Cochrane by even sending peons at times to his assistance.[16]

Throughout his period of contract, Cochrane had to face steady opposition from Yeates in various ways—for instance, prohibiting the weavers from fulfilling their contracts with Cochrane, purchasing the cloth meant for Cochrane, or offering higher prices to the weavers.[17]

By February 1788, Basil Cochrane realised that native merchants had a powerful hold over the weavers. These merchants could supply a large quantity of the Company's assortments in four months that he could not do even in 12 months.[18] He was apprehensive of a continual debasement of the Company's investment if they were allowed to provide cloth to private traders. In order to prevent such a situation, he proposed a plan by which the earlier native merchants could again enter the Company's arena, provided they fulfilled certain conditions. These were:

1. The merchants had to pay the weavers the prices established by Cochrane.
2. As most of the combs with which the cloths were woven were in poor shape, the merchants were asked to replace them at their own expense.
3. Agreements native merchants entered into with the weavers had to stipulate that cloths should be manufactured with these combs and no others and had to specify the full quantity of thread put in them in order to provide cloth of Company's established lengths and breadths. These agreements should contain particulars such as the stipulated time schedule for the delivery of piece-goods. These contracts had to be given to the Resident and the Superintendents of looms and entered in the public register to be kept for that purpose.

16 Yeates to BOT, 7 April 1788, with Cochrane's observation in the way of reply, *MDR* 2839, 178–80, enclosure, 1–23, especially 8.

17 Yeates' correspondence with the Board of Trade, 31 August 1787, *MDR* 2839, 12–13; Walter Balfour, letter to Board of Trade, 13 November 1787, *MDR* 2839, 13–14.

18 Cochrane to Dick, 13 February 1788, *MDR* 2839, 17–18.

4. The native merchants had to provide a monthly list of those weavers from whom they collected cloth, specifying even the quantities.
5. Adequate support and encouragement would be given to the native merchants by the Resident and the Superintendents of the looms in pursuing their contracts, provided they accepted the conditions specified.[19]

Regardless, the Resident at the Ingeram factory opposed the plan on the ground that it would lead to the merchants' incurring heavy losses.

In almost all cases, old merchants were not able to provide security for the money that they got as advance from the Company. The reasons for such inability or unwillingness varied from district to district. In Godavari district, the trade in textiles was only one among the many other business concerns they were engaged in. As Fullerton, the Commercial Resident, pointed out, they were the big merchants and were able to influence the rest. They might have registered in the Company's list mainly to secure its protection and the credit advanced by the Company annually. These merchants were unwilling to give the required security as it constituted a risk, and, besides, they did not really need the business. By the 1790s, however, the merchants lost many of the privileges, and had only a few monetary benefits besides the protection they could get.[20]

The Company had ultimately realised the necessity of conducting its operations through the copdars.

The Chay Goods Merchants

The European textile trade in Masulipatnam district was essentially in chay goods. Between 1766 and 1780, a group of eight merchants had catered to the demand for chay goods. They were referred to as the Company merchants or 'black merchants'.[21] Their attachment to the textile trade of the region was long-standing, dating back to the seventeenth century.[22]

19 Yeates to BOT, enclosure, 15.
20 Fullerton to Taylor, *GDR* 831, 41–49.
21 Samuel Statham, Warehouse Keeper, Masulipatnam, to Charles Floyer, Chief, Masulipatnam, 26 July 1786, *MDR* 2900 A, 5–19.
22 The diaries of Streynsham Master refer to a contract signed in March 1678 which mentions the names of Majeti Guruvanna and Mamidi Mallappa, whose family names also appear in the eighteenth-century list given in Statham to Floyer, *MDR* 2900 A, 5–19. R. C. Temple (ed.), *Diaries of Streynsham Master (1677–79)* (London: John Murray for the Government of India, 1911), 146–47, cited in K. Satyanarayana, *A Study of the History and Culture of the Andhras* 2 (New Delhi: People's Publishing House, 1983), 587.

The East India Company's procurement of chay goods was organised through the system of advances that rested on its contractual agreements with the merchants. The Company advanced money to the merchants, who were then responsible for the regular delivery of goods.[23] Elsewhere, the Company gave advances either in cash or as raw material, especially yarn for weaving, thus echoing more closely the so-called putting-out system or *verlag* system of Europe.[24] Here, in Masulipatnam, however, the Company offered only monetary credit.[25] The Company itself was in no way concerned with the balances in the hands of the weavers or about the mode of acquiring cloth.[26]

The procurement of manufactures through advances and the conditions attached to it in Masulipatnam were very similar to the *dadni* method that was widely prevalent in Bengal, Gujarat and other parts of India in the eighteenth century.[27] The English were continuing a practice probably introduced to the region by the Dutch.[28] In Bengal, the Company successfully eliminated the merchant intermediary and began to deal directly with the weavers through gumastahs.[29] In

23 A. Campbell, Fort St. George, to Charles Floyer, Chief, Masulipatnam, 27 February 1787, *MDR* 2900 A, 126–27.

24 For a discussion of the verlag system in Europe, see Hermann Kellenberg, "The Organization of Industrial Production", in E. E. Rich and C. H. Wilson (eds.), *The Cambridge Economic History of Europe* 5 (Cambridge: Cambridge University Press, 1977), 469–70.

25 The Company attempted to persuade the local merchants to accept English broadcloth in lieu of part of the advance. But they refused to agree to this, perhaps because the local demand for broadcloth declined considerably, especially after the forces of the zamindars and other magnates were disbanded. See Sadleir to Dent, *MDR* 2841, 58–66.

26 Campbell to Floyer, *MDR* 2900 A, 126–27.

27 For a discussion on the dadni system in Bengal, see Sushil Chaudhury, "Merchants, Companies and Rulers: Bengal in the Eighteenth Century", *Journal of the Economic and Social History of the Orient* 31, 1988, 74–109; Binoy Shankar Mallick, "English Trade and Indigenous Finance in Bengal and Gujarat in the Seventeenth Century: A Study of the Dadni System and the Rate of Interest", *Studies in History* 2, no. 1 (new series), 1986, 31–45; Hossain, *Company Weavers*, 85–87; Mitra, *Cotton Weavers of Bengal*, 45–47, 57. On the dadni system in Bihar, see Sinha, *Textile Industry in Bihar*, Chapter 4, 64–87.

28 W. Foster (ed.), *English Factories in India, 1622–24* (Oxford: Oxford University Press, 1907), 104, quoted in A. I. Chicherov, *India: Economic Development in the 16th-18th centuries: An Outline History of Crafts and Trade* (Moscow: Nauka Publishers, 1971), 120.

29 Mitra, *Cotton Weavers of Bengal*, 45–49.

Masulipatnam, however, it continued to follow the traditional system till 1814 when the factory itself was closed down.[30]

The Company worked through middlemen even two decades after acquiring political control over the region. Some of the weaving centres lay in the adjacent territories of the Nizam, and the Company was therefore compelled to employ agents or merchants for making its chay goods investment. Guntur district, known for its chay root and thread, and as a major area of residence of the weavers, was under the control of the Nizam till 1788. Any attempt by the Company to deal directly with these weavers may have led to political chagrin stemming from administrative disputes.[31]

A major obstacle in the Company's march towards complete commercial control was, however, the activity of private traders, in particular, the French merchants and the French East India Company.[32] They constituted a serious threat to the ambition of the English Company to acquire a monopsonistic position in the chay goods trade of Masulipatnam.[33] In order to check private-trading activities, the Company sought to impose tighter controls over its merchants. They were asked, for instance, not to make fresh contracts with any other company or private dealers, without seeking its prior permission.[34]

Nonetheless, merchant communities in the region began to take advantage of the expanding trade in chay goods. A new group of eight

30 The decline in chay goods investment, from 80,000 Madras pagodas in 1787 to a mere 7,194 in 1813, was one of the reasons for the 1813 decision to close down the factory at Masulipatnam. See extract of letter from Secretary, Board of Trade, Madras, 21 September 1813, *MDR* 2904, 1–4, and extract of a General Letter from England, 13 May 1813, loc.cit., 22–23.

31 The Chief's Minute on the question of balances due by the Company's merchants, nd, [1787], *MDR* 2900 A, 137–42.

32 Ian Bruce Watson, *Foundation for Empire: English Private Trade in India, 1659–1760* (Delhi: Vikas Publishing House, 1980), discusses the role of private traders in the seventeenth and eighteenth centuries.

33 For details of French activities in the Coromandel region during the late eighteenth century, see Arasaratnam, *Maritime Commerce and English Power*, 121–23. Similarly, for Bengal, see Hossain, *Company Weavers*, 79–82.

34 Corbrett to BOT, *GDR* 832, 412–40. Using the Company's advances to produce cloth and then to turn it over to private traders is akin to the "embezzlement" of raw material in the European putting-out system described in John Styles, "Embezzlement, Industry and the Law in England, 1500–1800", in Maxine Berg et al, *Manufacture in Town and Country Before the Factory* (Cambridge: Cambridge University Press, 1983), 173–210.

traders entered into contracts with the French through Manapaka Ramanah Naick, a prosperous and powerful merchant, who had been engaged by Moresein, the French Agent at Pondicherry, to supply chay goods. These dealers belonged, as can be seen from their family names, to the same groups who had already agreed to deal only with the English East India Company. They agreed to provide chay goods in alliance with merchants belonging to a different family and were held jointly responsible for the advances that they received from the chief merchant.[35] Such joint contracts must have been entered into to minimise risks and to get round the problems of limited capital.

These merchants appear to have operated in neatly demarcated spheres of commercial influence, with each having jurisdiction over some weaving villages. Caste and kinship networks also appear to have been limited to specific zones within the district.[36]

The weaver too was able to retain substantial economic freedom and often entered into contracts with more than one trader.[37] Such flexibility was possible because of the intense competition for chay goods encouraged by the entry of a multitude of companies and private individuals into the trade. Indeed, complaints were voiced by officials of the Company that weavers were supplying finer quality textiles to other European companies and to private traders. The new competition may have thus contributed to the demise of the symbiotic relationship between merchant and weaver that had existed in the seventeenth century.[38]

35 Consultation of 6 May 1786, *MDR* 2837, 46–74.

36 Information derived from statements for 1787 on balances due from the weavers to the Company's merchants, *MDR* 2900 B, 280–307.

37 Extract of letter, 2 June 1789, in BOT to Sadleir, 23 June 1789, *MDR* 2901, 7–38.

38 For a discussion on the paternalistic links between merchant and weaver, see Arasaratnam, *Merchants, Companies and Commerce*, 269–70. Ashin Dasgupta suggests that even in the pre-modern economy, the weaver was free to go to the highest bidder: "Indian Merchants and the Trade of the Indian Ocean" in Ray Chaudhuri, Tapan and Irfan Habib (eds.) *The Cambridge Economic History of India, c 1200–c 1700* (Delhi: Cambridge University Press in association with Orient Longman, 1987), 419. However, given the ideology of pre-capitalist relations exemplified in the paternalistic symbiosis referred to by Arasaratnam, it is unlikely that the weaver could have dared to exercise in practice the freedom he possessed in theory.

However, by 1786, the eight merchants trading in chay goods owed 18,000 Madras pagodas to the Company.[39] This was due to the non-fulfilment of contractual obligations by weavers to whom advances had been given, caused by factors such as war and related disturbances in the region.[40] While some of the merchants managed to hold their ground, others became virtually bankrupt.[41] The declining status of the regular merchants was reflected in the contemptuous manner in which they were treated by the Company and its officials. Their petitions were sometimes ignored, they received receipts for smaller amounts than they had actually deposited, and they were, on occasion, even treated with deliberate discourtesy.[42]

In 1787, the Company introduced the system of imposing a penalty on defaulters who failed to deliver goods and demanded a deposit from the merchants who wished to trade with the Company. The advertisement of the Company issued in 1787 stated, *inter alia*, that there should be more than one contractor, and that each contractor should agree to furnish security, and to pay a penalty if unable to fulfil the contract.[43] The old merchants as well as the emerging new merchants could not provide any security as that would have entailed further outlay of already scarce capital.[44]

The new clauses introduced by the Company, therefore, not only pushed the traditionally dominant merchant families out of the trading scene, but also appear to have fractured what must have been a much more cohesive mercantile community.[45]

39 Chief's Minute, *MDR* 2900 A, 139. For details of the amounts owed, see Statham to Floyer, *MDR* 2900 A, 5–19. Of this debt, the Company expected to recover only 3500 pagodas.

40 Statham to Floyer, 5–19; see also Chief's Minute, 138–42, especially 139, 140; Representation of the Company's merchants to Anthony Sadleir, Chief, Masulipatnam, August 1787, *MDR* 2838, 156–59.

41 Representation of Maumedi Lingiah, Company Merchant, to Anthony Sadleir, Chief, Masulipatnam, 24 September 1787, *MDR* 2900 A, 239–44 (also found in *MDR* 2838, 245). See also the evidence given by Kottagundu Ramiah, in Consultation, 6 May 1786, *MDR* 2837, 78–80.

42 See petition dated 10 September 1787 from Annam Lingiah and others to Anthony Sadleir, Chief, Masulipatnam, *MDR* 2838, 226-28 and also their undated petition, 228–29.

43 Anthony Sadleir, Chief, Masulipatnam, to A. Campbell, Board of Commerce [hereafter BOC], Fort St. George, 29 August 1787, *MDR* 2838, 185–88.

44 Representation of the Company's Merchants to Anthony Sadleir, Chief, Masulipatnam, *MDR* 2900 A, 171 onwards.

45 For a discussion on merchant guilds in the region, see Satyanarayana, *History and Culture of the Andhras* 2, 363–64.

The Company's commercial motives forced it to make some concessions to the new groups that were emerging in the chay goods trade. Out of the many proposals submitted in Masulipatnam for the investment of 1788, that of Sadasiva Naick, resident of Masulipatnam and a leading *sahukar* (native banker) and merchant, was accepted by the Chief and Council.[46] Sadasiva Naick did not agree to give any security, arguing that it would go against the principles of the sahukars, especially as it would diminish his credit worthiness in the community.[47] Even more significantly, he created a new trading precedent in the region by asking for a monopoly over the trade in chay goods, declaring that during the period of the contract the Company should not enter into any agreement with any other merchant nor directly trade in the goods.[48]

As Sadasiva Naick had extensive business contacts with the merchants of the Guntur circar, Company officials may have concluded that he would revitalise the critically deteriorated supplies of chay root and thread to the weavers. It may also have been hoped that the granting of monopoly trading rights to Sadasiva Naick would reduce competition, and thereby prices of the various chay goods. Moreover, because of the new commercial terms, the Company was not able to find bidders for the provision of the investment, despite the efforts of the officials to advertise and publicise the opportunities available. The situation was, in fact, so desperate that the Company attempted, although unsuccessfully, to persuade the Armenians and other local traders, who had been dealing in chay goods for a long time, but had refrained from participating in the new investment, to return to the business.[49]

The rise of Sadasiva Naick to a pre-eminent position as the sole trader in chay goods in the Masulipatnam region marked the virtual eclipse of the traditional textile merchants. However, his monopoly

46 Sadleir to Campbell, *MDR* 2838, 185–88. Naick, or Nayak, is a suffix or title given to an important Telugu warrior group that dispersed after the decline of the Vijayanagar empire. See N. Karashima, *South Indian History and Society: Studies from Inscriptions, AD 850–1800* (New Delhi: Oxford University Press, 1984), 159–65. See also J. F. Richards, *Mughal Administration in Golconda* (Oxford: Oxford University Press, 1975), 18–19. It is worth speculating whether some of these warriors transformed themselves into merchants. Thurston 5, 138–40, points out that some Telugu Balijas, among others, took the name Nayak. It is more likely that Sadasiva Naick belonged to this community.

47 Sadleir to Campbell, 185–88.

48 Proposal of Sadasiva Naick, 25 August 1787, *MDR* 2838, 180–84.

49 Anthony Sadleir, Chief, Masulipatnam, n.d. [September 1787], *MDR* 2838, 232–42.

position was shortlived. Although Naick fulfilled his contractual obligations, and that too to the complete satisfaction of the authorities, it was felt that the Company could minimise its risk by dividing the investment between Sadasiva Naick and another merchant. Sadasiva Naick initially did not agree to sharing the investment but was ultimately prevailed upon to do so.[50] Within a couple of years, the Company accepted the proposal of Manapaka Ramanah Naick, who agreed in 1791 to provide half the Company's total demand for chay goods.[51] He and Sadasiva Naick thereupon signed a joint contract by which they would receive 41,000 Madras pagodas each for the year 1791–92.[52]

Why did the local merchants meekly accept the hegemony of the Company? Lack of unity among them and the fact that the Company had become a monopsonistic buyer may be the key reasons. The similarly placed dadni merchants in Bengal were able to fend off the Company's efforts to impose controls to such an extent that they forced it to appease them with special incentives.[53] Even merchants of Godavari district, not far from Masúlipatnam, were able, partly because of their more diversified business interests, to resist the Company's attempts to insist on contractual clauses relating to the provision of securities and the payment of penalties.[54]

Some of the traditional merchant families in the chay goods business for a long time were peripheralised. Even more, the new mercantile atmosphere broke up existing caste, kin, and family networks, leading to a more individualised entrepreneurial system and increased competition.

The Mogul Merchants

While the chay goods merchants of Masulipatnam succumbed to the political and economic pressures exerted by the East India Company, there was one group of traders which steadfastly stood independent—Persian merchants, long domiciled in Masulipatnam, trading almost

50 Commercial Department letter, 21 April 1791, *MDR* 2841, 38–40.

51 Proposal of Sadasiva Naick addressed to Anthony Sadleir, 10 April 1791, *MDR* 2841, 40–42, and proposal of Manapaka Ramanah Naick, 10 April 1791, 44–54.

52 See the joint proposal of Sadasiva Naick and Manapaka Ramanah Naick, 20 April 1791, *MDR* 2841, 55–58.

53 For details, see Sushil Chaudhury, "Merchants, Companies and Rulers", 74–109.

54 Fullerton to Taylor, 45.

solely in chintz.[55] These Mogul merchants, as they were termed in contemporary records, controlled, along with their compatriots in Persia, the westward trade of Masulipatnam with the Persian Gulf.[56]

The role of such diasporic merchants, described by Philip Curtin as "cross-cultural brokers", appears to have been critical and significant in the building up of long-distance commercial networks and in the development of early modern trade.[57]

Persian merchants were known to have operated in Masulipatnam from at least the late sixteenth century.[58] With the support of the Qutab Shahis of Golconda, these immigrants settled down in Masulipatnam, becoming shipowners, administrators and merchants. Striking roots in the various localities of this port city, they slowly carved out a special place for themselves in the textile economy of the district by the latter half of the eighteenth century.[59]

From Bandar Bourchar on the west coast of Persia through Muscat to Surat, Bombay, and Goa, there were many markets for the multicoloured chintz fabrics of Masulipatnam.[60] By the second half of the eighteenth century, trade in Masulipatnam chintz was almost totally cornered by the Mogul merchants, their only major rivals being the other diasporic community in

55 In 1820, there were 12 Mogul merchants listed: Aga Syed Media, Hajee Ali Kherman, Aga Abdulla, Aga Mahomed Sadik, Aga Ali Khaja, Aga Syed Turkey, Aga Mahomed Nabi, Aga Caseem Ispahany, Aga Mahomed, Aga Media Ispahany, Meerja Abdulla and Meerja Abdul Kareem. These being the principal merchants, it may be presumed there were other lesser merchants, too, belonging to this expatriate community. See Agent to the principal Mogul merchants to Collector, Masulipatnam, 5 July 1820, *MDR* 3083, 197–98. For similar lists of Mogul merchants in 1812 and 1820, see William Thackeray to BOR, 29 December 1812, *PBR* 599 (1813), 18–58, and D. Hill to BOR, 30 January 1821, *PBR* 876 (1821), 997–1031.

56 G. Westcott, Sea Customs Collector, Masulipatnam, to Charles Floyer, Chief, Masulipatnam, 18 November 1786, *MDR* 2900 A, 94–95.

57 See Philip Curtin, *Cross-Cultural Trade in World History* (Cambridge: Cambridge University Press, 1984); A. J. Qaiser, "The Role of Brokers in Medieval India", *Indian Historical Review* 12, 1974, 225; R. W. Ferrier, "The Armenians and the East India Company in Persia in the Seventeenth and Early Eighteenth Centuries", *The Economic History Review* 26, nos. 1–4, 1973, 38–62; M. N. Pearson, "Brokers in Western Indian Port-Cities: Their Role in Servicing Foreign Merchants", *Modern Asian Studies* 22, no. 3, 1988, 455–72.

58 Sanjay Subrahmanyam, "Persians, Pilgrims and Portuguese: The Travails of Masulipatnam Shipping in the Western Indian Ocean, 1590–1665", *Modern Asian Studies* 22, no. 3, 1988, 503–30.

59 The 1871 Census gives the figure of 2074 Moguls, who, it may be assumed, were kin of the original Persian immigrants. Mackenzie, *KDM*, 383.

60 Westcott to Floyer, *MDR* 2900 A, 95–114.

the area, the Armenians.[61] They marketed the textiles internally, too, in places such as Poona, Aurangabad, Gujarat, Broach, and Cambay.[62]

In the seventeenth century, the chintz preferred in Persia was the expensive Golconda cotton paintings used as floor coverings and bedspreads in elite households, and as linings of coats.[63] By the second half of the eighteenth century, however, the more common, cheaper varieties of chintz, particularly those used by common folk, predominated, although the richer fabrics used as furnishings by the well-to-do continued to retain a share of the trade.[64]

The Mogul merchants, in attempting to monopolise the chintz trade, tried to control the production process as well. Unlike the chay goods merchants, these dealers supplied all the necessary raw material to the artisans and paid them a wage for their services. Quite clearly, the Mogul merchants were using an advanced form of the putting-out method, in which the seeds of a capitalist production system can be discerned.[65] The growing demand for chintz compelled these traders to look for other hubs of production besides Masulipatnam. They managed to get chintz produced for them at nearby centres such as Cocanada, Nursapur, and Palakollu.[66]

The Mogul merchants were able to organise the movement of cloth so efficiently possibly because of the existence of a large Islamic mercantile community.[67] They depended on their network of correspondents and business associates residing at different places such as Hyderabad and Bombay.[68] Some of them traded independently, others

61 R. W. Ferrier, "Armenians and the EIC", 38–70, 84. See also Chaudhuri, *Trading World of Asia*, 225–26; Westcott to Floyer, enclosures, *MDR* 2900 A, 99–112.

62 Westcott to Floyer, 94–95.

63 John Irwin, "Indian Textile Trade", 28–44.

64 For a list of chintz goods exported by the Mogul merchants to Persia, see Westcott to Floyer, 94–114; Discussions on chintz manufacture can be found in *Homage to Kalamkari*, especially John Irwin's "The Significance of Chintz", 79–85. Chaudhuri, *Trading World of Asia*, 227, suggests that the impoverishment of the affluent classes after the civil war in Persia led to the increase in demand for cheaper fabrics.

65 Hill to BOR, *PBR* 876 (1821), 997–1002.

66 Ibid., 997–1002, especially 1000.

67 For a brief description of the Islamic mercantile community in the region, see Arasaratnam, *Merchants, Companies and Commerce*, 218-19.

68 Representation of Hajee Mohammed, Mogul merchant, addressed to Thomas Oakes, Collector, 4th Division, Masulipatnam, 19 February 1798, *MDR* 3073 A, 135–36. See also the petition of Mogul merchants to George Edward Russell, Collector of Masulipatnam, 5 July 1820, *MDR* 3083, 197–98.

set up joint trade with cloth merchants at Persia, while some others acted as gumastahs or agents of merchants in Persia.[69]

Like many merchants of the early modern period, the Mogul merchants managed the financial aspects of their long-distance trade through sophisticated methods of fund transfers. The returns from the Persian market were in the form of gold and silver, both as coin and bullion. This was exchanged at Bombay for government bills drawn on Masulipatnam and Madras, so that payment could be credited quickly.[70]

Apart from the marketing advantages these traders enjoyed by virtue of their useful relationships and traditional linkages, their cloth was also cheaper than the cloth re-exported from Europe by the Company, thus rendering the competition unequal.[71]

The Company could have used its newly acquired political power to totally decimate this competition, as the Commercial Resident of Masulipatnam suggested it should.[72] Indeed, attempts were made by local officials to intervene in the chintz trade in various ways, with, presumably, the objective of controlling the competition. Company officials sought to systematically and deliberately cripple or, at any rate, hamper the trade of the Mogul merchants, but with no success. The major, perhaps the sole, reason for this was that the long-term imperial strategic considerations outweighed the short-term commercial gains that might have accrued, and effectively shaped the overall policy. It was this factor that was responsible, more than anything else, for the Company being prevented from adopting a harsher attitude towards the Mogul merchants.

There were two critical circumstances that determined the British attitude towards the Mogul merchants. One was the strategic consideration dictated by the geopolitics of the West Asian region.[73] The other was the increasing importance of Persia as an expanding market for imports from Europe as well as India. In the beginning of the nineteenth century, several missions to Persia undertaken by John Malcolm resulted, *inter alia*, in the signing of commercial treaties

69 William Thackeray, Chief Secretary to the Government, Fort St. George, to BOR, 29 December 1812, *PBR* 599 (1813), 27.

70 Hill to BOR, 997–1002.

71 V. Corbrett, Commercial Resident, Masulipatnam, to E. W. Fallofield, President, BOT, Madras, 4 February 1795, *GDR* 832, 403–11.

72 Ibid.

73 Ravinder Kumar, *India and the Persian Gulf Region, 1858–1907: A Study in British Imperial Policy* (Bombay, Asia Publishing House, 1965), 10–11.

securing better conditions for European commodities and the East India Company.[74] While the Company may have perceived the Mogul merchants as rivals in the Persian market, it could not afford to antagonise the Persian ruler by pressurising his people in Masulipatnam.

It was this realisation that prompted the Company to react with alacrity to the rumour that the Mogul merchants had sent a petition of protest regarding higher taxation rates to Persia, and that their agents in Persia had also complained to the British Ambassador at Teheran to the same effect. Quick to respond to such complaints and attempting to appease the merchants, the Company set up an inquiry committee, only to be told that no complaints had in fact been made.[75]

In 1814, the Mogul merchants represented to the Governor of the Madras Presidency that the newly introduced practice of subjecting their packed export goods to two inspections and two valuations, once for the land customs and once for the sea customs, was causing them undue hardship and delay.[76] The Governor-in-Council responded immediately and instructed the Board of Trade to ensure that "all reasonable indulgence and every possible facility" was extended to the merchants.[77] The Board of Revenue, to which similar instructions were issued, informed the Collector of Masulipatnam that he should "take such steps in conjunction with the Commercial Resident for the collection of the land and sea custom duties payable by these merchants as will relieve them from the charge and inconvenience of double packages."[78]

Similarly, when the merchants requested the Collector to accept some collateral as security in lieu of the duty they could not pay because of a temporary cash flow problem, the Board of Revenue authorised the Collector to do so, "in consideration of the expediency of encouraging the trade between the Northern Circars and the Persian Gulph." [*sic*][79]

74 John Malcolm's testimony, Minutes of Evidence before the House of Lords, London, 1813, in *Parliamentary Committee Reports / Minutes* (available at the National Archives of India, New Delhi), 17–24, 94, 684–702.

75 Thackeray to BOR, *PBR* 599 (1813), 18–58.

76 Representation of Mogul merchants at Masulipatnam to Lt. General John Abercromby, President and Governor-in-Council, Madras, 16 May 1814, *MDR* 2961, 293–96.

77 D. Hill, Chief Secretary to the Government of Madras, to the President, BOT, 31 May 1814, *MDR* 2961, 291–92.

78 BOR to Collector, Masulipatnam, 9 June 1814, *MDR* 2961, 289–90.

79 Secretary, BOR, to Collector, Masulipatnam, 30 May 1814, and Secretary, BOR, to the Chief Secretary to the Government, 30 May 1814, *MDR* 2961, 245–46 and 285–86.

Again, to avoid possible complaints from the Mogul merchants about overvaluation of their goods when customs duties were being levied, the Board of Revenue proposed that the Collector should be empowered to reduce the existing valuation if it exceeded the wholesale market price.[80] Thus, the Company, which could strongly assert its political power over other merchant groups such as the Telugu Nayaks, was virtually unable to make a dent in the trade of these Persian merchants.

Nevertheless, it did not desist from attempting to compete with them in the import of European chintz into the markets of Persia. In the beginning, the price advantage lay with Masulipatnam chintz, which was particularly popular with the Persian masses, European chintz being consumed only in small quantities by the elite.[81] By 1813, however, the situation had been reversed, and English chintz, now cheaper than the Masulipatnam product, flooded the Persian markets.[82] The English tried to increase their leverage in the market by copying Indian designs.[83] Interestingly, however, Masulipatnam chintz was able to hold its own till the 1830s, when, in fact, it was able to increase its share in the market by virtue of its greater durability and the fastness of the colours.

The Mogul merchants had to contend not only with the English competition but also with other factors that affected their trade, such as unstable political conditions and epidemics such as the plague in Persia during this period.[84] However, they were flexible and quickly adapted to changing conditions. For example, in 1849, they sent their chintz to Bombay through a circuitous route via Bellary only to avoid the payment of the frontier duties they would have been charged if the goods had been despatched by the direct route via Hyderabad.[85]

80 Secretary, BOR, to the Chief Secretary to the Government, 7 March 1814, *MDR* 2961, 143–45. Ultimately, the Madras Government made such a decision generally applicable, requiring Collectors to ensure that tariffs corresponded to wholesale prices, circular letter of BOR, 28 March 1814, *MDR* 2961, 164–70.

81 Malcolm's testimony, the House of Lords, 684–96.

82 I. Goldingham, Collector, Masulipatnam, to BOR, 21 November 1836, *MDR* 6318, 310–12.

83 The British, in fact, learnt the art of making chintz only in the eighteenth century. For a discussion on this, see *Homage to Kalamkari*, 29–79. The use of Indian designs, sometimes imported as chinoiserie, was not only to cater to the new taste for the 'oriental', it was also to compete with Indian fabric in world markets.

84 Goldingham to BOR, *MDR* 6318, 310–12.

85 R. T. Porter, Collector, Masulipatnam, to Collector of Bellary, 30 October 1849, *MDR* 6402, 213.

The Mogul merchants survived, therefore, into the 1840s, despite the increasing competition from Britain. They undoubtedly contributed to the perpetuation of the weaving and printing industry of Masulipatnam and its neighbourhood, even after the closure of the factory there.

It has been recently argued that political upheavals in Golconda contributed to the decline of the Persian merchants of Masulipatnam by the 1680s.[86] The evidence available from the East India Company records, however, indicates that even if they had indeed virtually disappeared, they had been buoyant enough to reappear with renewed vigour. In fact, as we have seen, the Mogul merchants proved to be more resilient and aggressive than other mercantile groups in Masulipatnam. This was, no doubt, partly due to the Company's desire to mollify them; at the same time, it was their commercial acumen that enabled them to perceive the possibilities of turning circumstances to their advantage and to display a remarkable and unparalleled staying power.

The early modern mercantile environment of Masulipatnam has been described as a constantly changing scene in which merchants and caste groups appeared and disappeared.[87] The emergence of the Naicks is an example of this, while the persistence of the Mogul merchants is a refutation of this proposition. Indeed, it can be argued that, overall, the merchants of Masulipatnam, chay goods traders as well as those who dealt in chintz, survived all the vicissitudes of economic and political changes. Elsewhere in India, merchant groups appear to have gradually lost their economic power, yielding place to other functionaries like gumastahs.[88] In Masulipatnam, however, although the Company made considerable inroads into the merchants' territory, they remained influential and viable till the end. The situation in the other districts of the region, especially in Godavari district, was markedly different, as the Company was much more successful here in eliminating the merchant.

Regional Markets and Merchants

The textile economy of Godavari district included Muslim merchants who controlled a sizable part of the region's trade. These merchants,

86 Subrahmanyam, "Persians, Pilgrims and Portuguese", 503–30.

87 Arasaratnam, *Merchants, Companies and Commerce*, 347.

88 Amiya Kumar Bagchi, "Merchants and Colonialism" in D. N. Panigrah (ed.), *Economy, Society and Politics in Modern India* (New Delhi: Vikas Publishing House, 1985), 12.

called Nursapur traders, played a very conspicuous role in the commercial activities of the early nineteenth century, and even up to 1853. A considerable proportion of these merchants traded with places in Burma, especially Rangoon and Pegu. This was a long-standing connection lasting from two to four decades. They dealt in textiles as well as articles such as betel nuts.[89]

There were some dominant families firmly entrenched in the textile trade of the northern Coromandel. These families did not restrict themselves to contracts with the companies, but often made individual or private trade agreements with a number of merchants. Besides textiles, they dealt in grain. The Maumedis were an important Komati merchant family in this region. Members of this family covered many trading activities in the late eighteenth century. Maumedi Lingiah, for instance, was in the Company's employment from 1766 along with seven other native merchants. Earlier, he had entered into contracts with the French and the Dutch for supplying textiles.[90] In 1786, his brother, Maumedi Reddy, proposed an agreement with the French Agent, Ramanah Naick, to provide chay goods.[91] This family enjoyed considerable economic status during this period. Maumedi Lingiah possessed an estate of about 5 or 6 thousand pagodas in 1766. Nonetheless, because of losses sustained due to non-payment by weavers, he was not in a position to maintain his family or discharge the balance he owed the Company. Even so, he offered to take up the Company's investment in 1787.[92]

Another aspect of the northern Coromandel textile economy was the inter-regional trade managed by a specific group of merchants. A considerable portion of the textile trade to the Nizam's territories during this period was in the hands of Muslim merchants such as Somma Khan, Emom Mohuddeen, Saib Hussain, Meseree Khan, Ebram Baig, Audeem Veig, and Akburally Saib. One of the hinterland trade routes ran between Hyderabad, Valegundu, Pendalapaka, and Battiprole and Addapully in Guntur district. The last two places were noted for red- and black-dyed cloth. In nearby villages such as Conatypooram, Iyalavaram, Doolepoody, and Rajavole, weavers produced piece-goods. The Muslim merchants

89 I. Prendergast, Collector, Rajahmundry, to G. D. Williams, Commissioner for the Investigation of Claims for Compensation by British Subjects in Burma, 7 December 1853, *GDR* 6746, 73–78.

90 Statham to Floyer, *MDR* 2900 A, 5–19.

91 Consultation, 6 May 1786, 46–74.

92 Ibid.

exported these varieties to Hyderabad, Bombay, and other towns, three or four times a year.[93]

The trade with Jalna and Masulipatnam passed through Tandicondah chowki, a major weaving centre. At Tandicondah, there were 50 looms and 20 Bania houses, whose weaving and trading activities enabled Guntur's trade with the rest of the region. Merchants from other districts came to this village for piece-goods, tobacco, ghee, and many other articles. This route was especially popular because transit duties could be paid at Tandicondah chowki itself.[94]

The nature of the trading networks used in the regional trade as well as for reaching more distant markets demonstrates clearly that merchants relied as much on custom, tradition, and family ties as on adapting quickly to a changing commercial environment. This was most evident in the case of the Masulipatnam merchants, who, as has been shown, were able to use their kinship linkages to maximum advantage. Ethnic ties too were an important element in traditional mercantile operations.[95] In Masulipatnam, this aspect was particularly visible in the case of the Mogul merchants and the Muslim Nursapur traders.

In the region as a whole, the traditional merchant communities were drastically affected by the Company's commercial strategies, most of them becoming marginalised and restricted primarily to regional trade. Some of them were, however, able to reap advantages even from this, and continued their business through all the colonial transformations, even into the twentieth century.

Even within the new commercial world constructed by the Company, merchants were powerful enough to seriously influence other elements. Among other issues, their operations may have contributed to the unrest and agitation of the weavers in the northern Coromandel during the period under study.

93 Arze addressed by merchants and sahukars residing at Battiprole and Addapally villages of Repalli division to I. Goldingham, Acting Collector, 30 September 1837, *gudr* 5393, 183–92.

94 Arze addressed by the Banias, weavers, ryots, of the four divisions of the village Tandicondah to I. Goldingham, Collector, Guntur, 8 October 1837, *gudr* 5393, 195–97.

95 Michelguglielmo Torri, "Ethnicity and Trade in Surat during the Dual Government Era, 1759–1800", *IESHR* 27, no. 4, 1990, 377–405.

SEVEN

Agitations in the Northern Coromandel

The restructuring and realignments in the textile economy of the northern Coromandel impacted greatly on the social and political relations of the weaver at the village level. From about 1765 to 1850, the Company had attempted to alter the processes and transactions of production in many ways, resulting in the virtual subordination of the primary weaver. In time the weavers countered the Company's steps and thereby created new tensions and strains.

The weaving community of the northern Coromandel had a tradition of reacting strongly to situations that it thought threatened its interests.[1] Elsewhere in India, handloom weavers expressed their discontent in a concrete form only when their industry was affected by the entry of machine-made goods from Europe.[2] Artisans were prominent in the riots in Rohilkhand and Benaras between 1809 and 1818. The resentment was directed not only against the Company and its agents but often at members of other communities and, sometimes, even at members of their own community. Weavers' struggles in Surat and Calcutta were "as much against the new British order as against the new Bania copdar."[3] However, in the northern Coromandel, especially in the Godavari and Visakhapatnam districts, evidence indicates that such unrest predates the import of mill-made fabrics. Company officials were particularly concerned by these disturbances because they tended to disrupt production and thus affect the massive investment that had been made in the textile industry of the region.[4]

1 Brennig, "Textile Producers", 336–53.

2 Bagchi, "Merchants and Colonialism", 14.

3 C.A. Bayly, *Indian Society and the Making of the British Empire: The New Cambridge History of India II* (Cambridge: Cambridge University Press in association with Orient Longman, 1988), 72.

4 For the total value of the Company's investment in the region, see Table 1.4 in Appendix.

Oppressive Practices

One of the more exploitative practices was *gadium* or *gaddem* by which a zamindar could compel non-agricultural groups under his jurisdiction to buy grain from him at artificially inflated prices. This dated back to the Vijayanagara period.[5] When there was a decrease in the price of grain or greater surplus in their stocks, zamindars would force weavers, and sometimes Banias, to take grain within a stipulated time.[6] Further, weavers had to pay a rate fixed at more than the market price. It ranged from ¼ pagoda per candi at one place to ½ and 1 pagoda at others.[7]

In the medieval period, such jajmani relationships were not always resented, since the reciprocities implied in such patron-client linkages provided a safety net in times of crisis. The new economic tensions, however, subjected these ties to oppressive situations when zamindars, hard pressed to meet revenue demands, took everything they could get by way of taxes. Even renters in zamindari areas took advantage of such a practice, and compelled weavers who had received cash advances from the Company to exchange cash for grain. This caused further hardship for the weavers as vendors of thread insisted on and accepted only cash payments. If weavers were given grain as advance, they had to sell it at a loss. This meant a smaller quantity and an inferior quality of thread, which, in turn, meant a substandard product. Malcolm, who was the Commercial Resident at Visakhapatnam, therefore, was not for the issue of grain.[8]

In August 1789, Company officials came to know of the undesirable practice of gaddem that was prevalent in 59 villages in the 2nd division of Masulipatnam district. Realising that weavers were being deprived of trading in a free market mechanism, they thought that one of the means through which they could secure their work exclusively for the Company was by abolishing this convention. They extended this concession essentially to those weavers registered for the Company's service.[9] The

5 Ramaswamy, *Textiles and Weavers*, 149.

6 Benjamin Branfil, Collector, 3rd division of Masulipatnam District, Rajahmundry, to Board of Revenue, 20 November 1795, *GDR* 842, 99–101.

7 John Rowley, Resident at Ingeram and Maddepollam, Mugalatoru, to BOR, 23 November 1795, *GDR* 841, 393.

8 Robert Malcolm, Commercial Resident, Visakhapatnam, to William Brown, Collector, Visakhapatnam, 25 August 1797, *VDR* 3709, 599–601.

9 Richard Dillon, Deputy Commercial Resident, Ingeram and Maddepollam, to William Fallofield, Board of Trade, 4 June 1796, *GDR* 830, 55–62.

Board of Revenue, in fact, passed a resolution authorising the abolition of gaddem and ordered zamindars to desist from this practice.[10]

In other instances, zamindars enhanced the taxes they traditionally collected from weavers. For example, according to a petition submitted by some weavers, the manager of the Peddapuram zamindari not only increased the house tax from 1 pagoda per house to 2, but also forced grain upon them at an inflated price. As a result, they quit their looms and assembled at the Company factory.[11]

A traditional tax that directly affected weavers was the loom tax. Recognising that its annulment would act as an incentive for weavers to produce only for the Company, the Board of Trade decided to exempt weavers in haveli lands from this tax as early as 1793. (For a detailed discussion, see Chapter 8.) The Board intended to extend a similar privilege to the weavers in zamindari areas whenever such became part of the Company's lands.[12] However, by 1802, the Company's attempts to control textile production led to the exemption of all weavers from paying the loom tax, provided they had registered for the Company's service.[13] The zamindars were, in turn, paid compensation for the loss of revenue.

With such privileges accorded to them, the weavers of the northern Coromandel freely expressed their grievances against zamindars, renters, and merchants. They sent representatives or submitted petitions to seek the assistance of the new juridical structures of the Company. In 1795, the Commercial Resident of the Masulipatnam factory received a petition from the weavers of Devee taluk stating that the Company's gumastah insisted on their clearing the balances owed by them.[14] From the accounts produced by the gumastah, it was seen that 30 weavers owed a balance of 33 pagodas; of these, 18 had died. The head weavers

10 Branfil to Edward Saunders, BOR, 30 April 1796, enclosing BOR's letter dated 18 April 1796, *GDR* 842, 60–62.

11 Rowley to Thomas Snodgrass, Collector, 1st Division, Rajahmundry and Eluru Circars, 19 March 1795, *GDR* 922, 122.

12 Extract of Government's letter dated 6 September 1793, in BOR to John Snow, Collector, Vizianagaram zamindari, 31 December 1795, *VDR* 3705, 43–46; interpretation of Government's letter dated 3 February 1794, in BOR to Snow, *VDR* 3705, 44.

13 D. Hill, Sub-Secretary to Government, to G. H. Barlow Bart, Governor-in-Council, Fort St. George, 27 September 1811, *MDR* 2960, 122–40.

14 V. Corbrett, Commercial Resident, to John Wrangham, Collector, 4th division of Masulipatnam, 10 July 1795, *MDR* 2991, 967, in *Guide to the Records of Masulipatnam District 1682–1833* 3 (Madras: Government Press, 1935), 57.

were, therefore, "ordered to discharge the balance of at least those who are living."[15] The Company also sought to control the zamindars who tried to use force to impose upon the weavers the custom of collecting a piece of cloth.[16]

It was not only zamindars who tended to oppress and exploit the weavers, they were subjected to the domination of other rural elites as well. In 1802, the Commercial Resident of Ingeram reported that the Kapus and the karnam of Pendalapaka were harassing weavers. The Company's copdar in Rajahmundry district sent a representation complaining against Seetaramoodoo, headman of Vaddasolaroo village. When there was a dispute between the weavers and the Kapus of the village, he had not taken any steps to reconcile the groups; rather, taking an active part, he had been offensive and antagonistic towards all the weavers. Consequently, 50 weavers stopped working and left the village. The Company's commercial officials immediately sought the assistance of other revenue officials by asking them to immediately release all weavers who were either confined by the officials or by zamindars. Seetaramoodoo was asked to account for his conduct, and orders were issued to encourage the weavers to return to the village and resume work.[17]

Nonetheless, while the Company cast itself in the guise of a benevolent jajmani when the weavers' hostility was directed against others, it had to face their intractable attitude against its own policies and practices. One of the main and recurrent problems faced in the early years of political control in the region was the evasion of balances by the weavers. In 1768, when the weavers working for the Company's merchants at the Ingeram factory owed large sums, Jogee Pantuloo persuaded them to move away from their locality and settle in villages falling under his jurisdiction. Further, he ill-treated the Company's sepoys and distributed dustacks all over the region.[18] When the Company attempted to introduce new duties, the weavers refused to work for its 1768 investment.[19]

15 Letter, 4 August 1795, *MDR* 2991, 150, in *Guide to the Records of Masulipatnam District*, 64.

16 Collector, Rajahmundry, to Commercial Resident in-charge, Ingeram, 11 February 1802, *GDR* 943, 131.

17 George Maidman, Deputy Commercial Resident in-charge, Ingeram, to Collector, 1st Division of the Masulipatnam District, 16 February 1803, *GDR* 944 B, 565–66; for further details, see Commercial Resident, Ingeram to Collector, Masulipatnam, 13 December 1802, *GDR* 946 B, 469–70.

18 Consultation of 17 May 1768, *PDC* 99 B, 340.

19 Consultation, 1768, *PDC* 99 A, 613.

Protests in Godavari Distict

The first serious protest was organised in 1775 by the weavers of the Ingeram and Maddepollam facories against the restructuring of the production process. Anthony Sadleir's measures introduced in 1774 led to the widespread impression that these new structural and intermediary arrangements would lead to oppression and curtailment of the freedom of weavers.

The weavers of mootahs producing fine cloth were forced to take up advances for coarser varieties. As such, they had to give up not only their expertise but also the profit that they had earlier earned. As some of the weavers did not know how to weave coarse cloth, they bought cloth elsewhere and gave it to the Company's gumastahs, consequently suffering a loss of between ⅛ to ¼ pagoda for each piece.

For instance, Appaguntaveeresha, the head weaver of Peddapatnam, testified that "four or five hundred fine cloth weavers told Mr. Sadleir and his servants that they never used to make coarse cloth and that they did not know how to make it. Mr. Sadleir in answer told them that they must now learn it." When the weavers refused to take up production of coarse cloth, the Company's gumastahs and other principal servants used stern action to cow them down.[20]

They were compelled to sell only to the English Company and were constrained to take advances. Consequently, they became indebted to the French. A number of weavers from different mootahs of the Ingeram factory bemoaned the deplorable situation in which they had been put under the Sadleir system.[21] They did not know whether cloth was kept or

20 Testimony of Appaguntaveeresha, head weaver of Peddapatnam, in Proceedings Relative to Sadlier, *PDS* 24 A, 12–19. Appaguntaveeresha went on to recount the fate of a weaver of Pedapundy mootah, who "wove a bad piece of cloth which the gumastah tied round his head, and in that condition he was made to walk round the town and then was made to bow down and a heavy stone was set upon his back. After he was released, they advanced him 4 pagodas for two other pieces of cloth which he tied at the end of his cloth with some accounts and going to a well put the cloth over the *pacote* and then drowned himself by jumping into the well." Appaguntaveeresha himself was kept a prisoner at Kopparapalem for 3 months along with several others. Some of them, such as Vesunnethele Sooroo, Tappiah Maloo and Moovooree Malloo (an old man), were put in fetters. The last named died a few days after he was released.

21 Testimony of Rustumpadah weavers, 9 December 1775, *PDS* 24 A, 106–10.

rejected. They were also unhappy with the low prices offered and the categorisation of 14-punjum cloth into four varieties.[22]

The weavers complained that because of the changes they became indebted to the Company. They ran away with their looms and families to the neighbouring French and Dutch factories at Yanam and Palakollu. Weavers from Amalapuram, Arrivatum, Hassanalibadah, and Rustumbadah moved to these places and declined to return to the Company's territories.[23]

The head weavers congregated to express their grievances to the Company's other officials. Weavers from various mootahs marched towards the Company's factory to present their position. The 4000 weavers who worked in Kottapalli tried to go to Ingeram to protest, but were attacked by Sadleir's peons and dispersed.[24] All this created a sense of discontentment among weavers, merchants, and private traders.

In March and April 1775, weavers quit their work, assembled at the village of Vellamarroo, and sent a verbal message to William Hamilton, a Company official at Maddepollam, that they wished to discuss their grievances with him. Hamilton sought instructions from Sadleir who forbade him to have any interaction with the weavers. A general mood of lethargy prevailed in 27 mootahs for a month or more. The rumour was that Simmadri Venkatachellem and Venkatachellem Chetty, the principal servants of Sadleir, had advised him to starve the weavers into submission as "hunger at length will constrain them to return to their looms." When Sadleir retaliated with violence and inflicted punishments, the weavers turned militant, and in some places attempted to injure the Company's servants and others. In Peddapuram, a crowd of weavers fell on the market, seized the Company's servants, beat up the sepoys, and destroyed their stores.[25]

22 Testimony of Whapuncundy Servoo, a head weaver of Amalapuram, *PDS* 24 A 25–26; Drugeon, Yanam, to Anthony Sadlier, 13 May 1775, *PDC* 114 A, 512–14.

23 Testimony of Hassanalibadah weavers, 2 December 1775, *PDS* 24 A, 29–31; Testimony of Arrivatum and Dungaroo weavers, 3 December 1775, *PDS* 24 A, 36–44. Only a few weavers returned because of persuasion by the head weavers. As the weavers of Hassanalibadah put it, "If you urge us further, we must drown ourselves in the river Godavari and that gentleman (Sadleir) may take our wives and families on board ships." The weavers of Arrivatum and Dungaroo mootahs also testified to the same effect.

24 Testimony of Amalapuram weavers, 4 December 1775, *PDS* 24 A, 44–46.

25 William Hamilton to Inquiry Committee, 22 November 1775, *PDS* 24 A, 4–8.

Realising the danger to its investment, the Company decided to inquire into the complaints against Sadleir. An Inquiry Committee with Peter Perrins, Alexander Davidson, and John Holland as members was set up. When Sadleir and the head weavers of the various mootahs were summoned before the Committee at Nelapalli, weavers from other mootahs took advantage of this opportunity and also went to Nelapalli primarily to record their complaints.

The remarkable feature about this particular uprising, seen repeatedly in the region, was caste solidarity, and the local units supported this. For instance, in February 1775 a letter was sent by the territorial assembly (*mahanadu*) of Jagannathapuram to that of Mandapeta stating that the main castes—Sales, Devangas, Karineelu, and Kaikolas—had formed a *samium* (association) and requesting that at least one man from each weaving family of Mandapeta be sent to join this alliance. They sought monetary and other pecuniary donations from the members of their community to consolidate this organisation.[26]

This organised protest of the weavers turned out to be a notable success when the Council reprimanded Sadleir, repudiated his methods, made peace with the weavers, conciliated the Dutch and the French, and, with their assistance, persuaded many of the weavers to return to their villages.

The victory of 1775 was however short-lived. The weavers resented the Company's increasing control of the production process and in particular its rejection of 'inferior' cloth. Sometimes the displeasure boiled over into militant action. In April 1795, John Rowley, the Commercial Resident at Ingeram, reported that weavers at the Pasalapoody mootah in Godavari district forsook their looms, prevented thread markets from functioning, and even attempted to get other weavers to join their strike, with the apparent objective of compelling the Company to accept the so-called inferior cloth.[27] These weavers invited those of the neighbouring mootahs to join them in their resistance, "threatening to cut from the looms the cloths of such as refuse to do so."[28] Rowley asked the Collector to take immediate steps to subdue the

26 Madras Public Proceedings 1775, 240/39, Reports of Special Committee, 7 April 1775, 12 July 1775, 30 August 1775, cited in S. Arasaratnam, "Trade and Political Dominion in South India, 1750–1790: Changing British Indian Relationships", *MAS* 13, no.1, 1979, 19–40.

27 Rowley to Branfil, 30 April 1795, *GDR* 921, 244–50; also Rowley to Snodgrass, 30 April 1798, *GDR* 924, 153–62.

28 Rowley to Snodgrass, *GDR* 924, 153–62.

"tumultuous assemblies."[29] Orders were issued to all revenue servants to keep a watch on the weavers and check their revolt. The zamindar of Peddapuram was also requested to bring the weavers to submission.[30]

A more serious insurrection occurred in 1798. There were three major reasons for this particular disturbance. First, the weavers under the Company's service were already discontented at not being able to get enough money for their work, specially when there was scarcity of thread. Second, the Company's attempt to introduce an efficient production system deprived the poorer weavers of whatever little they used to earn and also closed all the channels through which they could get loans from the merchants. The Company now insisted that the investment should be provided by the collection of balances from the advances made during the early part of the year. Third, consequently, the merchants used stern measures to recover outstanding dues from the weavers.[31]

The immediate cause for the flare-up was the action of Tumalapalli Appiah, a Company's merchant of Daaglooru village in Chentapooru mootah, who "pinched the ear of one weaver and pushed another weaver down", and who had also paid an unfair price for a piece of cloth and cut a patch out of one of the Company's looms. This flagrant display of power and arrogance was the last straw, as it were, and the angry weavers assembled at Daglooru to protest. The two head weavers of Daglooru village, Causiah Cimiah and Smithy Agusty, gathered together about 300 weavers, "entertained them with a supper and then prevailed on them to swear that they would never more weave for the Company."[32]

As in 1775, the weavers, backed by the strength and the solidarity of their caste leaders, moved from place to place to bring under their banner weavers of other villages too. First, they went to Maddepollam and Nursapur. Not finding enough provisions to feed the entire group, they left about 30 principal and head weavers behind and marched on to Relangi, where they were received by Punamachu Timmarauze, the *tanedar* (revenue collector).[33] Here, the number of weavers swelled to 500. They rejected all compromises offered by the Company officials and refused to return to work, because, according to the Commercial

29 Rowley to Branfil, *GDR* 921, 244–50.

30 Letter dated 10 May 1795, *GDR* 924, 212–14.

31 Richard Dillon, Deputy Commercial Resident, Maddepollam, to William Fallofield, Board of Trade, 19 January 1798, *GDR* 830, 20–41.

32 Ibid., 27–28.

33 Ibid.

Resident, they recognised their strength and "depended on perseverance and numbers for success.".[34] Issuing orders to weavers of their castes to join them, they declared that they will undertake work for any one but the East India Company, and, in fact, actually started producing cloth not of the Company's assortments. They also refused to liquidate their debts, to receive new advances on the present year's investment, or to employ themselves in the provision of the investment in future. They decided to hold out in the hope of achieving the same successful result obtained by the weavers residing in the mootahs under the Ingeram factory two years previously.[35]

From Relangi, a body of 200 weavers moved away and re-assembled in the village of Yellindrapurroo in Nidadavole pargana.[36] Later, another party consisting of about 20 weavers under the leadership of Sindanee Sivalingam of Commerroo proceeded on 17 January 1798 from Yellindrapurroo towards Masulipatnam. They passed through Moyaroo, Yendagandy, Mallapalam, Yelloopoora, Culdindy, and Toomedi. Despite being aware of the route through which the weavers intended to reach Masulipatnam, Company officials were not able to stop them on their way.[37] From Masulipatnam, they went also to Cayclapaud and Yellpoor in Assunta pargana in the 2nd division.[38]

The Company tried, in the first instance, to meet the weavers' discontent with a policy of appeasement and gave orders to the merchants to follow very mild tactics in collecting the balances.[39] But the weavers, on the verge of total revolt, did not respond to these measures, and the situation worsened. The Company, concerned about its investment, now attempted to use intimidation and severe methods through its local officials to subdue the militant weavers. For instance, it asked the tanedars to drive them out from their villages without any delay. The Company also seized some of the ringleaders who resided in the 2nd division, and hoped that the cold weather and lack of funds would compel the others to disperse.

Finding itself unable to satisfactorily deal with the refractory weavers even by such intimidating methods, the Company then adopted a much

34 Dillon to Branfil, 8 January 1798, *GDR* 847, 141–42.

35 Dillon to Fallofield, 19–44.

36 Dillon to Branfil, 16 January 1798, *GDR* 847, 168.

37 Dillon to Cornish Gambier, Collector, 2nd Division, Masulipatnam, 19 January 1798, *GDR* 847, 263–64.

38 Dillon to Gambier, 23 January 1798, *GDR* 847, 269.

39 Ibid., 37–38. Also, Dillon to Branfil, 8 January 1798, *GDR* 847, 141–42.

harsher policy. It now ordered placing the weavers' families under restraint, until the insubordinate weavers returned to their houses and accounted for their conduct.[40]

As a last resort, the Company used social constraints aimed at depriving and alienating the weavers from other structures and groups. The revenue officials in the weaving villages were asked to insist that the weavers discharge their balance in goods of the Company's assortments. Failing this, they were to be prevented from the enjoyment of those rights that were exercised by the rest of the inhabitants. These included the use of the village wells, pasturage for cattle, and the privilege of getting batta.[41]

Orders were issued to the native revenue officers to compel the weavers of their villages to return to duty and either pay off their balance in the Company's assortments or receive new advances. Agitating weavers were prevented from visiting the houses of those who had returned to work. They were also prohibited from collecting money from the working weavers, as it was feared this would go towards supporting those who had assembled in the 1st division.[42]

In 1800, there was yet another demonstration by the weavers of Vedurpaka village in the Dracharam mootah of Godavari district. Their main demand was that they be permitted to sell their pieces to any of the Company's merchants they wished to. They refused to meet the Commercial Resident in small numbers and were determined to see him as a "whole mob" either at Dracharam or Cauperpollam. At Vedurpaka, the scene of the unrest, 400 weavers had assembled (and a few in other villages) to stop the production in nearby places.[43]

This particular agitation, though short-lived and comparatively limited in its spatial influence, was significant for the fact that it created serious worries leading the Commercial Resident of Ingeram to request the higher authorities to despatch a contingent of 40 sepoys to Dracharam. "If it is not speedily done there will not be a loom at work in a short time... there are amongst the mutinuous weavers numbers actually armed with matchlocks, spears, swords and others." The Collector was asked to bring a small armed force for "I think these savages cannot disperse unless they view some sepoys with firelocks."[44]

40 Dillon to Branfil, 16 January 1798, *GDR* 847, 168–70.

41 Dillon to Branfil, 30 January 1798, *GDR* 847, 209; Gambier to Dillon, 29 January 1798, *GDR* 848, 20–22.

42 Dillon to Gambier, 5 March 1798, *GDR* 887, 316–17 and 321–24.

43 Charles Maxton, Resident, Ingeram, to Branfil, 27 March 1800, *GDR* 933 A, 101–06.

44 Ibid.

Visakhapatnam Disturbances

A serious insurrection among the weavers of Visakhapatnam district took place in 1796.[45] There were several instances of weavers complaining of economic oppression. The pervasive influence of Jaggapah over the production process caused discontent among the weavers. In order to complete his contract, Jaggapah applied "uncommon severity against them" and removed the gentoo cloth from their looms to compel them to work on salempores. The weavers were reluctant to undertake the production of salempores because of the high cost of thread. They were also unwilling to weave for the Company as this meant that they had to pay towards the upkeep of the Company peons. The low price paid for punjum cloth was another point of resentment. The Company demanded salempore piece-goods from Visakhapatnam in great quantities as the Ganjam district did not produce enough. Consequently, the Visakhapatnam weaver was prevailed upon to give up his specialisation.[46]

Thus, the Company's policies and demands threatened the relatively autonomous weaving environment of Visakhapatnam district. Weavers were forced to produce goods for which they had no sanction from their caste elites. Moreover, they had to give up alternative sources of employment such as producing fine varieties for private traders and gentoo cloth for local consumption. The rising importance of the native agency at the factory had resulted in the enforcement of these rules and regulations, because of which the weaver had to pay extra charges at a time when thread was scarce and the value of currency had diminished.

Such dissatisfaction and discontent culminated in a revolt that knitted together the weavers. The "fugitive" weavers in the region gave up their work and forced their counterparts from neighbouring villages to join them. The principal instigators of the disturbance were the senapatis and copdars at Ankapalli.[47] The ringleader, according to the kanakapillai, was Mulliah, the chief contractor.[48] Mulliah was known to be a leader

45 Malcolm to Webb, Collector, Northern Division, Vizianagaram zamindari, 27 July 1796, *VDR* 3706, 326–28.

46 W. Brown, Collector, Cossimcotah, to Malcolm, 24 July 1796, *PBOR* 162, 8058–73.

47 The senapatis were Anlunka Bogasha, Manam Basavannah, Yaluncabobanda Mulliah, Seela Tomiah, Manam Yamanah, and Tolica Bogasha, Gooty Veeranah, and Damtamasetty Reddy were the copdars who promoted this disturbance, Brown to Malcolm, 24 July 1796, *PBOR* 162, enclosure, 8082.

48 Brown to Malcolm, 26 July 1796, *VDR* 3706, 330–32.

among the Devangas as a popular proverb of the region says, "Allullalo Mallu peddah", meaning that among the Devangas, Mulliah was chief.[49]

The weavers proceeded from Cossimcotah to Tumapallah and on to Ankapalli. Here they engaged in a tussle with some of the kotwal's men, but did not stand much chance against the superior force.[50] Later, the kanakapillai of the warehouse, Jaggapah, complained that "some weavers of the Devangooloo caste from cusbah Ankapalli had forcibly seized a quantity of thread purchased at a neighbouring shandy by a certain number of weavers of the same caste, who were conveying it to their houses at Simprepilly for the purpose of working it into salempore...."[51]

The Collector summoned these copdars and senapatis to the cutcherry and warned them of the punishment they would get for their unwarranted conduct and for the confusion and improprieties they created in the region.[52] The senapatis maintained that they were not opposed to the Company or the new regulations per se, but complained of the "strictness and severity" with which the gumastahs enforced the orders.[53] The Collector, John Snow, hoped that the weavers would yield to reason and agree to the immediate terms prescribed to them. The way to secure this, he believed, was to insist that the senapatis of the several parties assembled should represent their grievances in a quiet, submissive manner, while the remaining weavers dispersed and returned to their work as usual. Further, the Resident was asked to prevent disorderly and intemperate meetings that disturbed and distracted the peaceful inhabitants of the district.[54]

On perusing the lists of agitators, it is evident that the insurrection was throwing up new leaders, because none of the weavers were senapatis.

The role of the extended network of caste and class among the weavers was reflected when weavers from other villages supported these movements. For instance, when the weavers at Cossimcotah were placed under detention for their active participation in the 1796 revolt, the weavers at Uppada retaliated and struck work until these confined weavers were set free.[55]

49 Carr, No. 1117.

50 Brown to Malcolm, *VDR* 3706, 330–32.

51 Brown to Malcolm, *PBOR* 162, 8058–59.

52 Ibid.

53 Snow to Malcolm, *VDR* 3706, 330–32.

54 Rowley to Brown, 9 February 1797, *VDR* 3709, 103–05.

55 Royalarapah Chenna Baupannah to Calesurgah Latchannah, 10 November 1798, *VDR* 3712, 204–05.

The weavers of this district had their own regulations and rules that were relaxed only with the common consent of their entire community. These economic privileges were guarded very jealously, and objections were raised whenever they were threatened. In 1798, Csalalungarh Latchanna forced some weavers of Kappaka and Rajupollam to manufacture 12-punjum cloth, for which he had advanced money. Such 12-punjum fabric was never made in the district. The weavers objected mainly on the ground that the order was not extended to the entire district, but only limited to two villages. "When all the weavers in the district are ordered we will be ready with them, now there is no order to anybody but to the people of these two villages."[56]

The next protest organised by the weavers of Visakhapatnam district was a massive but peaceful one in 1816. It continued for nearly two years, till they achieved their goals. More than 12,000 weavers assembled at the Vaishnavite pilgrim centre of Simhachallem to present a petition to Company officials.[57] It is possible that the size of the gathering itself, besides impressing the Company officials, drew more weavers to the cause. The weavers were acutely conscious of the possibilities for collective political and legal action to secure redressal of their grievances. Not only did they display remarkable organisational skills, they were also able to sense the ways in which the new juridical and state structures could be manipulated.

Since 1811 nearly 20,000 weavers had been chafing against the bullying tactics of Chinnum Jaggapah Chetty, the head servant and dubash at the Visakhapatnam factory. He and his relatives, Motumarry Paupadoo and Grandy Vencataramoodoo, attempted to control the entire production organisation of the textile economy. The weavers were very resentful of the domination of these Bania copdars and desired to bring their extortionary practices to the Company's notice. The listed grievances were the following:

- The copdars pay the weavers a lower price for their cloth than is allowed by the Company while at the same time inserting the full amount in their *wogetta*s.
- The copdars take on their own account the rejected cloth, paying for the same at a rate far below its value, with or without the consent of the weavers.

56 Ibid.

57 Petition of the Company's weavers in Visakhapatnam district addressed to George Strachey, Chief Secretary to Government, 19 March 1817, *CDC* 10, 1248–57, especially 1250–51.

- Advances are not given to the weavers till a considerable time after the cash has been received for such purposes from the Commercial Resident.
- Proportions of grain, cotton, and other articles of merchandise are substituted for advances that ought to be made wholly in cash.
- The weavers did not have access to the Commercial Resident to state their grievances because Chinnum Jaggapah's influence with him was such as to induce him to believe every mis-statement and they were eventually flogged without a hearing.
- Copdars Motumarry Paupadoo, Grandy Vencataramoodoo, and Maumedy Sooriah, all of the Bania caste, purchased readymade cloth with a proportion of the money they received for advances and affixed charcoal endorsements on such supplies, making it appear that every piece is the real manufacture of registered weavers of the Company.
- These said copdars exact sums of money from the weavers on all occasions of marriage ceremonies at their houses, and on various other pretences.
- Lastly, the general tenor of their conduct, aided by their powerful ally Chinnum Jaggapah, is so oppressive that the weavers were unable to follow their occupations in support of their numerous families.[58]

Weavers from Rajam, Parvadah, Dimili, Codoor, Goorvampallem, Boni, Nuckapilly, Payakarraopeta, Vamalapudi, and Uppada mocaums, cutting across territorial and administrative power structures, mobilised their groups into an organised force and assembled at Simhachallem. Interestingly, the weavers of Goorvampallem and Ankapalli and part of Codoor and Nuckapilly who were not in the Company's employ also participated.[59]

The huge gathering secured the Company's immediate attention. The Assistant Magistrate, Bird, and the Commercial Resident, Taylor, met the weavers and gave an assurance that their complaints would be heard and justice accorded. They wanted 20 representatives from among

58 Petition of Visakhapatnam weavers to Strachey, *CDC* 10, 1248–57, especially 1249–51.

59 For details, see list of mocaums under the Visakhapatnam factory with the names of the copdars and aummens signed by H. Taylor, Resident, Visakhapatnam, *CDC* 13, 570–71.

the body assembled at Simhachallem to testify before them. These leaders were, however, kept under the charge of the district peons at Visakhapatnam. At this point, Chinnum Jaggapah and the Commercial Resident persuaded the Assistant Magistrate not to hear the weavers' grievances. Accordingly, the Assistant Magistrate sent Meerum Saib, the *nazer* (inspector) of the court, with a number of peons to disperse the weavers. In spite of being flogged by the peons, and even though the nazer prevented their buying necessities such as rice, wood, and pots, the weavers, in a remarkable display of an early form of passive resistance, remained non-violent and peaceful.[60]

On the following day, Judge Pashe came to court and discharged the peons set on the weavers' representatives, and asked the representatives to give a statement detailing their problems. The agents submitted 8 petitions from 8 mocaums, with the hope that the judge would issue orders to prevent the oppression either by proclamation or petitions to Government or to the Board. But, "instead of doing so, he was pleased to return our petitions as wanting in the regular form of the court."[61]

Having failed to secure redressal of the inequities at the local level, the weavers, now clearly aware of their rights, attempted to influence the lower personnel by putting pressure on the higher authorities at Madras.[62] First, they lobbied the provincial administrators at Madras to intervene in the affairs of the district by dispatching petitions and retaining their agents at Madras for a long period. Second, when the investigation committee started its inquiry, they made well-ordered presentations of their grievances through their caste representatives and chief agents.

In the petition that they placed before the Board of Trade at Madras, they pleaded for (1) a new Resident at Visakhapatnam; (2) investigation and redressal of the charges specified in their petitions; (3) return of the sum withheld by the copdars on account of the punjum cloth taken by them from 1811.[63] The weavers further requested the Board to take

60 Ibid. Also, petition of the head weavers and weavers employed in the Visakhapatnam zillah, presented by the undersigned agents to the whole body, addressed to Hugh Elliot, 19 March 1817, *CDC* 10, 1259–60.

61 Petition of the agents to the Company's weavers in the Visakhapatnam district, addressed to the Board of Trade, 29 November 1816, *CDC* 13, 546–57.

62 Petition of the agents to the body of the Company's punjum cloth weavers in the district of Visakhapatnam, addressed to Robert Fullerton, Board of Trade, 29 November 1816, *CDC* 13, 546–56.

63 Petition of the head weavers and weavers employed in Company's punjum cloth investment in the Visakhapatnam zillah, addressed to Hugh Elliot, 19 March 1817, *CDC* 10, 1250–51.

measures to remove the said Chinnum Jaggapah from the commercial office and, if possible, from Visakhapatnam during the investigation. "He should not be in the smallest degree connected with any of his relations who were in the commercial department at Visakhapatnam, otherwise the Board would not come to know of the nefarious transactions of Chinnum Jaggapah." They maintained that they were, in fact, able to submit material in proof of the copdars' methods of oppression in their petition itself but for the fact that the Board could transmit an arzee to the Commercial Resident and thereby Jaggapah would be enabled to counteract their statement. Therefore, the weavers reserved their complaints to bring them forward before "the person who may be appointed from Madras to inquire into their complaints."[64]

The petition accepted that, "if the charges which they forwarded against Chinnum Jaggapah's relations Motumarry Paupadoo and Grandy Vencataramoodoo be proved to the satisfaction of the Board, the Board would be pleased to dismiss them from the Company's service. If the contrary would happen, then the weavers consented to undergo the punishment which the Board would think proper and also to pay off all the expenses which the Board would incur in course of these investigation."[65]

When the agents submitted the petition of the weavers to the Board of Trade, Henry Taylor along with Chinnum Jaggapah and the copdars, Grandy Vencataramoodoo and Motumarry Paupadoo, went to the mocaums. With the help of 130 Pariah peons expressly employed for the purpose, they seized certain weavers pointed out by the copdars. They forced these weavers to give *sunned*s attesting that (1) the proper price allowed by the Company was paid by the copdars; (2) the advances were not made in grain and other articles; (3) no damages were collected for the cloth which was rejected; (4) rejected cloth was always returned to them and not taken by the copdars, and (5) the weavers, through a want of prudence and sense, had assembled at the hill of Chinna Simhachalam.[66]

The poor were forced to give sunneds upon the threat that their houses and weaving looms would be auctioned. When the weavers refused, the copdars attempted to sell their property in order to clear their existing balances. As this ill-treatment was intensifying gradually, the weavers dispatched another petition dated 2 February 1817 to the

64 Ibid., 1252.
65 Ibid., 1253.
66 Ibid., 1252.

Board of Trade, this time by *tappal* (relay postal system), thus indicating their use of every available mode of communication with the provincial authority.[67]

In all these petitions, the weavers repeatedly drew the Company's attention to the long-standing economic oppression they were under and essentially sought relief from the Bania copdars.[68] Similar petitions continued to be sent until the Board took some decision on the issue.[69]

The Company initially attempted to resolve the entire matter of the revolt of 1816 by taking recourse to its judicial structure. The Company's legal and judicial procedures overruled the traditional systems through which weavers could secure redress.[70] The emergence of the new political authority and the subsequent consolidation processes, while leaving social and cultural problems to be solved by the communities, shifted all the disputes relating to the economic and production organisation directly to the new government. This was demonstrated in July 1816, when the weavers' petitions were not duly attended to on the ground that they did not comply with the existing judicial regulations.[71]

The Board of Trade proposed that the cases of assault be referred to the Magistrate, while the question of non-payment of dues be addressed to the Commercial Resident, in the first instance. If the weavers failed to secure justice from the Commercial Resident, they could appeal under Section XXVI of the 1806 Regulation to the zillah court. The Board was particularly keen that the weavers' representatives gathered at Madras return to their stations, especially since it could not "sanction combinations of weavers for the purpose of making general complaints," nor acknowledge "persons stating themselves to be agents for such combinations."[72]

67 Ibid., 1253.

68 Petition of the agents to Visakhapatnam punjum cloth weavers to Fullerton, 13 December 1816, *CDC* 13, 1257–65; 16 December 1816, *CDC* 10, 1269–73.

69 Petition of the Company's punjum cloth weavers in Visakhapatnam district, addressed to Board of Trade, Fort St. George, 2 February 1817, *CDC* 10, 1273–77; petition of the agents to the Company's punjum cloth weavers in the district of Visakhapatnam, addressed to Board of Trade, Fort St. George, 11 March 1817, *CDC* 10, 1277–86.

70 For this argument, see Hossain, *Company Weavers*, Chapter 4, 109–23.

71 Translation of a petition from Emunda Jagapa, Davluree Ramoodoo, Emunda Mulliah, weavers of Coderree mocaum in the district of Visakhapatnam, addressed to the Magistrate in the Visakhapatnam zillah, 30 July 1816, *CDC* 10, 1264–68, especially 1268.

72 Petition of agents to Visakhapatnam punjum cloth weavers to BOT, *CDC* 10, 1277–86, especially 1286, where the Board's reply to the petition was noted.

Quite clearly, the officials of the Company, and the Board of Trade in particular, were trying to impose the new rule of law and to negate the possibility of collective action. The weavers, aware of their position under the new legal procedures, however, refused to accept these proposals, because of the limitations that they had under the existing socio-economic forces that pervaded the factory environment. They could not send their complaints against the Resident to the Magistrate, as they had been harassed on earlier occasions and also as Chinnum Jaggapah's influence still persisted. Nor did it suit them to prefer their complaints to the Resident for the recovery of their just dues from the copdars. Besides, they did not have the time and money to send individual complaints to the district court. The only offer that the weavers appreciated was the Board's proposal "to issue orders to the Commercial Resident to investigate charges against his servants."[73]

The representatives of the weavers were, as a first step, asked to return to their respective villages and written orders were issued to punish severely those weavers who remained at Madras. However, the weavers who accepted the orders and returned to their villages were again treated harshly by the copdars. On one occasion, Bhogesam and his wife, and Sambia, Ankiah, Rama, and Ganga from Singavarem village were flogged for refusing to declare in writing that those weavers who went to Madras were rogues and that the copdars did no injustice towards them. Even Henry Taylor exercised pressure on some weavers to clear their balances by setting peons on them. Interestingly, weavers who obliged the higher authorities dared to act against them on provocation. The weavers of Visakhapatnam district, thus faced with renewed harassment both from copdars and the Commercial Resident, once again dispatched a common petition on 17 May 1817 to the Board of Trade with 201 signatures.[74]

The protest entered its next phase in October 1817. The Company, recognising that the weavers were in no mood to submit, had to retreat from its earlier intimidatory posture and set up a Committee of Inquiry with Savage and Fraser as members. The Company that had earlier rejected the idea of representatives now called for delegations of weavers to come forth and testify.[75]

73 Ibid., also see petition of Visakhapatnam weavers to Strachey, *CDC* 10, 1249–56.

74 Petition of weavers in the Visakhapatnam district, addressed to Board of Trade, 17 May 1817, *CDC* 13, 565–70, especially 568.

75 F. A. Savage, Commercial Resident, Ingeram, and W. A. Fraser, Deputy Commercial Resident, Maddepollam, to Hugh Elliot, Board of Trade, Fort St. George, 17 January 1818, *CDC* 13, 291–328.

Weavers from the Goorvampallem, Boni, Codoor, Rajam, Payakarraopeta, Parvadah, Dimili, Nuckapilly, Byavaram, and Uppada mocaums deputed 6 representatives each to present their case before the committee at Visakhapatnam. Authorisations to their representatives were forwarded by 3,018 weavers of these mocaums.[76] While empowering these delegates to speak on their behalf, the weavers depended exclusively on two chief agents—Jummundy Ammanah and Surumpoody Ramanah—who were assured of every assistance on written authority. When the Inquiry Committee started its proceedings, only Jummundy Ammanah was present at Visakhapatnam. Surumpoody Ramanah stayed at Madras, keeping in his possession all important documents, vouchers, etcetera, needed to substantiate the testimony, because of the fear that the documentary evidence may be tampered with or destroyed.[77] Jummundy Ammanah complained to the Committee against Motumarry Paupoodoo, Grandy Vencataramoodoo, Chinnum Jaggapah, and the Commercial Resident, presenting all necessary details.[78]

Interestingly, during the inquiry, the delegates took pains to point out that their main complaint was against the copdars and not against Chinnum Jaggapah. Obviously, this was because Jaggapah was very influential, and the delegates did not wish to offend him openly. It could also have been due to their strategy of focussing attention on the misdeeds of the three copdars who were "most oppressive", namely, Grandy Vencataramoodoo, Motumarry Paupadoo, and Maumedy Sooriah.[79]

Several side issues came up during the investigation. Some representatives said that they had not seen the circular letter of 23 October 1817 that announced the institution of the Inquiry Committee and asked weavers to send their representations. From the testimony presented by the delegates from Boni, Parvadah, Goorvampallem, Codoor, Rajam, and Dimili, it appeared that the copdars had refused to reveal the contents of the circular, unless they signed papers to say that

76 Statement showing number of weavers authorising delegates of their respective mocaums to testify before the Inquiry Committee at Visakhapatnam, *CDC* 13, 575–77.

77 Testimony of Jummundy Ammanah, 28 October 1817, in Savage and Fraser to Elliot, 17 January 1818, *CDC* 13, 353–66.

78 Testimonies of Jummundy Ammanah, 28 October 1817 and 19 November 1817, *CDC* 13, 353–66 and 418–20.

79 Ibid.

they had no complaints against Chinnum Jaggapah and the other copdars. Advances were not given to the weavers who refused.[80]

The weavers were often not forthcoming with more information than was necessary in their evidence. On 12 April 1817, 390 weavers of Rajam mootah forwarded a complaint that contradicted the opinion expressed by another group of 426 weavers, also of the same mootah. Cottamsetti Sunnassee, delegate from Maumedipolam village who figured in this list, explained the situation thus:

> "During my absence, some weavers came to my house by desire of the copdars and Jaggapah and compelled my sons to sign the paper, and on my return the same peons compelled me to sign but not until they had flogged me."
>
> Q: "Did these peons force the other weavers to sign the paper by the same means?"
>
> A: "I cannot say, I only speak about the way in which my signature and my sons' were obtained."
>
> Q: "Who presented this petition to Mr. Taylor?"
>
> A: "I do not know but I believe it to have been presented by the copdar."[81]

Apparently, it was not just the weavers of the mocaums controlled by Grandy Vencataramoodoo and Motumarry Paupadoo who participated in the movement of 1816. Weavers from other units took advantage of the situation and came forward to express their grievances too. For instance, on 28 October 1817, 5 weavers from Dimili came before the Inquiry Committee to complain that the *darogah* (native officer) of Dimili had insisted that they work as coolies to carry baggage. These weavers were asked to send their complaints either to the Commercial Resident or to the Magistrate.[82]

Similarly, 6 representatives from Uppada appeared before the Committee on 24 November 1817 with an authorisation from 284

80 For the names and the testimony presented by the weavers of Boni, Goorvampallem, Parvadah, Codoor, Rajam, and Dimili mocaums, see Proceedings of a Committee for Investigating Certain Complaints Preferred against the Principal Native Servants and Copdars of Visakhapatnam Factory by the Weavers of the District, 28 October 1817, *CDC* 13, 367–73.

81 Testimony presented by 6 delegates from Rajam mocaum, 15 November 1817, *CDC* 13, 393–96, especially 395, 396.

82 Testimony presented by 5 delegates from Dimili mocaum, 28 October 1817, *CDC* 13, 367–73.

weavers to place their complaints against their newly recruited Brahmin aummen (revenue official), Gauda Ramiah. He was a resident of Goorvampallem mocaum. He regularly charged ¼ of a rupee on each piece of cloth. If the weavers refused to pay the sum, their cloth was rejected and future advances were also withheld. He also collected one rupee from each village in his mocaum. The Company had given advances to these weavers on all but one or two looms for the current year's investment.[83]

Caste, needless to say, was an important element in this particular conflict. The weavers' demonstrations were provoked precisely because the new copdars were of a different caste. In fact, caste was a crucial element in all the protests and agitations, because it was the social bond that provided the framework of unity for the weavers and the rallying point for their mobilisation. The Company ultimately had to concede to the demands and bring about drastic restructuring and realignments in the weaving villages of the district. Under the new structural arrangements, caste leaders emerged triumphant, but with less power in their hands, having to share their position with other groups like gumastahs and senapatis.

Geographically, these protests and uprisings were limited to the northern districts of the region, suggesting that the weaver from Masulipatnam was a weaker and more passive element. This was primarily due to three reasons. First, the weavers of chay and chintz goods enjoyed the luxury of more marketing centres, and, thereby, their position was better off than the Godavari and Visakhapatnam weavers, whose specialised products reached only a few distinct markets. Second, the absence of strong intermediaries meant minimum interference by the Company in the production process. Third, the weavers were able to get enough for their living, and, therefore, they never attempted to revolt.

Fundamentally, the discontent of the weavers in the northern Coromandel needs to be seen as emanating from the two interacting structures in which they operated. One was the traditional, pre-colonial pattern of oppression and control which was undergoing transformation and the other was the new economic order being superimposed on the old.[84] The disturbances quite often had narrow, specific reasons that

83 Testimony presented by 6 delegates from Uppada mocaum, 24 November 1817, *CDC* 13, 437–41.

84 Hossain, "Alienation of Weavers", 329.

appeared to be unconnected. However, whatever the particular objective associated with each one, caste consciousness and solidarity among the weavers were two remarkable features that could be discerned throughout the period under study.

A general assumption in the literature is that the weavers meekly accepted the new order established by the Company. Artisans, it was assumed, were not as militant as peasants. This study reveals that not only were the weavers conscious of their situation and position under the changed circumstances, they also made full use of collective political and legal action.

It is observed that the Company itself viewed these struggles in a serious vein. That these were not just dismissed as unplanned acts of occasional and scattered violence is evinced by terms such as "refractory weavers", "mob", "insurgents", "mutiny" and "riotous conduct" used by Company officials in their dispatches. While not always violent, the weavers were well prepared for any eventuality. Evidence exists to show that even when they were protesting peacefully, they were "armed with matchlocks, spears and swords."

The weavers were opposed to all forms of control over their economic operations, whether by local elites or by Company officials. On different issues, they aligned themselves with specific groups, who, they felt, would be best suited to assist them in their agitation. Their alignments kept changing with the identification of new oppressors. Thus, while they sought the help of the new institutions against feudal forms of oppression, they looked to the regional leaders in their struggles against increased Company control over the production process. The weavers were not opposed to the Company per se, since after all it had opened up world markets to the Coromandel's textiles. It was the loss of control over their professional activities that they protested against.

The weavers also used a variety of ways and means in their agitations. Thus, during a period where methods of communication and organisation were practically unavailable, they showed remarkable skill in using caste networks to sustain and expand their insurrection both spatially and numerically. They frequently shifted from everyday, peaceful forms of protest to highly organised, coercive techniques. There was a marked continuity between the different forms of resistance, and the weavers demonstrated clarity, planning, and conscious action, based on evaluation of the possibilities of success of the different methods at different points of time.

Weavers in the northern Coromandel thus appear in several guises—passive and quiet as at Masulipatnam or militant and ever-conscious of their traditional privileges as in the Godavari and Visakhapatnam districts. In fact, it may be said, that these weavers were the first in the colonial period to protest against the new structures of dominance. This is not to attribute to them a proto-nationalistic or an anti-colonial sentiment. But, quite clearly, long before the western-educated middle classes adopted strategies of political action, the weavers of the northern Coromandel were protecting their rights by resorting to agitation.

EIGHT

External Influences on the Weaving World

The Coromandel weavers, as in any society, did not operate autonomously in a vacuum. Several elements constructed the many-layered world in which they were situated—price of food grains, the changing tastes of consumers, the taxes that they had to pay, or even the weather.

Artisan groups were tied to local alliances and rural structures through a wide variety of formal and informal taxes. The contribution of weavers formed a major component of the entire revenue system, next only to that of the agricultural groups. These remittances strengthened the landed elites and other local institutions, who were thus enabled to increase their hold over the weavers. The changes brought in by the Company into the traditional patterns of revenue administration affected indigenous links and paved the way for the incorporation of weavers into the colonial matrix. At the same time, the persistence of traditional cultural systems and the perpetuation of jajmani relationships helped to sustain some specialised weavers.

TAX COLLECTIONS

As seen in the earlier chapters, most of the weaving centres in the later half of the eighteenth century fell within the jurisdictional limits of the zamindari areas. These zamindaris depended to a considerable extent on the formal and informal taxes the weavers paid.

By the 1780s, most of the looms employed by the Company for its long cloth investment in Godavari district were under the Pitahpuram, Peddapuram and Cotah, and Ramachandrapuram zamindaris. In the Pitahpuram area of 127 villages, there were over 1147 looms.[1] The Peddapuram zamindari—the largest in the Godavari district, comprising

1 W. Robertson, Collector, Rajahmundry, to Board of Revenue, 25 June 1823, *GDR* 4637, 156–57; Circuit Committee Report, 15 February 1785, *MDR* 3009, 95–7.

14 parganas and 398 villages—had 2358 looms by 1787.[2] There were 508 and 162 looms respectively in Cotah and Ramachandrapuram.[3]

The annual loom tax and other kinds of exactions paid by weavers were an exclusive right enjoyed by the zamindar.[4] For instance, 6929 rupees were levied on the looms of the Company by the Peddapuram zamindar in 1802. Similarly, a large amount was collected by the other zamindars under the heads of moturpha tax and quit rent for the land occupied by the weavers' houses.[5]

Besides the loom tax and quit rent collections, the zamindars of Godavari district realised a variety of informal taxes such as *rusum*s (commissions), a customary *nuzzaranah* (gift of money) to the zamindar, or as a right in the shape of mirasi.[6] In Visakhapatnam district, the renters of the farms charged moturpha tax, imposts during weddings, presents on account of feasts and cloth *dalaty* tax.[7] Then there was also the practice of gaddem, under which a zamindar could compel non-agricultural groups under his jurisdiction to buy grain from him at artificially inflated prices.[8] [See Chapter 7.]

In Masulipatnam and Guntur districts, the relationship between weavers and rural elites was not so strong because of such factors as the scattering of the weaving villages over a wide area, the presence of a clearly demarcated power structure in the administrative set up, and the large-scale participation of non-traditional weavers in the textile economy. These weavers normally paid the taxes enjoined by their profession, "but in case any of them cultivates land, they receive their share of the produce in common with other inhabitants."[9] Their payments to the landed magnates and other village officials were formalised, and the forcing of grain on them was a rare phenomenon.[10]

2 Circuit Committee Report, 15 February 1785, *MDR* 3009, 98 and 114.

3 Petition from Rajah Ramachandrarauze, zamindar of Cotah and Ramachandrapuram, addressed to BOR, 20 June 1835, *GDR* 4648, 238–54.

4 Ibid, 238–39.

5 Ibid., 129–30. Also, an arze presented by Rajah Vencata Neeladry Rao, zamindar of Pitahpuram, to John Long, Collector, Rajahmundry, 28 June 1806, *GDR* 865, 176–80, provides information for 1804 and 1805.

6 Petition from Ramachandrauze, *GDR* 4648, 238–54.

7 W. Brown, Collector, Visakhapatnam, to BOR, 1 August 1790, *PBR* 162, 7698–7704.

8 Ramaswamy, *Textiles and Weavers*, 149.

9 John Wrangham, Collector, Masulipatnam, to BOR, 10 March 1796, *PBR* 149, 2441.

10 John Wrangham, Collector, Masulipatnam, to Edward Saunders, Secretary, BOR, 9 January 1796, *PBR* 143, 194–96.

In Masulipatnam district, taxes to the government were termed variously as professional taxes, fees or *tahareer*, and *sayer* (transit duty or customs toll), and *saderwareed* (incidental village expenses) payments. Moonavar rusums to the mirasidars and Karnam rusums were the extra exactions from weavers.[11] For instance, about 1787, mirasidars levied rusums on 211 looms of Mangalagiri village; in Vetapalam and Aumolly, kanakapillais used to collect fees; in Ulpooru, Coochannapadoo, Devi, Enoogoodoor, Gundoor, Accoolamaundo, Peddana, Cuppalapoody Polam, and Nundigamah, there were the Soornaynevary rusums; and loom tax was collected in the form of Deshmukh rusums and customs duties in Devaracotah, Gantasalah, Majagdoo, Cajah, Mungalapooram, and Peddapalli.[12]

In the later half of the eighteenth century, weavers in the Masulipatnam district were therefore situated in such a social structure where they were tied down to local officials in a linear fashion and were forced to pay these taxes.[13] It can be conjectured that the development of neo-political relations with the Nizams, and the subsequent changes associated with their revenue and administrative arrangements in the villages might have been responsible for creating a linear form of alliances and patterns of social relations even in the weaving world of the district. In other words, the central power was able to erect a politico-administrative system in this district extending down to the village economy, which, in turn, affected the relationship between weavers and the landed elites. Visakhapatnam and Godavari districts seemed to have largely remained outside the sphere of these changes.

In Guntur district, the traditional weavers were located in major zamindaries, and were fewer in number in the sequestered taluks of the district. The looms of the Pariah weavers and of those who supplied cloth to the natives, on the other hand, were spread over the entire district. The zamindar's right over the revenue collection also incorporated the right to collect moturpha tax from the weavers.[14]

In the ceded taluks, the village people were responsible for collecting moturpha from the weavers and paying the amount to the government. This tax was based on the total number of looms in a village. The villagers

11 Ibid.

12 Samuel Statham, Resident, Nizampatnam, March 1787, *MDR* 2838, 36–40.

13 In Masulipatnam district, the amount of taxes and extra sums to be paid by weavers were specified and each official of the district administration had, in fact, to take only that amount.

14 George A. Ram, Collector, Guntur, to BOR, 27 March 1796, *PBR* 151, 3345–3466.

usually made the weavers pay more.[15] The weaving communities that came under the purview of moturpha taxation included the Sales, the Malas, the Komatis, the Gavaravallu (arrack sellers), and the Gollavallu. On an average, the moturpha tax in Guntur district in 1796 was 1 pagoda and 36 cash on a hereditary weaver's looms and 14 fanams and 26 cash on Pariah looms.[16]

By 1796, out of the 2607 looms in the entire Guntur district, only 793 were employed for providing the Company's investment, the remaining looms catering to the local markets. Weavers registered with the Company in Chintapalli, Repalli, Rauchur, Chilakalurpadu, and Satnapalli paid nearly 1 to 2 pagodas towards the tax. The weavers for the natives paid ¾ pagoda and Pariah weavers, ¼ pagoda per loom.[17]

The Company, in the incipient stages of its political hegemony, had to rely on the local zamindars for the fulfilment of its investment, especially in the Visakhapatnam and Godavari districts.[18] The consent of the zamindars and head weavers had to be obtained when the prices of textiles were fixed.[19] Moreover, most of the Commercial Residents were dependent on these zamindars for creating and maintaining stability in the economy.[20]

The Company's attempts to minimise loss of investment and to secure a firm base in the textile economy of the region led it to discount many of the existing local alliances. To get them to work exclusively for itself in preference to other individuals and European companies, the Company tried to free the weavers from the traditional obligations that they resented. The first to come under the axe was the custom of imposing gaddem.[21] In 1796, the Board of Revenue passed a resolution seeking the abolition of this practice of forcing grain on weavers and other castes, not only at inflated prices but even at the current market rate.[22]

15 D. Hill, Sub-Secretary, to G.H. Barlow Bart, Governor-in-Council, Fort St. George, 27 September 1811, *MDR* 2960, 122–23.

16 Ram to BOR, *PBR* 151, 3345–3466.

17 Ram to BOR, 13 January 1796, *PBR* 143, 473.

18 Arasaratnam, *Maritime Commerce and English Power*, Chapters 2 and 3.

19 Basil Cochrane, Contractor for the Ingeram and Maddepollam investment, to Anthony Sadleir, 14 July 1787, *MDR* 2838, 118–20; Circular letters to the zamindars, Letter to Jaggeputty Rauze, zamindar of Peddapore, 17 July 1787, *MDR* 2838, 122–23.

20 Statham, *MDR* 2838.

21 For details on gaddem, see Chapter 7: Extracts from the letters of Rewell, Collector, Mugaltore, 15 December 1789, and the Secretary, BOR, 9 September 1793, to Chief and Council, Masulipatnam, in *GDR* 841, 386–88.

22 Extract of Government's letter, 6 September 1793, in BOR to Snow, *VDR* 3705, 43–46.

The Company brought in some internal changes to encourage weavers. These revisions, though, disturbed the traditional social and economic patterns of survival of many of the landed elites and renters in the region. The exemption from, or abolition of, loom tax was one such inducement offered by the Company to bring weavers under its control. A description of the nature and advantages of this loom tax was given in a letter of 1793:

> ....loom tax is that part of the quit-rent assessed on the weavers which all Handicrafts in the country pay a certain proportion to and that on this account, they are by the policy of the country's government exempted from the call of the circar to all duties of cultivation (except by old custom now obsolete they are esteemed as the Militia of the country, on the idea that having property in their houses they were most liable to stay and consequently best adapted to defend the general property). Further that if the (loom) tax were to be abolished in any degree, the authority of the Renter or Head of villages over a set of people, who most of all require subordination is at once destroyed, and an act of this kind to a set of men, who are known to be dissipated, turbulent, and consequently impatient of control, would at once overset the police of the country.[23]

Taxes paid by weavers employed only for the Company's investment were suspended, hoping that it would keep them from working for others.[24] In 1793, loom tax exemptions were extended at first to haveli areas and compensation was made to the renters on the loss of revenue to them on those looms registered for the Company's work.[25] These exemptions included abolition of moturpha and remission of quit rent for trees and cultivation within the compounds of houses.[26]

Weavers were provided the option to settle in haveli lands, moving away from zamindari areas. In order to make this attractive, the Company asked the commercial officers and renters to provide necessary building materials.[27] In zamindari lands, the collection of loom tax

23 Ibid., 44.

24 Interpretation of Government's letter, 3 February 1794, in BOR to Snow, *VDR* 3705, 44.

25 Hill to Barlow Bart, 27 September 1811, *MDR* 2960, 122–40, especially 125–27; General Letter to England, 16 January 1792, *CDDTE* 1 B, 370–71.

26 L. G. K. Murray, Collector, Vizianagaram, to Commercial Resident Visakhapatnam, 29 March 1804, *VDR* 3741, 70; Murray to the general zamindaries in the zillah of Visakhapatnam (Circular), 29 March 1804, *VDR* 3741, 71.

27 V. Corbrett, Commercial Resident, Masulipatnam, to Charles Hynox, Acting Collector, Masulipatnam, 19 July 1797, *MDR* 1947B, 664.

continued in an undisturbed manner.[28] The Company decided to extend the exemption privileges whenever a zamindari was ceded to it.[29] Thus, by creating differences between weavers residing in haveli areas and those in zamindaris, the colonial state was able to control the manufacturer more directly. By 1802, the Company was able to motivate weavers to stay away from the influence of the landed magnates by taking away the latter's right to collect loom tax.[30]

The Permanent Settlement of 1802 regularised the concessions to weavers. The Board of Revenue, in a letter to the Collector of Visakhapatnam dated 29 December 1803, maintained

> that although the zamindar was precluded by the Regulation from the levy of a professional tax, he had a right to levy a similar amount as a quit rent for the ground occupied by the weavers in their respective zamindaris. As per the rules and regulations of the Permanent Settlement of 1802, the Company ordered the zamindaris to desist from collecting any quit rent from the Company's weavers, for which they would be compensated by the Company. The zamindars were further requested to send these circulars to renters.[31]

Weavers were thus released from their financial obligations towards landed magnates and others. Nevertheless, the Company, through various regulations attached to the Permanent Settlement of 1802, did not entirely disrupt the dependent relationships between weavers and the agrarian elites. On the contrary, it balanced the removal of financial dependence by legitimising other kinds of subordination, again with the primary objective of protecting its investment.

Thus, one of the clauses attached to the permanent muchalika of the zamindars fixed for 21 years the quit rent for the land occupied by a weaver. The weaver, in turn, received a *cowle* (written agreement) from the zamindar by which he was entitled to a certain piece of land of specific measurements. For example, in 1804, Nodey Ḅasavappah executed a *ḳabooliat sunned* (counter agreement) to the zamindar of Cotah and Ramachandrapuram, whereby for an area 32 yards long and 13 yards wide, making 416 square yards, at Audevarapetah under

28 Board of Trade's order dated 17 March 1806 prohibiting the collection on the part of the zamindar of Vizianagaram of moturpha or loom tax in any shape, in Petition of Ramachandrarauze, 241.

29 Petition of Ramachandrarauze, 234–40.

30 Hill to Barlow Bart, *MDR* 2960, 127–47, Para 8.

31 Ibid., 131.

Dracharam mootah, he agreed to a rent of 4½ rupees including rusums for a period of 21 years. It was the responsibility of the weaver to carry out repairs at his own expense for houses situated on this ground. By this muchalika, a weaver was prohibited from leaving the village or shifting houses without the consent of the zamindar or his official. In the event of his doing so, the zamindar had the right to rent that house to some other weaver and could collect the tax.[32]

In all this, the Company was not so much strengthening the power of the zamindars as increasing its own. Through these muchalikas, weavers were in effect agreeing to abide by the regulations introduced by the Company, at least for a period of 21 years. This would, it was believed, introduce a degree of stability into an otherwise fluctuating demand system.[33] The Company was also trying to ensure stability for its investment operations by restricting the mobility of the weavers within the district. At times of economic depression and scarcity, weavers were prone to occasional migrations that led to fluctuating supply conditions. Thus, by constraining weavers both in time and space, the Company ultimately controlled them completely.

The Permanent Settlement of 1802 also made zamindars responsible for providing necessary facilities to weavers, such as constructing residential localities (pettahs) without any cess being levied.[34] Moreover, the decrees related to Section IV Regulation XXV of 1802 specified that "the revenue arising from moturpha as well as lands held exempt at the time of the settlement is reserved to Government."[35]

The same indulgence was extended to the Company's weavers in Guntur district.[36]

By the turn of the century, the Company's taxation policies were in for a change. When the decision was taken to stop the export trade in chay goods in 1814, the taxation structures introduced in the 1790s came to be revised. As the Company's object was to maximise revenue collections from all economic sectors, it saw no need to grant any concession to weavers. Therefore, moturpha loom tax collections were reverted to, even from those weavers who worked for the Company's

32 See kabooliat sunned executed and delivered by Nodey Basavappah to Stree Rajah Ragnathanarauze Maharauze, Sunday 7th of *Margah Bahoolum* in *Raktakshee* [February 1804], enclosed in Petition of Ramachandrarauze, 234–40.

33 Ibid, 239–40.

34 Ibid, 253–54.

35 Ibid, 253–54.

36 Hill to Barlow Bart, 122–40.

investment. The decision for such a change was based essentially on three grounds. First, if the exemption was continued, it would destroy the ultimate spirit of private trading activities; second, it would reduce the price of these goods as against those sold by weavers paying moturpha tax; and third, the Company had to forego a lot of revenue on account of this exemption.[37]

The Company, nonetheless, exempted some weavers from remitting moturpha tax. In Guntur district, five heads of the Sale caste in Repalli, Perala, and Rajahpeta were absolved from tax on some of their looms. This indulgence was granted as a token of appreciation for their efforts in collecting the taxes in the district. In 16 villages, the looms of 70 Pariahs were cleared because their owners were employed in assisting the Company's post and travellers in crossing different *nullah*s (watercourses) during the rainy season, conveying the baggage of travellers, accompanying the escorts who carried money from outstations to the *huzzoor* (respectful term for the public official), and from village to village, preserving the avenues of trees and performing other duties of a public nature.[38]

Between 1817 and 1818, however, weavers complained that zamindars, without any authority, were extracting money from them besides the moturpha, and that karnams were making extra collections under the head of village charges. The Collector of the district introduced a new arrangement based on the circumstances of the individuals possessing looms. By this system, all extra collections were added to the *circar dowle* (official revenue assessment) and pattas (revenue documents) were granted to the weavers specifying a fixed amount as taxes. From this, 10 per cent was granted to karnams in each village as remuneration for their service. The rate of tax varied between half a rupee and seven rupees.[39]

Another interesting feature associated with the new tax structures was the equalising of the rate on all Pariah looms. Till 1820–21, the tax on such looms ranged between 1 and 3½ rupees per loom. But, after taking into consideration the poverty and economic distress of this

37 Revoking of exemptions in favour of the Company's weavers was considered by the Government in 1814, as reflected in correspondence from T. A. Oakes to the Chief Secretary, in *Consultation*, 20 February, 1814. For extracts of this correspondence, see *GRBOR* 10, 11 and 12, 237–38.

38 Collector, Guntur, to BOR, 14 September 1832, *gudr* 3988, 40–44.

39 Ibid.

class of weaver, the entire tax liability was reduced to 1 rupee throughout the district.[40]

With the resumption of moturpha collections by the Company in 1814, all the weavers in Masulipatnam district again subscribed to this tax. It was levied only on the looms, and not upon the houses of weavers. In a few villages, the head weavers were exempted from paying tax on one or two of their looms, but had to pay for the other looms in their possession. In some villages, moturpha was collected by the landed elites. The tax was imposed on the looms at different rates, essentially following the old system of levy.[41]

In Masulipatnam, the Company resumed the imposition of moturpha only after its factory there closed down. In Godavari district, it attempted to collect tax on its weavers even before the shutting down of the factory.

> The Governor-in-Council is fully convinced that the exemption of the Company's weavers from the moturpha tax is both illegal and injudicious. It is illegal, because it is contrary to those statutory provisions by which it was intended to place the Company's trade on the same footing with respect to taxation as that of private merchants, and it would be injudicious, even were it legal, on account of the facility given by it to fraudulent evasion of the tax. The Governor-in-Council therefore desires that the exemption be wholly abolished.[42]

There was a continual increase in revenue on account of loom tax collection in Masulipatnam district, though the factory was abolished as early as 1812.[43] In the case of other factories, the external demand for textiles started declining from the 1820s and was completely over by the 1830s; but within a decade it showed signs of gradual improvement and the revenue from the looms reached the earlier situation by the 1840s.

To what extent did the loss of loom tax affect the landed estates? The decline and fall of the zamindari system has often been attributed to the mismanagement of estates and the nature of the agrarian economy. What has not been recognised, however, is that the artisan played as crucial a

40 I. D. Gleig, Collector, Masulipatnam to BOR, 1 April 1833, *PBR* 1359, 3506–08.

41 Ibid.

42 Extract from letter from the Secretary to Government to Collector, Visakhapatnam, 18 July 1826, *VDR* 4752, 225; regarding resumption of moturpha in the 2nd Division of the Visakhapatnam district, see A. Robertson, Collector, Visakhapatnam, to the Commissioner, Northern Circars, Waltair, 27 September 1852, *VDR* 6655, 156–70.

43 Ibid.

role in sustaining zamindars as the agriculturist. Quite often, zamindars depended on the revenues they collected through moturpha taxes to pay their annual revenue debts to the Company. Sometimes, they used the compensation they received on the loss of loom tax to liquidate the balances. For instance, in 1835, when the zamindarini of Peddapuram had to clear the 1,87,562 rupees she owed the Company, one of the sources which she utilised was the loom tax due up to 1819–1820, an amount of 95,633 rupees. Thus nearly 50 per cent of the outstanding balance was paid off.[44] Similarly, in the same year, the Cotah and Ramachandrapuram zamindar had put forth a claim for 65,611 rupees. Out of this amount, 60,385 rupees, comprising four-fifths of moturpha revenue, was due from the looms employed for the investment of the Ingeram factory.[45] In fact, in certain villages, a large percentage (often more than 50 per cent) of the revenue collections came from taxes on looms or on weavers' houses.[46]

Some estates were dependent on the economic activity of the weavers who lived and worked there. A decline in the fortunes of the weavers adversely affected the worth of these estates. The negative valuation in the estates of Gunnerupoody, Kumudavalli, and Cheyyera in Godavari district from 1802 to 1832, for instance, was attributed by the Collector to the decline of the prosperity of the weavers there.[47]

Owing to the abolition of all informal taxes and the grant of exemption from loom tax payment, weavers slowly drifted away from the linkages that they earlier had with zamindars and other landed magnates. More specifically, these measures drastically affected the avenues of revenue for the zamindar as now he had to depend entirely on the resources of his lands. Further, weavers started to move towards market mechanisms, as the earlier practice of receiving foodgrains at an inflated rate was abolished altogether.

On the other hand, a more direct way of incorporating weavers into the matrix of the colonial economy was created through reverting to the imposition of loom tax, but this time the right to collect tax was made the prerogative of the Company. The ultimate effect on the weaver was that his economic position more or less remained the same with an occasional improvement. The crucial change, however, was that the

44 M. Lewin, Collector, Rajahmundry, to BOR, 24 September 1835, *GDR* 4648, 186–87.

45 Petition of Ramachandrarauze, 238–54.

46 Read to Patrie, 10 November 1800, *MDR* 2998, 121–23.

47 Crawley, Collector, Rajahmundry, to BOR, 1 April 1835, *GDR* 4648, 54–65.

Company's policies effectively disrupted the traditional relationships between the weaver and his rural overlords. This supposedly freed the weaver, making him a more autonomous artisan but, in reality, this semblance of independence only drew him deeper into the textile economy now being evolved by the Company.

Cultural Determinants

While the changes initiated by the Company in the established patterns of revenue administration affected the economic links between weavers, landed elites, and local institutions, the persistence of long-standing cultural systems helped to sustain the weavers. That a textile economy is intricately linked with the social fabric is perhaps a truism. Indeed, it may even be possible to argue that certain cultural practices—with origins in other domains such as ideology and attitudes, religion, castes, social ritual, or court traditions—supported specific textile production activities. Many sanctioned rituals, sacred and secular, elitist as well as those of the common people, required the use of particular types of cloth, and their impact on the textile economy could not have been insignificant.

Interestingly, the fashions and styles of the various societal groups of this period were strikingly similar. Social differences were indicated not by style, but by quality and type of cloth. Sometimes, the use of a particular pattern and size of fabric denoted economic difference. The popular proverb, "*Kaligite kallu muyya, lekapote mokallu muyya*," spoke of the economically disadvantaged groups wearing a garment that extended only to the knee, while the richer classes could afford a full-length one.[48]

Men usually wore garments that were mostly unstitched, namely, *dhovati or dhoti* (a man's lower garment), *kanduva* or *jamavaru* (upper garment), and *pagah* (turban). A plain length of cloth, usually white, the dhovati was passed between the legs after a couple of turns round the waist and tucked under the folds behind. On all religious and ceremonial occasions, this was the simplest indigenous fashion adopted by all groups including the rich landed magnates.[49] However, a social message could be discerned not only in the quality but also in the specific patterns of the borders. The wearing of dhovatis with particular designs and colours

48 Narasimha Reddy, *Telugu Sametalu*, 309.

49 Maclean 3, 275.

in the borders was considered a privilege associated with wealth and political power. White dhovatis with red borders, saffron-coloured dhovatis, dhovatis with Latchminarayana *anchu* (selvage or border), Soundaryamani anchu, were some of these special varieties.[50]

The kanduva or jamavaru was an upper garment. A pagah, also termed *kullayamu* or *talapagah*, was a narrow scarf wound round the head to form a turban. Even though the use of pagahs was common among all sections, the size and shape of turbans were determined by the caste of the wearer.[51] The higher classes wore pagahs of silk or fine cloth, with some of them having embroidered or *zari* (gold thread) edges. In addition, some garments like *jamah* (a long gown), *neemah* (a waistcoat with sleeves), and fabric like *sash* (muslin turban cloth), soosi, and taffeta were exclusively worn by the elite groups.[52]

Sometimes, specific costumes went with particular administrative positions. Thus, the village karnam, usually of the Brahmin caste, generally sported a white dhovati, kanduva, *chokkayi* (shirt) and pagah. This traditional costume of the karnam persisted well into the eighteenth century and even later.[53]

Fernand Braudel has, in fact, suggested that in India (as in China), costumes remained unchanged till the Mughal conquest led to the rural elites' seeking to emulate the culture of the conquerors.[54] We find this at work in the northern Coromandel, where the landed magnates and, to some extent, the rich communities of merchants imitated the fashions and cultures associated with the new rulers. The various garments adopted by the zamindars to meet ritual, social, civil, and courtly obligations illustrate the conscious effort on the part of the local elites to imitate the styles of power groups, but without giving up the traditional indigenous character.

50 See the list of the property of Cocherlakota Venkata Jugnudarow, minor son of the late Cocherlakota Ramachandra Venkata Krishna Row, proprietor of Polavaram and Paattiseema estates, examined on 16 May 1846, *GDR* 6742, 235–46; the literature of this period, *Hamsavimsati* and *Suka Saptati* also contain descriptions of the varieties of dhovatis worn by different caste groups.

51 For a detailed description of pagah as an item of dress, see Maclean 3, 721.

52 Property List of Jugnudarow, *GDR* 6742, 231–47.

53 Tallapaka Tirevengalanadudu, *Parama Yogi Vilasamu*, 455. A similar description is found in *Hamsavimsati*. See for details, Pratapareddi, *Andhra Sangheeka Charitra*, and Nanduri Venkata Satya Rama Rao, *Andhra Sahityamu Sangheekha Jeeveena Pratipalamu (A.D. 1022 – A.D. 1856)* (Pentapadu: Srivaishnava Press, 1979).

54 Braudel, *Civilization and Capitalism*, 311–23.

Evidence from the proprietary estates of Pattiseema and Polavaram shows a wide variety of fine textiles in the wardrobe of the former zamindar, Cocherlakota Ramachandra Venkata Krishna Row. Besides gold and silver items, brass and metal utensils, inventories of his property list 104 pieces of fine textiles with gold thread designs.[55] Dhovatis, kanduvas, pagahs, and romals making up the bulk is sufficient indication of the importance of traditional styles. Nevertheless, the presence of certain garments such as jamah, jackets, waistcoats, pantaloons, and half trousers show that the rich and privileged easily adopted the lifestyles of the Muslim ruling class.

A similar fusion of styles seems to have been at work for female costumes as well. Brocade jackets and colourful silk shirts embroidered with gold thread, imported from China as well as West Asia, were popular with affluent womenfolk. At the same time, the attire of Hindu women influenced that of their Muslim counterparts.[56]

These consumption patterns helped the survival of those weaving villages that depended greatly on the support and strength of the landed magnates. Many fine varieties of zamindari consumption included local textiles such as the dhovatis of Uppada and Tautipaka, as also fine handkerchiefs produced in the Mangalagiri village of Masulipatnam district.[57]

The presence of textile varieties like broad cloth, locally called *banathu*, and velvet was an indication of the way long-distance trading networks were stimulated by the adaptation of new cultural styles.[58] The broad cloth of Europe journeyed a long way to the markets of the region.[59] Much of the broad cloth appeared to have been used as decorative symbols for legitimising the pomp and power of landed and rural elites. The civil and ritual authority of zamindars was signified by palanquins embellished with velvet and broad cloth with silk and gold thread hangings, as was seen in the Pattiseema and Polavaram zamindar's

55 Property List of Jugnudarow, *GDR* 6742, 231–47.

56 Ibid., 235–37.

57 Moti Chandra, "Costumes and Textiles in the Sultanate Period", *JITH* 6, 1961, 5–61; Moti Chandra, "Indian Costumes and Textiles from the Ancient to the Twelfth Century", *JITH* 5, 1960, 1–41.

58 Property List of Jugnudarow, 235–37.

59 "Rajam Kaifiyat" in *Grama Kaifiyatlu: Srikakulam Zillah* of the Mackenzie Collections (Hyderabad: Andhra Pradesh State Archives Publications, 1990), Glossary, 31–32.

list.[60] Sometimes, these fabrics were used for garments as in pantaloons made of velvet for the Polavaram zamindar. However, broad cloth was essentially used for military and furnishing purposes.

This kind of demand for broad cloth ultimately resulted in the importation of different varieties into Masulipatnam district in the later half of the eighteenth century. Superfine broad cloth—scarlet, thick and thin, green thick, blue thick, white, buff, yellow, and fine and ordinary varieties of yellow, blue, green, red, and popinjays—and crimson, green and white velvet up to an amount of 1130 rupees were imported into the district between May 1789 and 30 April 1790.[61]

The disbanding of military forces attached to the estates of landed magnates in the pre-Permanent Settlement period and the decline of the zamindars consequent to the introduction of the Permanent Settlement with the subsequent reduction in the numbers of their retainers led to a change in the overall consumption pattern and a decline in the fondness for broad cloth.

The styles and preferences of the zamindari class for a particular textile variety made for regular trading between the northern Coromandel and the Bengal Presidency during this period. From distant places such as Sylhat, Assam, Cossimbazar, Roodanagore, Seorpony, and Dakka, dhovatis of *muga* silk (special to north-eastern India), raw silk of different sorts, silk and cotton piece-goods were imported into Masulipatnam district.[62] This continued well into the first half of the nineteenth century.

The consumption patterns of the various groups of people in a zamindari was another factor that affected textile production. The expenditure on cloth constituted a major budget item, as the zamindar

60 Broad cloth was considered very precious and luxurious by the common people, and the early Europeans widely used this item as a gift to Indians. For instance, in 1679, Streynsham Master presented different sizes of broad cloth to those natives who extended their hospitality towards him. He presented broad cloth to merchants at Masulipatnam and Petapoli when arranging their commercial contracts. See "A Memorial of Streynsham Master, Agent of the Coast and Bay Company, his journey from Fort St. George, Madraspatam, to Machillipatam and Parts to visit those Factories, 19 March 1679", Appendix to Chapter V in Mackenzie, *KDM*, 130–46; Property List of Jugnudarow, 235–37.

61 William A. Dobbyn, Sea Customs Collector, to Anthony Sadleir, Chief and Council, 9 October 1790 (accounts of sale of broad cloth from 1 May 1789 to 30 April 1790), *MDR* 2840, 118.

62 Cloth imported at Masulipatnam for 5 years from 1 January 1785 to 31 December 1789, in Dobbyn to Sadleir, 9 October 1790, *MDR* 2840, 112–17.

provided all the requirements of the service groups attached to his family.[63] The list of expenses on cloth incurred by Jugnudarow's family is illustrative. (For more details and the list, see Potukuchi Swarnalatha 1986.) The sharp distinctions between the ordinary and luxury expenditures and the desire of the zamindars to distinguish themselves from other social groups is evident in the payments for people other than members of their immediate family.[64]

Traditional rituals were as important as the established institutions in furthering the production of specific kinds of textiles. Particularly significant were those ceremonies identified with power groups and local landed elites as large amounts were spent on fine textiles. An important event that called for special varieties of valuable textiles was the marriage ceremony. Gifts of cloth were exchanged between the wedding parties—this was a crucial ritual obligation.[65] For instance, out of the expenses of 395 rupees on the marriage of the sister of Cocherlakota Venkata Jugnudarow to Paunnugappally Venkiah, 191 rupees were spent on cloth provisions. Presents in the form of cloth on the wedding day included a pair of *arse* (silk) cloth with gold thread border, a pair of upper cloth with gold thread border, and a turban to the bridegroom Venkiah; a pair of arse cloth for his father; two pieces of gold thread bordered cloths for his mother and sister; and one piece of cloth bordered with gold thread for the bride, Venkata Chellammer.[66]

The arse cloth played a significant part in social and religious rituals. Arse is a *pattu vastram* or silk cloth, ordinarily called *madiceru*.[67]

The cloth gifts in the above case were the bare minimum as there were strict limits on the overall marriage expenses, keeping in view the straitened circumstances of the estate. On similar occasions in the past, an amount of 1000 rupees was spent, a reflection of splendid and lavish patterns of consumption. Established norms relating to the quantity and value of cloth bought on marriage occasions created problems for the declining aristocracy. In 1824, the minor zamindar of Nuzividu,

63 Read to Patrie, 15 May 1800, *PBOR* 252, 4418–24.

64 Ibid., 4422.

65 Arze from Daumarauz Cammarauz, guardian of the Polavaram taluk, to T. Prendergast, 9 May 1847, in T. Prendergast, Collector, Rajahmundry, to BOR, 16 June 1847, *GDR* 6743, 166–71.

66 Ibid.

67 This is based on the definition provided in Konduri Iswara Dutt, *Sasana Subdha Kosamu Andhra Pradesama (Inscriptional Glossary of Andhra Pradesh)* (Hyderabad: Andhra Pradesh Sahitya Akademi, 1968), where medicera is defined as *madichira pattu vastram* (silk cloth) and the equivalent of this is *arṣinam*.

whose estate was placed under the Court of Wards, had requested the government to sanction an amount of 1,20,000 rupees towards marriage expenses. Of this, 14,550 rupees were meant for the purchase of cloth.[68]

In the eighteenth century, the influence of the Mughal wars on the Deccan was noticed in the traditions insisted upon in Nizam-ul-Mulk's court. Lalamangaram's *Khanaun-i-Durbar*, also called *Risalapi-Durbar-i-Asif*, describes styles of attire that were to be followed if an entry into the court was sought.[69] These included rules such as:

1. Anyone not wearing headgear was prohibited entry into the *diwan-khana*.
2. In the court, no one could enter without a belt on the waist and carrying something like a shawl (*dupatta*) over the shoulders.
3. The length of the cloth for making a full dress was to be at the most 7½ yards (*pats*); and the short dress had to be of 5 yards.
4. The cost of the cloth was also to be taken into consideration in making the dress so that everyone could easily afford it; the cloth of the headgear and the dress had to be of superior quality.
5. The dress was to be such as to have a long extension in front, in order to receive and tie in it any gift, if presented by the Nizam.

Headgears were of different styles such as Arabi, Mughlai and Khuridar. However, those of a light colour were never worn in the presence of Nizam-ul-Mulk.

Among the economically less powerful groups, too, the marriage ceremony was associated with the demand for specific kinds of cloth. There was a connection between the variety of textile prescribed and the caste or community in which the marriage was being celebrated. For instance, the *madhuparkam* was an essential item in a Brahmin marriage.[70]

It was not only during weddings that cultural prescriptions were made. Specific designs, colours, textures were ordained for almost every significant event in life, especially for women. A pregnant woman was expected to wear a sari of a deep red colour (*rakta katreku koka* or *rakta pinjari chira*) at a particular time. The unadorned, plain saris decreed for widows are well known.[71]

68 Prendergast to BOR, *GDR* 6743, 166–71.

69 For a description of the institutions at Nizam-ul-Mulk Asaf Jah's court, see M. A. Nayeem, *Mughal Administration of Deccan under Nizam-ul-Mulk Asaf Jah, 1720–48* (Hyderabad: Jaico Publishing House, 1985), 84–87.

70 Krishnamurti and Dakshinamurti, entry under *Madhuparkam*, 304.

71 Ibid, 328.

The sacred and religious rituals of the higher castes prescribed wearing particular textiles. One such was the use of *madi* apparel, which was the name given to ceremonially pure garments worn at home during auspicious or sacred occasions.[72] It was an indispensable item, essentially for Brahmins, to procure which they would even if necessary go without food, as in the proverb: "Miss the meal but not the madi cloth."[73]

The persistence of traditional attire among all segments of society was yet another factor in maintaining the specialised craftsmanship of weavers. The hill people in the Visakhapatnam region wore the colourfully striped rough cotton fabric that was the speciality of the weavers of Rajam.[74] Even the simple dhovati and turban of the ordinary ryot, because of their continuance over generations, sustained the textile economy. Descriptions of the dress codes of the Reddis and the Kapus in Telugu literary works of the period, such as *Parama Yogi Vilasamu* and *Suka Saptati*, indicate that hardly any changes had taken place in the styles of the cultivating groups. Interestingly, the combali entered the common dress mores of cultivators in this period, worn especially when they went to their fields.[75]

At another level of production, the presence of jajmani and institutional relationships at the village level determined the endurance of lower class consumption patterns associated with groups such as the Palerus, bonded agricultural labourers. These workers received payment not only in cash but also some in kind such as unthrashed paddy at the end of the year, a new piece of cloth, and tobacco in some areas of Godavari district. In Guntur district, a Paleru—whether Gentoo, Pariah or Chucklar—was entitled to 5 maunds of grain and a cloth, if he had worked for one year. After three or four years, if he desired to attach himself and his family hereditarily to a particular ryot, then his emoluments contained a number of allowances on various ceremonial and ritual occasions. Besides, he was entitled to 1 seer of *jonna* a day and a combali annually, whether his employment was in the fields or in some other business.[76]

The foregoing discussion underlines the important role culture played in determining the stability and vitality of the textile industry. It

72 Hemingway, *GGD*, 102.

73 Narasimha Reddy, 310.

74 Havell, *Arts and Industries of Madras Presidency*, 19–20.

75 Tallapaka Tiruvengalnadu, *Parama Yogi Vilasamu*, 478 and 531; and Kadirapati, *Suka Saptati* 2, 413 in Pratapareddi, 229–30 and Rama Rao, *Andhra Sahityamu*, 320–21.

76 Hemingway, *GGD*, 90–91.

is evident that the social prescriptions of dress and the persistence of tradition helped the Coromandel weaver to work with a degree of security that could not have been achieved solely by the economic value attached to cloth. In the post-1830 period, the Collectors of the region were unanimous in their view that the decline of the zamindars and other landed elites was perhaps the most crucial factor in the loss of the market for silk and cotton of both fine and superfine varieties. Traditional weavers appeared to have had no choice but to shift towards the production of coarser and ordinary texiles.[77]

Price of Cloth

The Company's attempts to reorganise the structural arrangements of the weaving villages, the extension of various legal procedures, and the granting of tax exemptions to control the entire production organisation of the weaving world were manifestations of its commercial motives. By the turn of the eighteenth century, having virtually acquired a monopsonistic position over the textile trade, the Company manipulated the prices of the various assortments intended for export markets. The Court of Directors consistently tried to procure textile varieties at the lowest possible price.[78]

The prices offered by the Company for Masulipatnam chay goods showed a declining trend between 1786 and 1816.[79] Earlier, allegars, callowpores, sastracundis, red and blue ginghams, and Masulipatnam romals of different assortments, were largely produced on the requirements of private traders.[80] The prices which the Court of Directors offered fluctuated often, depending on the intensity of competition created by other European traders or when a rise in costs occurred because of dislocations in the economy such as famines in the region.

The Company effected price reductions continually in chay goods mainly by carrying all the varieties in its investment lists, including those in the Spanish, French, Dutch and Armenian musters, which not only reduced the competition of private traders but also effectively

77 R.T. Porter, Collector, Masulipatnam, to T. Pycroft, BOR, 20 October 1845, *PBR* 1992, 14242–55.

78 See Letters from Court of Directors, *CDDE* 1–40.

79 Table 1.1 in Appendix has details on prices.

80 For details on private trading activity, see Chapter 9.

reduced the bargaining capacity of the Masulipatnam weaver.[81] The Company's pricing policy for Masulipatnam cloth was determined by two opposing factors. There was the need to encourage weavers by offering an attractive price. On the other hand, as most of the Masulipatnam cloth was intended for the rural markets of Europe, the prices could not be pegged at too high a level. The final amount, therefore, was somewhere between the two.[82] Conflicts between the chief and under-contractors of chay goods were utilised by the commercial officials at Masulipatnam to offer a low price. The recovery of the district from the effects of famine, the virtual eclipse of private competition, and the availability of more weavers were the grounds on which the Board of Trade resisted the demand of the contractors for a higher remuneration.[83]

The value of punjum cloth and salempores from the Visakhapatnam, Ingeram, and Maddepollam factories followed a vacillating course between 1787 and the 1830s. In Visakhapatnam district, the price of long cloth, as fixed by the Court of Directors, increased from 38 pagodas per corjee in 1793 to 47 pagodas per corjee by 1800. In the decade following 1800, the price offered was only 46 pagodas, but after 1811, it rose to 51½ pagodas. A similar trend could be seen between 1787 and 1817 in the case of middling and fine varieties too. Ordinary salempore, when introduced in 1799, was valued at 23½ pagodas, but increased continually up to 26 pagodas till 1810, and later on declined by 1 pagoda. Although the middling variety remained at 28 pagodas between 1805 and 1810, it went up to its original price of 30 pagodas by 1817.

Prices went up on all the varieties primarily because of the severe famine that engulfed the region from November 1790 to November 1792. The principal dietary item of the weavers, jonna, was sold at 25 pagodas per candi. Consequently, most of the weavers left the area, causing a decline in the provision of the Company's investment.[84]

Weavers also had to spend a higher percentage of their earnings on raw materials. Therefore, the Company had to increase the value of piece-goods and chay goods.[85] This had to be continued for some years, as the decrease in the population of the region during the famine period,

81 Letter from Court of Directors to Board of Trade, Fort St. George, 3 July 1795, *CDDE* 8, 83–85.

82 Letter from Court of Directors to BOT, 28 May 1794, *CDDE* 7, 63.

83 Letter from Court of Directors to BOT, *CDDE* 11, 51–53.

84 Revenue Consultation, 5 August 1790, *MDR* 2794C, 622–32.

85 Sadleir to BOR, 26 April 1793, *MDR* 2798, 467–74.

especially in Godavari district, led to scarcity and dearness of thread. Despite the increased availability of cotton in 1794, the cost of thread was still high, as most of the inhabitants gave up spinning for agricultural activities.[86] Political disturbances, unusually severe monsoons, and famine conditions in the last decade of the eighteenth century, were all responsible for the Company's inability to effect reduction in prices.

The prices fixed by the Company for coarser varieties of punjum cloth and salempores registered a continual decline from 1820 onwards because of the low profits these goods obtained in the London market. This led to a decrease in demand for the textiles of the northern Coromandel. The Company insisted that the estimated costs and charges of every description of cloth should not exceed the price fixed by the Court of Directors, and warned that any rise in the price of piece-goods would ultimately lead to the withdrawal of its textile investment:

> ...If the goods shall be charged at a higher rate every motion for a Future Indent will cease and we shall be under the necessity of directing the abolition of the Visakhapatnam Commercial Establishment ....[87]

The critical issue, however, was the effect of these, mostly downward, price fluctuations on the weaver. It had grave consequences for him as his earning capacity depended primarily on the real wages he got. The severe famine in 1794 drastically affected the earnings of the weavers at the Ingeram factory. They had to pay more for thread, which meant lesser profits. By 1799, their net gain, after deducting the cost of thread, was only a small proportion of the total price offered by the merchants.

At Ingeram, the monthly earnings of a weaver were considered adequate to support himself and his family of three.[88] In 1796, in Visakhapatnam district, a weaver and his family consisting of his wife and two children needed about 75 rupees a year, and the taxes he paid may have been about 5 per cent of the whole.[89]

Since the vast majority of weavers working for the piece-goods investment of the Company at the Ingeram, Maddepollam and Visakhapatnam factories were under the control of the copdars, they had hardly received any profit from their production, rarely beyond

86 Rowley to Fallofield, 22 May 1794, *GDR* 831, 5.

87 Letters from Directors, 2 May 1821, *CDDE* 34, 129–30; 26 June 1822, *CDDE* 35, 35–36; 10 March 1824, *CDDE* 36, 229.

88 Rowley to Fallofield, *GDR* 831, 5.

89 W. Brown, Collector, Visakhapatnam, to BOR, 1 August 1790, *PBR* 162, 7698–7704.

subsistence levels. Combined with the Company's policy of maintaining moderate prices, this caused dissatisfaction among the weavers who consistently revolted against such oppression.[90]

At Masulipatnam, however, the recommended prices of the Company seemed adequate. It appeared the weavers had no complaints, a fact remarked upon in 1803 by Vincentio Corbrett, the Resident there:

> ...For a term of 10 years there was no complaint on the records (of recourse to compulsion nor of the smallness of the gains of the weavers or insufficiency of the price paid them for the goods, ... indeed they [seem] well satisfied with their lot): the more surprising and unexpected in a district where provisions of all kinds were generally higher priced than further north, at a period the weavers in the neighbouring factories have been in a state of revolt.[91]

In Visakhapatnam, the price of punjum cloth went down greatly from 6 rupees to 3 rupees and 8 annas after the closure of the factory in 1830. Consequently, the weaver's profit decreased from two rupees on each piece of cloth to a meagre 4 to 6 fanams, which was hardly enough to maintain his minimum standard of living.[92] The wages earned by weavers and other artisan groups in Visakhapatnam district were less in 1839 (I *dub* for one cubit of cloth) than during the first decade of the nineteenth century (2 to 3 dubs).[93] The fall in wages coincided with a general declining trend in the economy of Visakhapatnam district. As the cost of grain increased to twice its usual level, the price of gold and silver fell from 16 rupees per *tola* in 1806 to 14½ rupees in 1839.[94]

In Godavari district, however, a different effect of the economic dislocation was noticed. The declining position of weavers because of the winding up of the factory in 1830 further deteriorated owing to a general regression in the status of the zamindars and landed magnates. The demand for fine and expensive cloths consequently decreased. Yet another decisive factor that distressed weavers as well as other classes was the recurrence of adverse climatic seasons.

90 Ibid.

91 Corbrett to BOR, 14 October 1803, *GDR* 832, 412–26, especially 417.

92 W. U. Arbuthnot, Collector, Visakhapatnam, to BOR, 3 October 1837, *PBR* 1584, 14914–16.

93 Arbuthnot, letter dated 5 January 1838, *VDR* 6643, 10.

94 Arbuthnot to C. R. Cotton, Secretary, BOR, Madras, 5 January 1839, *VDR* 6643, 3–18.

From 1824 onwards, the Company's demand was primarily for coarser varieties (like 12, 13, 13½ and 14) of punjum cloth, but after the closure of the factories at Ingeram and Maddepollam, these assortments were rarely bought. Nevertheless, private traders in the region continued to deal in these varieties. While private merchants bought large quantities of 13- and 14-punjum cloth till 1839, 16-punjum cloth was demanded by them only up to 1827. Private trade in 18-punjum cloth completely ceased by 1830. More than 3 or 4 pieces at a time of the middling and superfine varieties, varying from 20- to 50-punjum, were also hardly ever bought.[95]

Thus, in Godavari district, the position of weavers deteriorated in the decade between 1830 and 1840. The termination of factories, declining private trade, instability in the political economy of the district, famines and other natural calamities—all these had deleterious effects on the weaving economy. Table 1.8 in Appendix provides details on the number of weavers, looms, houses, and the production capacity of each of 33 villages, at four different average periods between 1824 and 1843.

The number of looms in Amalapuram taluk registered a drastic decline by the 1840s because weavers, faced by economic uncertainty, sought new avenues of employment in Moulmein and other places. Some weavers also died in the famine.

The weavers from Pitahpuram and Komargeri villages lost their employment and opted for temporary migration to Payakarraopeta and other villages of Visakhapatnam district, and a few went to Yanam.

At Mandapeta, Artamoor, Vedurpaka, Cookoodooroo and Nelatur of Mandapeta mootah, punjum cloth of coarse and middle varieties (i.e., from 12 to 24 punjums) were manufactured. Here, although the textile economy worsened, an increase in the number of looms in four of the villages (except in Artamoor) was primarily due to the movement of weavers from nearby villages.

The effect of the Company's withdrawal of its investment was hardly noticed in Samulcotah and Bheemavaram villages of Cocanada taluk, and there was no decrease in the number of looms from 1824 to 1844.

In the Peddapuram zamindari, reduction of looms and weavers could be attributed to deaths and migration to other villages for want of livelihood; the increase was due to arrivals from other villages.

95 Bird to BOR, 15 January 1845, *PBR* 1950, 1146–48. Page 1148, in fact, includes a number of enclosures concerning the textile investment, the prices of the various cloths, and the effect of the Company's withdrawal from the textile economy of the district; Bird to BOR, 15 January 1845, *GDR* 6741, 6–11.

Famine casualties and the emigration of some weavers to Mauritius and other places led to the fall in the number of looms in Palakollu.

Some weavers of Tuni mootah actually took up work as agricultural labourers and a few went to Visakhapatnam district, where they did not need to pay moturpha tax. Despite these adverse circumstances, there was an increase in the number of weavers employed, as there were new arrivals from other villages. On the whole, over several decades, the weavers in Godavari district were forced into a low-profit situation, and their economic status rapidly worsened.

In all the major textile production villages, the crisis started in the 1820s and reached its worst point in the years between 1829 and 1838. Between 1814 and 1830, nearly 15,000 weavers were employed by the Company and 5000 weavers worked for private traders. From 1814 to 1845, the number of looms in the district came down from 15,000 to 4000. Recovery in quantitative terms was noticed from the end of the 1830s, when weavers went back to work on their looms. Further, the looms paying moturpha tax increased in number by the 1840s. This was due to the opening up of new textile markets in Asia where the demand was mainly for medium and coarse varieties. Consequently, the value of cloth produced in the district was not much, although the number of weavers overall was more.

Migration

We have talked about weavers moving away from their villages in response to situations of coercion or during economic crises. Besides such temporary migrations, weavers, like cultivators and agricultural labourers, also moved on a more permanent basis to foreign shores, to escape oppression at home.

The contraction in the production of cloth motivated weavers to migrate more often in the 1830s. In the new territories in which they located themselves, they often accepted work totally different from their traditional occupation. The weavers of Godavari district, for instance, migrated in the 1830s to Bourbon and Moulmein where they had to labour as coolies on sugar plantations. The number of coolies engaged from this district in 1828–29 for Bourbon was about 3000 and they had to remain at Bourbon for at least 3 years. They were paid a wage varying from 7 to 12 rupees per month besides food. They were to be given, according to the official contracts, a seer of rice and a sufficient quantity of meat or fish for curry every day. They were also to be provided 2 pairs of trousers, 2 shirts and 2 red handkerchiefs annually. When their contract began, they were to have three months pay in advance, and from 3 to 6 rupees per month were to be paid to their families every month.[96]

During this period, nearly 500 weavers moved to Pondicherry, while some originally bound for Bourbon went to Penang. They were generally well treated here, partly because the Dutch were more responsible in seeing that the terms of their agreement had been "more conscientiously fulfilled." The Dutch government intended to employ many more, to the extent of some thousands, especially weavers and artisans.[97]

In the years 1828 and 1829, the French Agent, M. Argand entered into contracts with two parties of the Coromandel coast to employ them at Bourbon as labourers. The first party consisted of 150 men, the second of 300. By 1834, nearly 5,000 persons migrated, mostly from Yanam but also some from Pondicherry and Calcutta. The number of natives from Rajahmundry who lived in Bourbon in 1834 was about 3,000. Owing to various reasons, this was not considered an advantageous idea and no more coolies were hired from this region.[98]

Price of Food

While the price of cloth decreased continually, affecting the earnings of weavers, the monetary and other allowances accorded by the Company were withdrawn from 1830 onwards. With his limited earnings, how did the weaver maintain his basic standard of living? Of particular relevance to this question is the price of foodgrains.

By a selective study of agrarian products, a correlation between the position of the weaver and the agrarian economy of the region can be discerned. Sharp increases in costs affected the weaver's subsistence levels, as there was no corresponding rise in his earnings.

The first half of the nineteenth century was characterised by a general decline in agricultural prices in almost all the districts of the region. By 1843–44, prices had fallen to one half of the average level during the first decade of the century. The rise in agricultural prices was recorded only in the 1860s.[99]

96 Porter to Pycroft, *PBR* 1992, 14242–55.

97 A. Crawley, Collector, Rajahmundry, to the Officiating Secretary to Government in the Judicial Department, Fort St. George, 14 April 1834, *GDR* 4647, 72–73.

98 Officiating Secretary to Government, Sea Customs Office, Fort St. George, to Crawley, 14 March 1834, *GDR* 4659 A, 181–83.

99 John Antsey, Rajahmundry, to BOR, 5 September 1827, *GDR* 4641, 177; Crawley to BOR, 7 July 1831, *GDR* 4644, 15.

The downward trend in food prices affected ryots more than urban dwellers.[100] Weavers actually benefited by this development as they could buy more provisions even with their meagre earnings. There was continuous fluctuation in the economy for about two decades from the 1820s. Cultivators were forced to abandon their land and move to other places to work as coolies or casual labour.[101] The demand for cash crops and food products was at such a low ebb that it was not possible for the producers to even reap the cost of cultivation. The colonial policy of dumping Arakan rice into the region that began at this time was held to be one of the chief factors contributing to the difficult situation.

Zamindaries and proprietary estates were affected alike, and had ultimately to pay up their taxes. The result was that a great number of estates were put up for sale. The decades marked a nadir in the fortunes of the intermediate elements as well as Banias and money-lenders. This was due to contraction on all sides—contraction of production due to the closure of the factories and contraction in exports due to favourable conditions outside the area.

The cost of raw material went up but the wage rate did not. Malas and other groups involved in the spinning of thread were the worst affected lot as they lost their immediate source of livelihood.[102] The ranks of the Rangiraju painters were also decimated because of the acute scarcity and famine conditions.[103]

An active trade in rice between the south-eastern markets and the northern region mitigated the effect of the extraordinarily adverse seasons on weavers. The nature of the trade was diverse. Rice and paddy were imported entirely or exclusively from Arakan and Chittagong into Visakhapatnam district, whereas the exports from the district were directed to Penang, the Malay Straits, and Pondicherry.[104]

Rice exported to Bourbon from Rajahmundry district brought in great profits, while the people of the region commonly depended on Arakan rice, an inferior and cheaper variety. Moreover, Cocanada rose to importance mainly owing to this trade. Nevertheless, in 1845, the rising price of rice made it no longer a profitable item for export. This led to

100 G. N. Rao, "Stagnation and Decay of the Agricultural Economy of Coastal Andhra", *Artha Vignana* 20, 3, 1978, 221–43.

101 Crawley to BOR, 26 July 1832, *GDR* 4645, 126–31.

102 Crawley to BOR, 6 September 1833, *PBR* 1379, 11225–28.

103 Goldingham to BOR, *MDR* 6318, 310–11.

104 W. U. Arbuthnot, Collector, Visakhapatnam, to T. Pycroft, Board of Revenue, 29 November 1845, *PBR* 2001, 16797–805.

a glut of foodgrains in the local market, though the import of rice from Arakan continued as it was still cheaper.[105]

Although this trade disastrously affected cultivators and owners of land, it turned out to be a great relief to weavers because they were

> able to obtain a market at Moulemein, Arracan, Hyderabad and other places for cloths where they could not formerly, in consequence of the very cheap rate at which they can afford to make and sell them... within the last five years however there have been many more houses occupied by weavers and many more people and looms at work, and yet the price of the whole quantity of cloth made has been less. That is, more people have been able to live upon a less income, and at this moment there is a prevailing opinion that the weavers have more to do and are in better case than they have been in for a way long while, and yet there is no rise that I know of in the price of cloths.[106]

Konrad Specker was, however, of the opinion that "even though the low prices of food stuffs which prevailed since the Great Famine of 1833–34 alleviated the misery of the weavers, it failed to eliminate the basic evils responsible for their plight and prospects for the future were uncertain and bleak..."[107] The more devastating effect on the socio-economic position of weavers really occurred only after 1850, when the competition from Manchester textiles made it hard for them to cope with the rising agricultural prices.

The weavers in the northern Coromandel were thus affected by a multitude of factors, thereby demonstrating the way in which they were locked into a wider world that shaped their destinies. The East India Company and its commercial policies—and even more, the industrialisation of Britain—were elements in this broader environment that had a dramatic impact on the Coromandel weaver during the 100 years this study has been investigating.

105 Prendergast to T. Pycroft, Board of Revenue, 11 December, 1845, *PBR* 2004, 17464–69.

106 Bird to BOR, *GDR* 6741, 12.

107 Konrad Specker, "Madras Handlooms", 156.

NINE

The Textile Economy: 1750–1850

No study of the textile economy of the northern Coromandel will be complete unless one examines the various circumstances that affected the production and consumption of textiles. In the century that this study has focused upon, numerous factors—some emerging within the local economy, others having more distant origins—impinged upon the world of the weavers. Cumulatively, these, in the first instance, produced fluctuations in the local economy, and, in the end, contributed to the marginalisation of the region's cloth production, and ultimately subordinated it to the British textile industry.

Between 1750 and 1850, the interaction between metropolitan economies and those of the periphery led to drastic fluctuations in the demand for the textile varieties of the northern Coromandel region. Dislocations in this trading connection occurred because of the political turmoil in the European continent, technological developments in England, and changes in colonial policy. Internal factors such as the political and economic disturbances caused by the colonial wars of the Company, and the persistent domination of landed elites even after two decades of political hegemony in the region also, to a large extent, influenced the pattern of textile production and use.

One illustration of the manner in which political events radically influenced the textile economy was the steep decline in the East India Company's investment at Masulipatnam between 1770 and 1780. The Company's efforts to establish orderly administration and cohesiveness in its controlling structures failed because of the political turmoil that engulfed the Deccan during this period. Therefore, the Company's investment was adversely affected. The "calamitous war" in the Carnatic distressed the weavers of Masulipatnam district to such an extent that they moved to adjoining territories.[1]

1 Chief's Minute, *MDR* 2900A, 137–42.

Apart from political events, which, in any case, tended to diminish in importance as the Company's hold over the region strengthened, another major factor that shaped the course of the textile economy was the activities of private traders.[2] The popularity of the northern Coromandel textiles in Europe and the West Indies created intense competition among the private merchant community. By 1780, the European demand for chay goods spurred private mercantile activity in Masulipatnam to a considerable degree.[3]

Particularly significant was the role of the French agents and the French East India Company in catering to the requirements of the West Indies market, especially for the romals of Masulipatnam.[4] The European wars and Napoleon's continental system, however, radically affected French trading activity in the Coromandel region, and thereby provided a chance for the East India Company to corner the textile trade.[5] From 1793, onwards, for instance, Commercial Residents were authorised to purchase all those goods being provided by the French at Pondicherry, Yanam, and other places.[6]

The investment of foreign traders other than the English East India Company amounted to 1,50,000 Madras pagodas in Masulipatnam district at this time. Although the goods supplied to these private agents were distinct from those of its assortments, the Company, nevertheless, saw in these operations an inducement to weavers to leave its service. To guard against such intrusion into the weaving world, the Company introduced other textile varieties also in its indent by 1795. The concerned commercial authorities were asked to furnish necessary details that would ultimately help to include all those varieties "permanently" into the Company's investment indents.[7]

The war in Europe, instead of depressing the market for Indian cloth, actually created new opportunities. The West Indian markets, which

2 For a detailed discussion of the role of private traders in the seventeenth and eighteenth centuries, see Watson, *English Private Trade in India*.

3 Statham to Floyer, *MDR* 2900A, 5–19; Letter from BOT, *MDR* 2901, 7–38; Letter from Court of Directors, 29 November 1788, *CDDE* 2, 72.

4 Letter from Court of Directors, 28 May 1794, *CDDE* 7, 59–129. For a discussion of French activities in Bengal, see Hossain, *Company Weavers*, 79–82; Watson, *English Private Trade in India*. The Company's indent lists of textiles in Madras Presidency include details on colours, designs, quality and measurements of each variety of cloth to be provided at various factories of the Presidency. See *CDDE* 1–40.

5 Directors to BOT, 28 May 1794, *CDDE* 7, 63–98.

6 Ibid.

7 Directors to BOT, 8 June 1796, *CDDE* 10, 26–27.

were earlier being supplied mainly by France, now opened up for the products of the Coromandel coast, especially for the manufactures of Masulipatnam. The Company, therefore, allotted 3,00,000 pagodas for the appropriation of the West Indies trade.[8] But the European market itself remained uncertain. In 1797, the Court of Directors reported the difficulties faced in selling textile goods in the European markets.[9]

The Company evolved strategies to respond sensitively to the changing demand in its far-flung market. (Table 1.1 in Appendix sets out the demand for chay goods between 1787 and 1815.) Thus, the 1800 indent for the investment of 1801 also included calico cloth as this was becoming popular.[10] Orders for coloured textiles for the African and West Indian markets were not increased as the demand was low and the market had been inundated by the earlier season's supply.[11]

The chay goods investment of Masulipatnam received a setback by 1801. The looms of the district could supply chay goods to a value of 3,50,000 pagodas, but because of the lull in the external markets, the Company ordered only for an amount of 1,00,000 pagodas, inclusive of the new patterns of handkerchiefs. In order to provide employment to the weavers, the Court of Directors suggested getting the required supplies of calico from the looms of Masulipatnam, and allocated an amount of 50,000 pagodas for the first season.

The Company found it extremely profitable to continue to supply cloth to other European purchasers, private as well as organised. For instance, it provided varieties of chay goods to the Dutch and the French as well as the Philippines companies.

Masulipatnam district's textile trade with France ceased from 1793 onwards. Subsequently, the Company tried to take over the French investment wherein various kinds of coloured handkerchiefs constituted highly profitable items. Contemplating large profits on the French assortment, the Court of Directors sent repeated orders for these varieties from 1795 onwards. Strangely, however, for a few years, the orders do not seem to have been met nor was there any information on these items.

It was only in July 1800 that the first sale of "French" goods took place, with the Company offering considerable quantities. However, this was a fiasco as the market had already been supplied with these assortments. It became evident that, though the French trade with India was suspended,

8 *CDDE* 10, 27; Directors to BOT, 1798, *CDDE* 11, 20–21.

9 *CDDE* 11, 23, 24; Directors to BOT, *CDDE* 13, 34–36.

10 Directors to BOT, 18 March 1807, *CDDE* 14, 36–45.

11 Ibid, 56

handkerchiefs were still available for private merchants such as the Armenians. They bought these on a large scale and furnished them to the French markets at a time when the Company was under the impression that there was no foreign competition on the Coromandel coast.

The Company initiated what was thought to be a clever plan to assess the market as a whole. It imitated almost all of the patterns sent from America on British looms. Exported to the West Indies, these goods were sold at exorbitant prices with a fraudulent tag declaring them to be "the products of India".[12] However, in course of time, these imitated fabrics were found to be of very inferior quality, especially as to the colors "which soon fade both in the sun and in the wash; the consequence is not only that the market is glutted with such articles, but that the genuine Indian and British being nearly similar in appearance, the whole assortment is fallen into disrepute, and the prices have undergone a great consequent abatement."[13] Even when the goods were offered at a reduced rate at the sale of 1801, the quantity sold was very low, because of the reduced material condition of buyers.[14] The Company had necessarily to decrease the order for such items.[15]

Technological improvements in England completely marginalised the chay goods industry of Masulipatnam district by 1810. The Company stopped its investment by 1814 as it could supply similar fabrics from its looms in England.

The impetus for the trade in long cloth of different varieties from the Visakhapatnam factory continued till the 1830s. The specific varieties of long cloth sold in the European markets were the ordinary kind ranging from 13½ to 16 punjums and middling 17- and 18-punjum cloth.

The demand for fine varieties such as 20, 22, and 24 punjum existed for some time, but because of cost factors and the non-availability of good quality thread, it was found expedient to shift these assortments to the Ingeram and Maddepollam factories.[16]

A new variety, salempore, found its way into the Coromandel textile economy from 1800 onwards as the Company could not procure it from Ganjam district. Initially, weavers were not keen on producing

12 Directors to BOT, 3 July 1795, *CDDE* 8, 71–72.

13 Ibid.

14 Directors to BOT, *CDDE* 14, 47–48.

15 I. Smith, Collector, Visakhapatnam, to Board of Revenue, 12 April 1814, *VDR* 3752, 111–20, especially 114, para 7.

16 Directors to BOT, *CDDE* 14, 47.

salempores as the available loom technology had to be adapted.[17] The Company, therefore, excluded this variety from the factory investment. However, in course of time, the weavers of Visakhapatnam district started producing salempores too.

The Company's investment on these long cloth and salempore varieties continued, even though on a lesser scale, till 1830. Interestingly, weavers from the districts of Visakhapatnam and Godavari were the last to succumb to Britain's Industrial Revolution. While Masulipatnam weavers lost out on the export trade as early as 1815, Visakhapatnam weavers retained their pre-eminent position for a longer period, because of the demand for long cloth that could not be manufactured on the new looms of the English industry.

In 1814, the Collector of Visakhapatnam stated that nearly 80 per cent of the looms were employed for the production of 14- and 18-punjum cloth. Demand was increasing because of the constraints on the British textile industry of the time. As the Collector put it:

> It being the description of heavy, coarse, but well-made cloth that is not likely to be manufactured in Europe to advantage, the enhanced price of the raw material there not admitting of profitable competitions, it will therefore at all times meet purchasers.[18]

Even Visakhapatnam cloth had, nevertheless, to face competition from Manchester goods by the 1830s and this ultimately caused a decline in the price of punjum cloth. In 1840, the Collector of Visakhapatnam district contemplated a total stoppage of this trade as mill-made cloth completely displaced the Indian products in the London market. Subsequently, cloth usually meant for this outlet was diverted to Calcutta for shipment to eastern markets.

In Godavari district, a large quantity of long cloth and other plain textiles were provided to meet the investment of the Ingeram and Maddepollam factories. Depending on their specialised production, weavers lost out on export opportunities with the gradual decrease in the Company's investment during this period. The direct impact of this was felt most heavily by those weavers producing finer sorts of cloth, especially fine and superfine long cloth. Textiles such as bettelles, dungarees, percaules, etcetera, were no longer included in trading. The reason perhaps was the development of British manufactures that could

17 Ibid.

18 Smith to BOR, *VDR* 3752, 111–20, especially 114, para 7.

replace these varieties as early as 1800.[19] It was evident that the Company's demand was mostly for coarse and middle varieties of punjum cloth. The new kinds that were added were much below the ordinary 12½ and 13 punjums.

Between the 1780s and the 1830s, the Company's textile operations reached a high peak. Between 1786 and 1820, the Visakhapatnam, Ingeram, and Maddepollam factories (and the Masulipatnam factory up to 1815) provided nearly half of the investment of the entire Madras Presidency. Interestingly, between 1820 and 1830, Ingeram, Maddepollam, and Visakhapatnam provided almost the full investment, as long cloth from these factories still retained its hold in the European market. This phenomenon was not perceived in the case of the southern factories, which were gradually amalgamated or closed down, starting from 1815. It has recently been argued that "textile exports from the northern Coromandel region peaked in about 1700 and declined thereafter. Specifically, within this picture of stagnation in the exports from the Coromandel, there is further perceptible a shift from procurement in the northern part of the region to more southerly areas. This suggests that, while the Company exports from the Coromandel as a whole stagnated, exports from the Krishna-Godavari and the Warangal-Khammam areas actually declined."[20] The evidence on the total investment operations of the East India Company in the entire Madras Presidency and the contribution of the northern Coromandel region to the total demand suggests that textile exports continued till the closure of the factories.

Another curious picture that emerges from a careful examination of district records is that the decline in exports cannot be solely attributed to a reduction in demand from the Company. On the contrary, when one looks at the data on indents and the actual amounts supplied, it becomes apparent that often there was a considerable shortfall in supply. Between 1821 and 1827, for instance, there was a total deficit of 11,842 bales from the Visakhapatnam and Godavari districts.[21] Evidently the weavers were not always able to satisfy the demand. This could have been due to the constraints of the production system and/or the problems of raw material costs and availability.

19 G. A. Smith, Collector, Rajahmundry, to BOR, 16 October 1837, *PBR* 1599, 13649–52.

20 Subrahmanyam, "Rural Industry and Commercial Agriculture in Late Seventeenth Century South-Eastern India", *Past and Present* 126, 1990, 105.

21 Gwatkin to Chief Secretary to Government, *CDC* 48, 953–59.

One of the commonly held notions of the impact of colonialism is that decline in the Company's requirement of finer varieties of cloth adversely affected the weavers of such fabric.[22] It may be correct to argue, as G. N. Rao does, that the diminution of the rural aristocracy contributed to a reduction in the orders for finer pieces in the first half of the nineteenth century. In a sense, this was an indirect result of the colonial penetration of the regional economy, a process that contributed to the undoing of the traditional aristocracy. Nevertheless, did the Company directly contribute to the decrease in the production of fine textiles by curtailing its demand for such fabrics?

The evidence we have for this region does not permit us to argue that this was a universal phenomenon. On the contrary, it would appear that even in the last quarter of the eighteenth century, the Company did not always want the finer assortments; rather, it was more interested in the middling and coarse varieties of textiles. The export trade of various factories under the East India Company is clearly indicated by the figures shown in Tables 1.5, 1.6, and 1.7 in Appendix.

The Company's commercial policies and associated administrative strategies had thus not only managed to extinguish all competition, but also, in the process, drew the primary weaver into the world economy. Therefore, colonial policies and market shifts elsewhere too had their impact on the weavers of the northern Coromandel. But, these were not the only factors at work. Weavers produced not only for the overseas markets, local and regional ones were as important.

Cloth Trade and Regional Markets

The centres producing cloth to meet local needs were not drastically affected by the various changes occurring during this period. Trading activity in the different fabrics in Visakhapatnam district can be taken as an index of the circulation of textiles within the micro region. One can perceive a clear pattern of location and growth of centres

22 See Rama Chatterjee, "Cotton Handloom Manufacturers of Bengal, 1870–1921," *EPW* 22, 1987, 988–97 and G. N. Rao, "Changing Conditions and Growth of Agricultural Economy in the Krishna and Godavari Districts, 1840–1890", Ph.D. diss., Andhra University, 1973, 73; Bird to BOR, *GDR* 6711, 6–11, attributed the continual declining position of weavers in the district to the general failure of zamindars and landed proprietors. *CDC* 41, 518, indicates that the Company was willing to accept 12-punjum cloth whereas the coarsest variety accepted earlier was of 13 punjum.

demonstrating the social determinants of textile production. For instance, the price of cloth consumed by ordinary people never went beyond 1 rupee. Often, if they also bought cloth worth 2 rupees, the piece was cut into two, each piece valued at a rupee. The common ryots as well as coolies and labourers usually wore these cloths.[23]

There was an extensive movement of textiles through chowkis such as Bobbili, Rajam, Ullajanghy, Seereepuram, Poondoor, Boddavaram, Lacavaram, Veeragottam, and Parvathipuram that were concentrated in a small area.[24] Most of these toll posts were situated near district limits and the amount of duty collected on piece-goods was a clear indication of the internal trading activities of the weaving world. For instance, between 1815–16 and 1824–25, there was a remarkable increase in the collection of duties on piece-goods from Visakhapatnam district.

The impact of mill-made cloth on local trade appears to have been very little, as no cloth of foreign manufacture was available in the market. On the other hand, the demand for coarse and middling assortments whose value did not extend beyond 2 rupees might have gone up with the increase in population during this period. In 1837, commercial officials recommended an exemption of duty on those textiles of value of not more than 2 rupees, because these cloths were generally used by cultivators and labourers, and the exemption would also benefit the manufacturer and merchant alike.[25]

In Godavari district, the ordinary sections of society seldom used cloth more than a rupee in value. Out of 54 chowkis where transit duties were collected, 25 contributed revenue exceeding 100 rupees on cloth valued below 1 rupee as well as varying from 1 to 2 rupees.[26] Incidentally, the chowkis also represented major textile production centres such as Tuni, Pitahpuram, Uppada, Peddapuram, Amalapuram, Ambazepeta, Peddapatnam, Mumedivaram, Kottapeta, Rajahmundry, Mandapeta, Dracharam, Nellapalli, Amravatum, Penumadum, Penugonda, Attili, Nadervapally, Bandarlanka, Mulkepolam, Ramachandrapuram, and Assunta.[27]

In Godavari district, duties collected on essentially the coarsest varieties increased by almost 100 per cent in the decade between 1815 and 1825, leading to the inference that internal trade in piece-goods was growing.

23 Arbuthnot to BOR, 3 October 1837, *PBR* 1584, 14914–16.

24 Ibid.

25 Lewin to BOR, 30 April 1835, *GDR* 4663, 93–102; Bird to BOR, *GDR* 6741, 6–11.

26 Smith to BOR, *PBR* 1599, 13649–52.

27 Ibid.

There were distinct production centres in Masulipatnam district producing chay goods, white piece-goods, and chintz.[28] The fluctuations in the trading activities of Persian merchants was a crucial factor in determining the fortunes of weavers and painters of cloth, the two essential elements in the textile economy here. The growing importance of Masulipatnam port depended largely on this trade. The production centres of the district usually produced textile varieties such as table linen, towels, handkerchiefs, printed and painted articles, turbans, palampores, and chintz. It was this branch of the industry that continued into the nineteenth century, showing some promise, even with being exposed to competition from British mills in the 1820s.[29]

In the 1830s, the chay goods industry was servicing markets in Persia, Hyderabad, and Masulipatnam. The customers for these goods were mainly Muslims.[30]

Piece-goods also continued to be produced. By 1837, there were 14 customs posts in the district that collected duties on piece-goods. Nearly half the total land trade was concentrated in and around the Bandar chowki. An extensive business in ordinary and painted textiles, the value of which did not extend beyond 2 rupees, passed through this chowki as did all the chintz trade.[31] The dealings in lower cost varieties, especially of those below 1 rupee, was limited to a few chowkis such as Eluru and Relangi. Most of the weaving centres of Masulipatnam district thus depended on those varieties meant for middle-class consumption.[32]

The survival of weaving villages in the region was, therefore, interlinked with the nature of the consumption patterns at distant receiving centres. For instance, socio-political factors that persisted in Persia had a direct repercussion on the chintz trade. The decline in the Persian demand for chintz directly affected the urban economy of Masulipatnam town.[33] This was further compounded by the shortage of painters without whose skill chintz could not be produced. Many of these painters had died during the famines of the 1830s.[34]

28 Goldingham to BOR, *MDR* 6318, 310–11.

29 Ibid.

30 Ibid.

31 Roberts to BOR, 19 April 1826, *PBR* 1061, 3827–32.

32 I. C. Wranghton, Collector, Masulipatnam, to BOR, 27 October 1837, *PBR* 1582, 14442–44.

33 Goldingham to BOR, *MDR* 6318, 1–23.

34 I. Blame, Acting Collector, Masulipatnam, to Board of Revenue, 9 April 1838, *MDR* 6320, 295–323, especially 298.

A major aspect of the Masulipatnam cloth industry was the trade with the Nizam's Dominions. From 1838–39 onwards, there was a gradual increase in the total value of cloth exported to this region. Moreover, textiles contributed nearly 50 per cent of the total trade.[35]

Weaving centres in and around Jaggaiahpeta, Tirwoor, Goodjoor, and Chintalapudi chowkis primarily depended on trade with the Nizam's Dominions. These four chowkis constituted major frontier posts through which the trade was conducted.[36] The textiles from Masulipatnam district that went to the Nizam's territory included raw silk, cotton, cotton twists, silk thread, and thread twists. The level of such trading activity can be seen in the actual transit duties collected on piece-goods.[37]

The trade link between the Nizam's territories and Masulipatnam was reciprocal and interdependent—the Masulipatnam weaver depended for his survival on exports to the Nizam's territories and it was from this region that the raw materials for his fabrics came.

In Guntur district, there were two categories of weavers, one catering to local demand and the other to export trade. The most important centres from where cloth of low value (that is, up to 1 rupee) were obtained were Guntur, Tadicondah, Mangalagiri, Rayapudi, Prattipadu, Amaravati, Chebrole, Nundipadu, Tenali, Modukuru, Ponnur, Colleparah, Rajahpeta, Chilakalurpadu, Innacondah, Narasaraopeta, Nauikel, Repalli, Battiprole, Dhulipudi, Kurapadu, Atchempettah, Kondavidu, Sattenapalli, Dutchapally, Joolacalloo, Machavaram, Macherlah, and Maudogaleh. The weavers at these places specialised in dhovatis, *punchalu* (dhotis), *cheera*s (women's garments), *buchakani*s (woven fabric), coarse cloths, *angavastramu* (upper garment/shawl), talapagahs, jamavarus, *chela*s (scarves or mantles), *ravekalu* (woman's blouse), *ootariyalu* (upper garment), kanduvas, and *voneelu* (half saree). Although these items were usually purchased by the poorer sections of

35 "The Frontier Duty consisted of two duties, one the General Transit Duty at 5 per cent collected on 36 articles and the other, the Frontier Duty strictly collected on specific articles at the rates specified in clauses 1st and 2nd, section XIV, Regulation I of 1812. The collection on account of inland or transit and frontier duties in the Frontier Divisions are so much blended with one another that they cannot now be separate," Porter to BOR, 25 October 1843, *MDR* 6326, 320–25, especially 321.

36 Ibid.

37 Goldingham to BOR, 18 October 1837, *PBR* 1599, 13655–56.

people, they contained two varieties that were meant for Brahmins and Komatis. Production of high-quality textiles centred around interior places such as Guntur, Tadicondah, Mangalagiri, Rayapudi, Chebrole, Amaravati, and several other places, and border villages such as Pedugulah, Gottemokala, and Gottepallah.[38]

Weaving centres such as Mangalagiri, Perala, Vetapalam, Tenali, Rajahpeta, Battiprole, and Kanagalah produced for external markets. Weavers established trade links over a widespread area in the Deccan and in the Masulipatnam and Chittoor districts, and in distant places like Bombay, Jalna, Colombo and Ankolah.[39]

Weavers working for a growing mass market were benefited when an exemption on inland duty was accorded in 1824. All weavers, including Pariahs and barbers who had looms, were absolved from paying duty on those pieces meant exclusively for their personal use. In 1826, when the Company intended to abolish sayer duties on cloth valued below 1 rupee, such a step was seen as an impetus to the manufacturer too.[40]

The fall in external demand would have led to a glut in the local markets and consequently to a reduction in the price of textiles. This did not, however, immediately distress the weavers, especially those producing for local consumption, since there was a simultaneous decrease in the price of grain.[41] This meant that there was no substantial cutback in their standard of living.

Though weaving for local markets was not challenged by mill-made cloth till late in the century, the chief centres producing for export markets were severely affected by the 1840s. The profits of the trade declined greatly, because the competition for their products was in those markets where the specialised products of these centres were traditionally sold. Vetapalam handkerchiefs and other goods were displaced by European products by virtue of their lower prices.[42] Interestingly, such competition could not be waged at the price level

38 Ibid.

39 Ibid. The value of cloth turned out at these places for varieties meant for external trade was high. See Tables 1.5, 1.6, and 1.7 in Appendix for details.

40 Goldingham to BOR, *PBR* 1599, 13655–56.

41 H. Oakes to BOR, 28 August 1844, *gudr* 5402, 296–99.

42 Ibid.

alone. British goods sought to capture the markets commonly dominated by Indian textiles by turning out imitations.[43]

Thus, initially at least, the trade wars were waged in markets fairly distant from the production centres. This can lead us to the inference that textiles from the mills of England did not adversely affect local consumption. In fact, the data for the period from 1820 to 1850 clearly shows an overall increase in the number of looms, though this may appear specially paradoxical because this was a time when the Company was withdrawing from the textile economy, and when the region was being racked by famines and adverse seasons.

Can we conclude that the increase in the number of looms reflected a growth trend in the textile economy? G. N. Rao has argued against drawing such an inference, pointing out that the number of looms and weavers was not an accurate pointer. However, he suggests three possible explanations for the rise in the number of looms. One, textile imports from Britain could not penetrate interior markets; second, there was a shift to coarser varieties, production of which could have increased; third, Rao argues that the agrarian situation was in a state of stagnation and decay, pushing low-caste cultivators and labourers into the weaving profession, thus swelling the number of looms and weavers.[44]

Rao also dismisses the arguments of Morris D. Morris who suggested that population growth was a factor.[45] This can, no doubt, be subject to controversy and dispute.[46] Nevertheless, there is reason to believe that

43 Goldingham to BOR, *MDR* 6318, 310–12, describes this phenomenon in the Persian market. However, the Persian customers were apparently quite shrewd and prudent, as the Collector reported that Indian goods soon regained the ground lost because they were more durable than English mill fabrics. Britain, in fact, learnt the art of making chintz only in the eighteen century. See *Homage to Kalamkari*, 20, 79. The use of Indian designs, sometimes imported on chinoserie, was not only to cater to the new taste for the 'oriental' but also to compete with Indian goods in the world markets.

44 Rao, "Stagnation and Decay", 232–33.

45 Morris, D. Morris, "Trends and Tendencies in Indian Economic History", *IESHR* 5, no. 1, 1968, 381.

46 See the discussion relating to this by Pravin and Leela Visaria, "Population: 1757–1947" in *Cambridge Economic History of India* 2, 463–69.

the high levels of artisanal activity in the eighteenth century may have sustained a growth in population.[47] Such an increase would, it can reasonably be assumed, support the weaving industry by maintaining or increasing the demand.

While population growth was an important factor in the region as a whole, there were various factors at work in the different districts of the northern Coromandel which affected the weaving industry. In the Rajahmundry district, there was a brief setback to the weaving industry in the 1830s. G. N. Rao has suggested that this was caused by the competition from British mill-made cloth as well as famine and adverse seasons.[48] An equally important reason was the declining position of the rural elites.[49]

To what then could the upswing in the number of looms in the 1840s be attributed? One major explanation was that the district resumed its textile trade with Asian destinations such as Penang, Mauritius, Rangoon, Pegu, and Sumatra. This trade showed a significant increase, as Tables 1.5, 1.6 and 1.7 in the Appendix indicate. In fact, the increase was of such magnitude that the Company did not deem it necessary now to protect the weaver through tax concessions. As the Collector of Rajahmundry pointed out:

> The Board invited an opinion regarding the measures which may appear proper to be adopted for the encouragement of the cloth trade. I fear it is not in the power of government to do anything to place it to its former prosperity and I am afraid to think that it is not expedient at this period of time to extend any particular indulgences to weavers. Some fifteen years ago when the demand for the Company's investments and those of private merchants were suddenly stopped and persons were thrown out of their employ, a remission of the moturpha on looms and of transit duties on cloth would no doubt have been a material alleviation of the privations and hardship which must have been extensively and severely felt, but since then time has restored the balance which was

47 The proto-industrialisation theory suggests a connection between industrial activity and rise in fertility levels because of lowering of the age of marriage. See D. C. Coleman, "Proto-Industrialisation:A Concept Too Many", *Economic History Review*, 2nd series, no. 36, August 1983, 435–48. It needs to be examined whether this argument can be applied to this region too.

48 Rao, "Stagnation and Decay", 232–33.

49 Bird to BOR, *GDR* 6741, 5–12; Bird to BOR, 20 October 1844, *PBR* 1950, 1146–48, along with its enclosures provides details on data pertaining to the position of the weaving economy.

disturbed. The superfluous hands have been taken from the looms and occupied in agriculture and many persons have gone to seek employment at Moulmein, and even it is said emigrated as coolies to Bourbon and Mauritius. A new business has sprung up for the weavers in cloths suited to the Asiatic market of a kind not brought to the country from England and their circumstances are perceptively improving under its influence. I thus look upon the present class of weavers as quite distinct from those who existed in the days of the trade with England and as it is so long since that set has passed away and the present one seems to require no particular fostering I do not perceive that it is in any way incumbent on government at present at least to make sacrifices of any kind in their favour.[50]

Another argument raised in this context is that, although the number of looms may have increased, the value of cloth produced was decreasing.[51] It is evident, however, that this was merely a reduction in totals. The decrease was not uniform, either over the entire region or over the range of fabrics.

Exports to the territories of the Nizam were also important for the textile economy of Masulipatnam district, as already indicated. More crucial here was the large-scale textile trade of the district with Persia. Loom tax collections show a drastic fall in 1831–32 and an increase thereafter. The fall could be attributed to the famine in the region. The increase was due, it can be suggested, to the continuation of the trade with Persia, despite increasing competition from British mills. This, in fact, helped to compensate for the cessation of the chay goods trade in 1810. Moturpha collections in 1855–56 were greater than the amounts collected in 1821–22.

The situation in Guntur district was also the same. Here too, by the 1850s, the tax collections virtually reached the position obtaining in the 1820s.[52]

The tax figures thus show a slow but perceptible growth. But this increase did not uniformly affect all the categories of weavers. The number of looms operated by the low-caste Mala weavers grew at a slower pace, implying, therefore, that the benefits of the new prosperity went primarily to the traditional weaver.

50 Bird to BOR, *GDR* 6741, 10.

51 Rao, "Stagnation and Decay", 221–43; Specker, "Madras Handlooms", 153–55.

52 Even in Masulipatnam district, loom tax collections reached an earlier position by 1854. J. I. Knox, Collector, Masulipatnam, to BOR, 20 October 1857, *MDR* 6344, 312–57.

While the textile economy showed clear growth in the 1840s and 1850s in Guntur and Masulipatnam, the situation in the Visakhapatnam district was in stark contrast. Ironically, it was here that the weaver continued to produce punjum cloth till 1840. After that, however, the industry declined rapidly.[53] Visakhapatnam, unlike the other districts of the region, had very few export markets other than the European ones. Once these were closed to it, the textile industry collapsed.

The other major factor in the textile economy of the region was the import of British textiles.

IMPORTS

What was the nature of textile imports into the region? There were, towards the end of the eighteenth century, two major kinds of imports. One was the import of textiles from other production centres in India, the other was that of European textiles.

Indian textiles that came into Masulipatnam district included Mogga dhovatis from Sylhat and Assam, raw silk of fine sort from Cossimbazar, *mucotal* (raw silk) from Cossimbazar and Radnagore, silk piece-goods from Radnagore, Maldeved, Seorporny, and Cossimbazar, cotton piece-goods and twist from Dakka and coarse cloth from other places.[54]

Around 1830, it was mainly the silk piece-goods and white piece-goods of Madras and Calcutta that were imported such as *Ballacheny bottadar*s (patterned fabric from Bengal), 15 to 22 cubits long and 2¼ broad, valued at 20 to 40 rupees; Ballacheny *cootney*s valued from 3 to 5 rupees; damasks per yard from 4 to 5 rupees; Bengal taffetas from 8 to 12 rupees; raw silk per bundle of 2¼ pucca maunds from 850 to 1000 rupees; raw silk check muctoal per bundle of 2¼ pucca maunds from 180 to 750 rupees.[55] All these items were mainly consumed by the elites for whom they were as much symbols of status as functional fabrics.

A similar cultural function was served by the European imports, which, in this period, mainly consisted of broad cloth. Earlier, Company officials had gifted broad cloth to social groups such as, merchants, dubashis and zamindars who were the primary intermediaries in their commercial activities. The presence of large military forces necessitated

53 Arbuthnot to BOR, 24 September 1840, *VDR* 6644, 345–57.

54 Dobbyn to Sadleir, 9 October 1790, *MDR* 2840, 112–17.

55 T. H. Crozier, Assistant Collector, Masulipatnam, to Board of Revenue, 6 April 1836, *MDR* 6318, 34–73.

and stimulated the import of broad cloth of different varieties into the region. But this trade received a setback after the Settlement of 1802, with the reduction of the zamindars' clout and the disbanding of their forces.[56]

By the turn of the eighteenth century, there was a near total decline in the imports of broad cloth at Masulipatnam as merchants also refused to receive these varieties in lieu of money advances.[57]

What was the situation in the first half of the nineteenth century? The data on sea customs suggests that only a limited quantity of European thread was coming in and no mill-made cloth was being imported. By the 1840s, imports of European thread were seen as a threat to weavers' profits, as they ordinarily used country cotton thread in their manufactures.[58]

The impact of the East India Company's textile trade on the economy of the northern Coromandel was thus highly disparate—in terms of time, textile varieties, and locations. For example, chay goods investment declined completely by 1815 while piece-goods continued till 1830. Regional trade evidently persisted till the 1840s. It was after this period that European fabrics began to compete with local products, not in the localities of production but in the destinations where they were marketed.

The persistence of traditional markets and the remarkable resilience they repeatedly displayed were not enough, however, to protect weavers of the Northern Coromandel from the overwhelming tide of the products of the mills of England that started in the middle of the nineteenth century.

56 Dobbyn to Sadleir, *MDR* 2840, 112–17.

57 By 1786 itself, the demand for broad cloth declined completely at wholesale as well as retail markets. Statham to Floyer, *MDR* 2837, 131–34.

58 Porter to BOR, 31 January 1845, *MDR* 6329, 259–61.

TEN

Conclusion

The weaving communities of the northern Coromandel were subjected to a wide range of forces in the hundred years between 1750 and 1850, during which the East India Company began to create new structures of dominance in the area, and, finally, when its power was consolidated, to radically transform the region. This book has attempted to delineate the broad contours of the world of the northern Coromandel weaver at this time.

Earlier studies of the textile economy of the Coromandel, most notably that of S. Arasaratnam, have examined the varying fortunes of the weavers of the region in the context of the growing interaction of the regional economy with the expanding colonial enterprise of the European powers.[1] This survey has sought to trace the course of the consequences that flowed from the imposition on the region of a new political hegemony, and, in particular, to explore the restructuring and realignments that resulted from the consolidation of the colonial system.

The study, thus, has explored the way in which the social and political patterns of the weaving world interacted with the colonial polity and economy. It has attempted also to examine the areas in which changes occurred and to determine the factors that influenced the patterns of adjustment.

The evidence at our disposal reveals that the policies adopted by the Company tended to blur the finer nuances of social, especially caste, distinctions and to extinguish hereditary caste specialisations. Traditionally, weaving communities had evolved a high degree of distinct skills, and virtually each sub-caste had a specific textile variety associated with it. Under the new dispensation, however, they were compelled to produce not what they preferred, but what the Company—that is to say, distant markets—demanded. Long cloth production in Visakhapatnam district was a particularly conspicuous example of the Company being able to bend the will, as it were, of the weavers, and to yoke their specialised skills to produce what the market required.

By facilitating the increased participation of non-traditional weavers in the textile economy, the Company's textile trade contributed to the blurring of caste boundaries in yet another way. Customarily, low-ranking

1 Arasaratnam, *Merchants, Companies and Commerce*.

communities, especially the Malas and the Madigas, had spun thread or produced textiles. This was a phenomenon that can be traced back to at least the fifteenth century, when it was possibly aided and reinforced by the emergent egalitarian ideology of SriVaishnavism. But the creation of new demands by the arrival of the European companies may have given an impetus to their growth, and the operations of the East India Company further increased the possibilities of the Malas being recruited into the textile economy of districts such as Guntur and Masulipatnam. The fractures in the traditional boundaries between castes did not, of course, mean the total eclipse of their various institutions, rites and rituals. In fact, paradoxically, the Company, which through its commercial policies was contributing to the undermining of caste specialisation, was also, through administrative necessity, reinforcing caste structures. Dependent as it was on caste heads for mediating with the primary weavers, the Company had to strengthen their power, implicitly and explicitly. Then again, caste came to the fore when weavers organised themselves to protest against oppression, although, here too, there was a degree of ambivalence since some of these groups of weavers cut across the traditional lines of caste cleavage.

Nevertheless, many established caste institutions seem to have persisted, despite the numerous social changes that occurred in the region. The manner in which marginalised sects were transformed into mendicant communities attached to, and protected by, the weaving castes, is an illustration of this.

Another socio-cultural phenomenon that undoubtedly helped weaving communities to survive in the face of radical changes in the production processes was the significant relationship between clothing and cultural/ritual practice. The cultural codes of traditional societies, which prescribed particular varieties and modes of dress for specific occasions, were evident in the northern Coromandel too. The survival of the weaver in this region was, in no small measure, dependent on these cultural codes, which must have helped to maintain the skills of groups specialising in the production of specific varieties of cloth required under the various prescriptions. The political economy of rituals determined, as it were, the durability of certain segments of the textile economy, local as well as regional.

As noted by many scholars, the East India Company was not always able to impose its will on the society or the economy.[2] Indeed, in the

2 R. E. Frykenberg, *Guntur District 1788–1948: A History of Local Influence and Central Authority in South India* (Oxford: Oxford University Press, 1965).

beginning, in the eighteenth century, the Company tried to shore up traditional networks of production and trade to protect its investment, supporting, for example, the activities of the Banjara traders and the copdars. It was only in the nineteenth century that the Company began to look for ways of more directly controlling the production and distribution of textiles as well as raw materials such as indigo, chay root, and cotton. In this search for dominance, the Company necessarily came up against the problem of the intermediaries.

Intermediaries were long-standing commercial buffers between the external markets and the weavers, managing the marketing of the finished fabric. The Company attempted to extinguish the power of go-betweens such as the copdars. In trying to control the production process, it also created new administrative divisions primarily aimed at reducing the power of the intermediaries by redrawing their constituencies. However, this was not a success. The Company was not able to curb the power of the copdars, nor was it able to otherwise effectively manage the regional mediators.

The Company did prevail, however, in reducing the power and influence of the merchants of the region. There were several kinds of merchants who operated in the northern Coromandel. The local merchants were men of wealth and status who could hold their own against the constant attempts of the Company to restructure the economy and commerce in the region, although there is no indication of the presence of great merchant princes. In fact, one of the local problems seems to have been an acute shortage of capital. Merchant families who had been hereditarily dominant in the textile economy proved to be very resourceful and adaptable and tried to cope with the new conditions. There were setbacks to some of them, and there appears to have been a breakdown of the traditional extended family commercial operation and the emergence of a more individualised and competitive mercantile world. But, on the whole, they survived the vicissitudes of time. One group that weathered the commercial storms well and took advantage of the strategic concerns of the colonial state to further their interests, was that of the Mogul merchants—expatriate Persian traders operating from Masulipatnam.

The evolution of a new economic, social, and political order caused strains and tensions, with manifold consequences. Weavers responded to these pressures, often in a militant manner, and did not hesitate to give expression to their discontent. A general assumption is that once the Company established its hold over the region, the weavers became quiescent and meekly accepted the new dispensation. Artisans, in distinction to the peasantry, have been assumed to be non-aggressive. What emerges from this study is that the weavers were acutely aware of their situation and of the possibilities for collective political and legal action to secure redressal of their grievances. Not only did they display remarkable organisational skills, they were also able to sense the ways in which the new juridical and state structures could be exploited.

The militancy of the weavers was, no doubt, tempered by the ways in which they were locked into the entrenched social, political, economic, and legal matrices. One of the ways in which the artisan groups were tied to local alliances and rural structures was through a variety of formal and informal taxes reflected in the revenue collections. The contributions of weavers formed a major component of the entire revenue system, next only to that of agricultural groups. The changes in economic administration brought in by the Company affected the indigenous links and paved the way for the incorporation of weavers into the matrix of the colonial economy. At the same time, the persistence of traditional cultural systems and the perpetuation of jajmani relations helped to sustain certain specialised activities of groups of weavers.

One aspect that affected weavers, and, therefore, their social environment, was the demographic factor. In times of crises such as famines or significant population shifts caused by large-scale migration, the textile economy tended to be markedly disrupted. For instance, death or migration of low-caste weavers created scarcity of thread in the region.

A major question that confronts the historian of this period is with regard to the impact of the colonial economy on the Coromandel weaver. What was the extent to which the weaver was affected, first by the closure of the Company's factories, and second, by the importation of British textiles? The evidence from the districts of the northern Coromandel indicates that even as the Company was shutting down its purchasing operations, the production of textiles did not decline drastically because of the support provided by regional, local, and newly emerging Asian markets. On the contrary, we find that there was an apparently anomalous increase in the number of looms paying moturpha tax after 1830, the year by which all the factories were closed. This could be due to the fact that the increasing imports of British textiles did not reach this region, leaving the weavers free to cater to the local and transregional demand. Moreover, weavers were shifting towards the manufacture of coarser varieties of cloth. Traditional groups, who had earlier produced for export, had to turn to weaving ordinary varieties and limited quantities of finer sorts.

The stagnation and decay in the agrarian economy of the region further complicated the process. In this context, how does one explain the continuation of textile production and trading, though on a reduced scale, till the middle of the nineteenth century? The evidence presented in this book supports the argument of Konrad Specker, that, in studying developments in the textile industry in the nineteenth century, one has to consider the "the quantitative, product and region specific" dimensions of the problem.[3] In this case, intra-regional and re-emerging Asian trading activity were factors sustaining the demand for Coromandel cloth.

The immediate social consequence of the economic changes in the nineteenth century was the marginalisation of the Pariah or Mala weaver. In the wake of the Industrial Revolution, the traditional weaver began to return to the coarser cloth that he had relinquished to the Mala weaver several centuries before. This meant, in turn, that, to a large extent, the Mala weaver was now pushed out of the textile economy. As David Washbrook has pointed out, the "golden age of the Pariahs" that existed in the late eighteenth and early nineteenth centuries seemed to have disappeared owing to the greater integration of the northern Coromandel region into the world economy. From this time onwards the Pariahs became heavily dependent on agricultural activities for their sustenance and began "their march into 'modern' destitution and despoilation."[4]

Although this study was primarily an investigation of the weavers of the northern Coromandel, a pertinent issue that confronts any researcher of this period needs to be addressed, even if only in an indirect manner: What was the impact of the emergent colonial state on the society and economy of the region? It is suggested that, in general, the new dispensation did not—perhaps because it could not—radically alter the basic agrarian structure, at any rate, in the first century of its rule.[5] In the case of the textile economy and the world of the weavers, there were some significant changes in the organisation of the production process, supply of raw materials, in the alliances between the landed elites and weavers, and so on. Here too, the colonial power was compelled to retreat for a time from radical departures from past practice, and to recognise, and thus reinforce, traditional elites and customary practices. Indeed, even this withdrawal was, ultimately, to subserve the commercial goals of the Company.

3 Specker, "Madras Handlooms", 131–66.

4 David Washbrook, "Land and Labour in Late Eighteenth Century South India: The Golden Age of the Pariah?". In Peter Robb (ed.), *Dalit Movements and the Meanings of Labour in India* (Delhi: Oxford University Press, 1996), 68–87.

5 Vasanthi, "Agrarian World of Masulipatnam".

At the same time, the operations of the Company did alter the way in which the indigenous mercantile communities functioned, both by eliminating customary traders and accelerating some developments as in competition and individualism that had already begun to emerge. Again, administrative re-organisation of the territorial spaces within which weavers functioned earlier, leading to a breakdown of an older focal point of power, was an important new factor. It was this, perhaps, that helped the Company also to break the rigidities of caste specialisation and to force the weavers to produce its requirements.

Elements of continuity, then, contended, even in the world of the artisan as in the world of the peasant, with elements of change. As in the case of the agrarian economy, here too, it would seem, the new commerce and the new polity created conditions in which some elements of the traditional weaver's world could reap a rich harvest, for we do find many substantial weaving families continuing into the twentieth century, though now in the new guise of prosperous textile merchants. This is not to imply that the emergent state was facilitating the growth of domestic capitalism. On the contrary, what was a thriving industry—and one that could have been the basis for indigenous industrial development—was in the end stifled and extinguished.

Thus, the major argument set out in the study is that the process of incorporating India into the international economy in the course of the hundred years from 1750 transformed the world of the Coromandel weaver in many significant ways. Yet, by the end of the period, the weaver remained an integral constituent of the economy, continuing to produce and, to a limited extent, export textiles, surviving, thus, into the 1850s, when the flood of industrial products from Lancashire was to radically alter his world.

Appendix

Table **1.1**
Company's Investment at Masulipatnam Factory, 1787–1816

Years	Allegars			Callowpores			Sastracundis		
	Pieces	*Price*	*Value*	*Pieces*	*Price*	*Value*	*Pieces*	*Price*	*Value*
1787	4800	22	5424	2400	22	2712	6000	24	7260
1788	4800	22	5412	2400	22	2706	6000	25	7623
1789	4800	22	54724	2400	22	2712	6000	25	7623
1790	2400	22	5424	2400	22	2712	6000	25	7623
1791	2400	22	2712	2400	22	2712	6000	25	7623
1792	2400			2400			6000		
1793	2400			2400			6000		
1794	2400			2400			6000		
1795	4000			4000			6000		
1796	4000			4000			6000		
1797	4000			1000			6000		
1798	1000			1000			2000		
1799	1000	19	975	1000	19	975	2000	22	2225
1800	1000	19	975	3000	19		4000	22	4450
1801	4000	19	3900	3600	19	3405	6000	22	6675
1802	12000	19	11700	12000	19	11700	12000	22	13350
				3000	16	2400			
1803	12000	19	11700	12000	19	11700	12000	22	13350
				3000	16	2400			
1804	12000	19	11700	12000	19	11700	12000	22	13350
1805	4000	19	3900	4000	19	3903	6000	22	6675
				1000	16	800			
1806				2000	19	1950	2700	22	3006
				350	16	250			
1807									
1808	1000	19		1000	19	975	1400	22	1557
				200	16	160			
1809	1000	19		1000	19	975	1400	22	1557
				200	16	160			
1810	1000	19		1000	19	975	1400	22	1557
				200	16	160			
1811	2300	18		2400	19	2340	3200	22	3559
				500	19	487			
1812	2300	18	2156	2400	19	2340	3200	22	445
				500	22	487			
1813	400	18	376	200	19	195	400	22	445
1814	400	18	376	200	19	195	400	22	445
1815									
1816	400	18	376						

Note: Till 1817, value was in pagodas. From 1818, value was in rupees.

(*Continued*)

Table **1.1**

(*Continued*)

Years	Allegars Gingham Red			Callowpores Gingham Blue			Sastracundis Masulipatnam Romals Patterned (21 Punjums)		
	Pieces	*Price*	*Value*	*Pieces*	*Price*	*Value*	*Pieces*	*Price*	*Value*
1787	600	16	495	600	16	495	10000	32	16225
1788	600	16	495	600	16	495	10000	38	16225
1789	1000			1000			10000		
1790	1000			1000			8000		
1791	1000			1000					
1792									
1793	1000			1000			8000		
1794	4000			1000			5000		
1795	2000			2000			8000		
1796	4000			4000			8000		
1797	4000			4000			8000		
1798	500			500			8000		
1799	500	15	381	500	15	381	8000	28	11292
1800	500	15	381	500	15	381	8000	28	11292
1801	400	15	305	400	15	305	12000	28	16939
1802	2400	15	1831	2400	15	1831	36000	26	48177
1803	2400	15	1831	2400	15	1831	36000	26	48177
1804	2400	15	1831	2400	15	1831	36000	26	48177
1805	2400	15	1831	2400	15	1831	36000	26	48177
1806	800	15	610	800	15	610	15000	26	20114
1807							15000	26	20114
1808	200	15	152	200	15	152	8000	26	10718
1809	200	15	152	200	15	152	8000	26	10718
1810	200	15	152	200	15	152	7000	26	9366
							14000		
1811	500	13	343	400	13	275	14000	26	18735
1812	500	13	343	400	13	275	14000	26	18735
1813							3000	26	4012
1814							2000	27	2700
1815									
1816							1400	29	2052

(*Continued*)

Table **1.1**

(*Continued*)

Years	Masulipatnam Romals Large (18 Punjums)			Romals Ab1			Romals 2		
	Pieces	*Price*	*Value*	*Pieces*	*Price*	*Value*	*Pieces*	*Price*	*Value*
1787	4800	44	10340	1000	59	2956	2000	67	6710
1788	4800	44	18560	1000	59	2956	2000	67	6710
1789	5000								
1790	-								
1791	-								
1792	-			1000			1000		
1793	5000			1000			800		
1794	4000			800			1400		
1795	6000			1400			1400		
1796	6000			1400			2000		
1797	6000			3000			1500		
1798	6000			2000			1500		
1799	6000	38	15920	2000	51	5142	1500	58	4378
1800	6000	38	15920	2000	51	5142	1500	58	4378
1801	10000	38	19140	2000	51	5142	1500	58	4378
1802	30000	36	54512	6000	49	14800	6000	51	15567
1803	30000	36	54512	6000	49	14800	6000	51	15567
1804	30000	36	54512	6000	49	14800	6000	51	15567
1805	30000	36	54512	3000	49	9403	3000	51	7783
1806	6000	36	10902	2000	49	4935	2000	51	5189
1807	6000	36	10902	2000	49	4935	2000	51	5189
1808	3000	36	5454	1000	49	2467	500	51	1297
1809	3000	36	5454	1000	49	2467	500	51	1297
1810	2600	36	4724	900	49	2221	400	51	1037
1811	4000	36	7268	2100	49	5182	900	51	2335
1812	4000								
1813	1000	36	7268	2100	49	5182	900	51	2335
1814	1000	36	1825						
1816	1000	36	1262						

(*Continued*)

Table **1.1**
(*Continued*)

Years	Romals 3			Romals 4			Romals 5		
	Pieces	*Price*	*Value*	*Pieces*	*Price*	*Value*	*Pieces*	*Price*	*Value*
1787	2000	64	6490	2000	51	5170	2000	47	4730
1788	2000	64	6490	2000	51	5170	2000	47	4730
1789	2000			2000			2000		
1790									
1791									
1792									
1793	1000			2000			2000		
1794	400			1600			1600		
1795	800			2500			2500		
1796	800			2500			2500		
1797	2000			2000			1400		
1798	1500			2000			1400		
1799	500	60	1500	500	44	2880	1400	41	2880
1800	500	60	1500	1000	44	2880	1400	41	2880
1801	1000	60	3001	1500	44	3373	1400	41	2880
1802	3000	51	7703	6000	40	12260	4200	38	8033
1803	3000	51	7703	6000	40	12260	4200	38	8035
1804	3000	51	7703	6000	40	12260	4200	38	8035
1805	1500	51	3851	3000	49	6130	2000	38	3825
1806	700	51	1798	1500	49	3065	700	38	1339
1807	700	51	1798	1500	49	3065	700	38	1339
1808	1000	51	2569	700	49	1747	200	38	382
1809	1000	51	2569	700	49	1747	200	38	382
1810	900	51	2311	600	49	1496	200	38	382
1811	2100	51	5392	1400	49	3490	500	38	956
1812		51							
1813	2100	51	5392	1400	49	3490	500	38	956
1814									
1816									

(*Continued*)

Table 1.1
(*Continued*)

Years	Romals 6			Romals 7		
	Pieces	*Price*	*Value*	*Pieces*	*Price*	*Value*
1787	2000	27	2722	800		
1788	2000	27	2722	800		
1789	2000			800		
1793	1000			1000		
1794	800			800		
1795	1400			1400		
1796	1400			1400		
1797	2000			1400		
1798	1500			1400		
1799	1500	23	1776	1400	27	1090
1800	1500	23	1776	800	27	1090
1801	2000	23	2368	1400	27	1090
1802	6000	21	6455	2400	27	3270
1803	6000	21	6455	2400	27	3270
1804	6000	21	6455	2400	27	3270
1805	3000	21	3227	1200	27	1635
1806	1500	21	1613	300	27	408
1807	1500	21	1613	300	27	480
1808	700	21	754	100	27	136
1809	700	21	754	100	27	136
1810	600	21	645	100	27	136
1811	1400	21	1506	200	27	272
1812	1400	21	1506	200	27	272

Source: CDDE, 1–40

(*Continued*)

Table 1.1
(*Continued*)

Years	Romals 8			Romals 9			Romals 10		
	Pieces	*Price*	*Value*	*Pieces*	*Price*	*Value*	*Pieces*	*Price*	*Value*
1787	2000	26	2640	2000	22	2200	800	20	835
1788	2000	26	2640	2000	22	2200	800	20	835
1789	2000			2000			800		
1793				2000			2000		
1794	2000			1600			1600		
1795	1600			2500			2500		
1796	2500			2500			2500		
1797	3000			1500			1500		
1798	2000			600			600		
1799	2000	23	2396	1500	19	1435	1000	18	908
1800	2000	23	2396	1500	19	1435	1000	18	908
1801	2000	23	2396	1500	19	1435	1500	18	1363
1802	3000	20	3126	4500	18	4088	4500	17	4033
1803	3000	20	3126	4500	18	4088	4500	17	4033
1804	3000	20	3126	4500	18	4088	4500	17	4033
1805	1500	20	1563	2500	18	2271	2500	17	2240
1806	700	20	731	1000	18	908	1000	17	896
1807	700	20	731	1000	18	908	1000	17	896
1808	1000	20	1045	500	18	454	500	17	448
1809	1000	20	1045	500	18	454	500	17	448
1810	900	20	937	500	18	454	500	17	448
1811	2100	20	2188	1200	18	1090	1100	17	985
1812	2100	20	2188	1200	18	1090	1100	17	985

Table 1.2
Company's Indented Piece-goods from the Ingeram Factory, 1787–1820

Years	Longcloth Ordinary			Longcloth Middling		
	Pieces	*Price*	*Value*	*Pieces*	*Price*	*Value*
1787	15000	46	34000	10000	52	26000
1788	15000			10000		
1789	20000			10000		
1790	20000			10000		
1791	20000	46		10000	52	
1792	20000	50		10000		
	10000	50	25300	5000	57	14300
1793	30000			15000		
1794	30000			15000		
1795	50000			25000		
1796	50000			25000		
1797	50000			25000		
1798	40000			20000		
1799	40000	54	108538	20000	61	61349
1800	50000	54	135673	25000	61	76686
1801	50000	54	135673	25000	61	76686
1802	55000	54	149240	25000	61	76686
1803	55000	54	149240	25000	61	76686
1804	55000	54	149240	25000	61	76686
1805	55000	54	149240	25000	61	76686
1806	37000	54	100434	17000	61	52167
1807	37000	54	100434	17000	61	52167
1808	19000	54	51574	8000	61	24549
1809	14000	54	37988	6000	61	18414
1810	14000	54	37988	6000	61	18414
1811	27000	51	69525	12660	58	37030
1812	27000	51	69525	12660	58	37030
1813	45000	51	115875	25000	58	73125
1814	39000	51	100425	21000	58	61425
1815						
1816	30000	51	77700	16000		46840
1817	30000		195940			
	52500		50944			
1818	24000		190606			
	40000					
1819	16000		169449			
	40000					
1820						

Note: Prices shown are per corge, in Madras pagodas.
Source: CDDE, 1–40

(*Continued*)

Table 1.2
(*Continued*)

Years	Longcloth Fine			Longcloth Superfine		
	Pieces	*Price*	*Value*	*Pieces*	*Price*	*Value*
1787	6000	67	20100	600	205	6150
1788	6000			600		
1789	4000					
1790	4000			400	220	4400
1791	4000	70	14080	400		
1792	5500	70	5599	400	31	319
				200	28	288
				200		
1793	5500			400		
1794	5500			400		
1795	7000			400		
1796	7000			400		
1797	8000					
1798	6000					
1799	6000	75	22635			
1800	6000	75	22635			
1801	6000	75	22635			
1802	6000	75	22635			
1803	6000	75	22635			
1804	6000	75	22635			
1805	6000	75	22635			
1806	4000	75	15090			
1807	4000	75	15090			
1808	2000	75	7545			
1809	1000	75	3772			
1810	1000	75	3772			
1811	2340	72	8424			
1812	2340	72	8424			
1813						
1814						
1815						
1816						
1817						
1818						
1819						
1820						

Table 1.3
Company's Indented Piece-goods
from Maddapollem Factory, 1787–1819

Years	Longcloth Ordinary			Longcloth Middling		
	Pieces	*Price*	*Value*	*Pieces*	*Price*	*Value*
1787	11500	46	26450	16000	52	41600
1788	11500			16000		
1789	10000			16000		
1790	15000			16000		
1791	15000	46	34500	16000	53	11600
1792	15000			16000		
1793	15000			16000		
1794	15000			16000		
1795	20000			16000		
1796	20000			16000		
1797	20000			16000		
1798	20000			10000		
1799	20000	54	54269	10000	61	30674
1800	25000	54		15000	61	46008
1801	30000	54	81400	15000	61	46008
1802	40000	54	108533	18000	61	52210
1803	40000	54	108533	18000	61	52210
1804	40000	54	108533	18000	61	52210
1805	40000	54	108533	18000	61	52210
1806						
1807	27000	54	73285	12000	61	3680
1808	14000	54	38000	6000	61	18403
1809	11000	54	29846	5000	61	15336
1810	11000	54	29846	5000	61	15336
1811	24000	51	62100	12000	63	37800
1812	24000	51	62100	12000	63	37800
1813	55000	51	142312	23000	58	67275
1814	45000	51	116437	19000	58	55575
1815						
1816	36000	51	93240	14000	58	40988
1817	82000		246884			
1818	64000					
1819	56000					
1820						

Note: Prices shown are per corge in Madras pagodas. *(Continued)*
Source: CDDE, 1–40

Table **1.3**
(Continued)

Years	Longcloth Fine			Longcloth Superfine		
	Pieces	*Price*	*Value*	*Pieces*	*Price*	*Value*
1787	6000	67	20100	400	207	4100
1788	6000			400		
1789	3000			400		
1790	3000			400		
1791	3000	70	10560	400	225	4512
1792	3000			400		
1793	3000			400		
1794	3000			300		
1795	3000			300		
1796	3000			300		
1797	3000			700		
1798	5000			700		
1799	5000	72	18018	700	187	6545
1800	5000	72	18018	2500	187&162	22125
1801	5000	72	18018	2500	187&162	22125
1802	5500	72	19820	1600	187&162	14210
1803	5500	72	19820	1600	187&162	14210
1804	5500	72	19820	1000	187	9350
1805	5500	72	19820	1000	187	9350
1806						
1807	3700	72	13334	700	187	6545
1808	1800	72	6487	300	187	2805
1809	1800	72	6487	300	187	2805
1810	1800	72	6487	300	187	2805
1811	3600	68	12375	700	192	6737
1812	3600	68	12375	700	192	6737
1813						
1814						
1815						
1816						
1817						
1818						
1819						
1820						

Table 1.4
Company's Investment at Visakhapatnam Factory, 1787–1826

Years	Longcloth Ordinary			Longcloth Ordinary 2		
	Pieces	*Price*	*Value*	*Pieces*	*Price*	*Value*
1788	35000	38	67375			
1789	35000					
1790	35000					
1791	35000					
1792	35000					
1793	35000					
1794	35000					
1795	60000					
1796	60000					
1797	60000					
1798	60000					
1799	60000	47	141570			
1800	60000	46	139500			
1801	60000	46	139500			
1802	90000	46	209250			
1803	90000	46	209250			
1804	90000	46	209250			
1805	90000	46	209250			
1806	60000	46	139500			
1807	60000	46	139500			
1808	30000	46	69950			
1809	20000	46	46500			
1810	20000	46	46500			
1811	43000	51	110725			
1812	43000	51	110725			
1813	60000	51	154500			
1814	50000	51	128750			
1816	36000	51	92571			
1817	40000			38000		
	38000		222000			
1818				32000		
1819				24000		
1820				1000	165	247500
1821				1000	165	247500
1822				1000	165	247500
1823				1500	163	368543
1824				1250	165	307118
1825				1600	163	393000
1826				1500	163	368437
1827				1200	163	294750

Note: From 1819, the investment was in Madras rupees. *(Continued)*

Table 1.4

(*Continued*)

Years	Longcloth Ordinary 3			Longcloth Middling			Longcloth Fine		
	Pieces	*Price*	*Value*	*Pieces*	*Price*	*Value*	*Pieces*	*Price*	*Value*
1788				10000	53	26950	3000	63	9461
1789				10000			3000		
1790				12000			3000		
1791									
1792				12000			3000		
1793				12000			3000		
1794				20000			3000	300	
1795				25000			3000		
1796				25000					
1797				25000					
1798									
1799									
1800				25000	57	71428			
1801				25000	57	71428			
1802				32000	57	91442			
1803				32000	57	91442			
1804				32000	57	91442			
1805				32000	57	91442			
1806				24000	57	60000			
1807				21000	57	60000			
1808				11000	57	31434			
1809				9000	57	25714			
1810				9000	57	25714			
1811				23000	60	69000			
1812				23000	60	69000			
1813				34000	60	102000			
1814				26000	60	78000			
1816				26000	60	60000			
1817									
1818	32000								
1819	32000								
1820	1500	150	337500						
1821	1500	150	335500						
1822	1500	150	337500						
1823	2250	155	523125						
1824	2000	155	665000						
1825	1200	150	270000						
1826	1100	150	247500						
1827	900	150	202500						

(*Continued*)

Table **1.4**

(*Continued*)

Years	Salempores Ordinary			Salempores Middling		
	Pieces	*Price*	*Value*	*Pieces*	*Price*	*Value*
1798	7000	23	8225	4000	30	6100
1799	7000	23		4000		
1800	10000					
1801	10000	24	12250	16000		24400
1802						
1803						
1804						
1805						
1806	3000	26	3910	3000	28	4230
1807	2000	26	2606	2000	28	2820
1808	2000	26	2606	2000	28	2890
1809	1000	26	1303	1000	28	1410
1810	1000	26	1303	1000	28	1410
1811	1000	26	1303	1000	28	1410
1812	2300	25	2932	2360	30	3540
1813	2300	25	2932	2360	30	3540
1814	16000	25	20400	14500	30	21750
1815	13000	25	16575	10500	30	15750
1816	16000	25				
1817	10000	25	12857	8200	30	12300
1818						
1819						
1820						
1821						
1822						
1823						
1824	500	82	650	75		
1825	750	81	975	77		
1826						
1827						

(*Continued*)

Table 1.4
(*Continued*)

Years	Salempores Ordinary 2			Salempores Ordinary 3		
	Pieces	*Price*	*Value*	*Pieces*	*Price*	*Value*
1798						
1799						
1800						
1801						
1802						
1803						
1804						
1805						
1806						
1807						
1808						
1809						
1810						
1811						
1812						
1813						
1814						
1815						
1816						
1817						
1818						
1819						
1820	500	82	123750	650	75	147225
1821	500	82	123750	650	75	147225
1822	500	82	123750	650	75	147225
1823	750	81	184269	975	77	226688
1824	1000	81	245695	1225	77	284812
1825	2000	81	491250	1200	75	270000
1826	1900	81	466687	1100	75	247500
1827	1500	81	368437	900	75	202500

Table **1.5**

Piece-goods Exported from Visakhapatnam District between 1 May 1835 and 30 April 1845

	14-Punjum Cloths				12-Punjum Cloths			
Years	*Qty.*	*Value*	*Qty.*	*Value*	*Qty.*	*Value*	*Qty.*	*Value*
1835 & 1836								
1836 & 1837								
1837 & 1838								
1838 & 1839								
1839 & 1840								
1840 & 1841								
1841 & 1842	8968	57566	687	1975-2	28	140	666	1255
1842 & 1843	19167	110210	1093	3142-6	2612	13060	2352	3935
1843 & 1844	11901	4769	–	–	9543	38172	7791	1200
1844 & 1845	14578	58312	61	122	3178	127158	1629	4115
Total	54614	267692	1841	5329-8	4397	178530	5426	10505

Note: Quantity in numbers. Values in rupees

Source: VDR

Table **1.6**

Cloth Exports from Godavari District to South-East Asian Markets from 1821–1844

Years	*Total value*	*Pegu*	*Batavia*	*Penang*	*Bourbon*	*West coast of Sumatra*	*Persian gulf*
1835/36	116675	67800	5931	4006	18469	19858	611
1836/37	125250	79767	611	16333	2432	24330	2187
1837/38	266566	92222	9117	32135	61059	67920	4413
1838/39	215930	86842	12166	441	62525	42188	11768
1839/40	158540	133293	12300	---	---	10075	2872
1840/41	180377	157063	21503	---	1640	---	171
1841/42	184385	163865	84	14928	308	84	1513
1842/43	258815	129202	14630	---	103650	14630	7511
1843/44	274027	121525	62	4825	98791	2850	43456
1844/45	452082	165716	4775		252661	5000	22927

Source: Prendergast, Collector Rajahmundry, to Pycroft, BOR, 11 December 1845, PBR 2004, pp. 17465–490

Table 1.7
Quantity and Value of Exports from
Masulipatnam District 1834–35 to 1843–44

	Arakan		Chittangang		Mouleimen	
	No.	*Value*	*No.*	*Value*	*No.*	*Value*
1835–36						
1836–37	108	148–4			27	62–8
1837–38			639	210		
1838–39					847	2316–12
1839–40	1838	2698–2	146	716–4	956	1721–4
1840–41			907	2983–2		
1841–42	752	1017–8	143	263–2	187	304–8
1842–43	3300	4782–12	51	121		
1843–44						
Total	5598	8646–10	1886	6184–8	2044	4405

Source: R.T. Porter, Collector Masulipatnam to T. Pycroft, 20 October, 1845, PBOR, 19

Table 1.8

Number of Looms, Weavers, and Value of Cloth Produced in 34 Villages of Godavari District from 1824 to 1844

	Name of Estates	*Village Names*	*I*	*II*	*III*	*IV*
				1824–1828		
1.	Peddapuram	Peddapuram	203	203	238	10670
2.		Vettalapallam	69	69	79	11826
3.		Cautravoolapall	67	67	90	13453
4.	Nagaram	Chintapalli	30	40	50	3600
5.		Morey	30	42	33	2556
6.		Jaggempettah	75	75	77	5545
7.	Amalapuram	Amalapuram	45	118	118	7877
8.		Bandarlanka	70	203	168	13626
9.		Pollaccora	30	37	107	9106
10.	Coconada	Samulcotha	57	59	62	5952
11.		Beemavaram				
12.	Valugabandah	Mundapetah	180	350	210	25882
13.		Artamur	100	182	93	11462
14.	Bicavole	Vadurpaka	80	140	74	9120
15.		Caucodau	60	108	61	7518
16.	Vyaghempeteh	Nalatore	150	280	143	17624
17.	Pennugondah	Marteru	20	24	24	1506
18.		Pundetavitloor	30	35	35	2376
19.		Chintaparro	27	37	37	2433
20.	Tanuku	Velpur	100	51	51	4560
21.		Atteley	18	20	22	2100
22.		Tiropatepuram	22	30	26	2500
23.	Mugal Tore	Policole	150	256	256	30339
24.		Narsapore	15	15	15	17269
25.	Pithapuraam	Pitahpuram	40	40	40	3480
26.		Uppadah	167	194	201	20100
27.		Komaragiri	40	30	30	3600
28.		Rapurty	30	30	30	2400
29.	Tuni	Tuni Pettahs	250	162	172	15996
30.	Drakcharam	Angarah	134	134	168	22921
31.		Pedapudi	41	41	40	5325
32.	Rajahmundry	Rajamundri	71	71	71	12607
33.		Dollah	129	129	130	12612
34.		Cautaroo			74	7325

Note: Value of cloth in rupees

(*Continued*)

I Weavers

II Weavers Houses

III Weavers Looms

IV Value of Cloth Produced

Source: C.I. Bird, Collector to BOR, 15 January 1845, *PBR* 1950, pp. 1148

Table **1.8**
(*Continued*)

	Name of Estates	*Village Names*	*I*	*II*	*III*	*IV*
				1829–1833		
1.	Peddapuram	Peddapuram	192	192	230	9523
2.		Vettalapallam	59	59	59	7195
3.		Cautravoolapall	49	49	53	6696
4.	Nagaram	Chintapalli	35	50	54	3434
5.		Morey	25	41	34	2386
6.		Jaggempettah	85	85	90	5724
7.	Amalapuram	Amalapuram	60	94	88	5671
8.		Bandarlanka	60	117	114	8610
9.		Pollaccora	30	53	53	3032
10.	Coconada	Samulcotha	58	57	57	5120
11.		Beemavaram				
12.	Valugabandah	Mundapetah	166	373	167	16783
13.		Artamur	60	141	63	6331
14.	Bicavole	Vadurpaka	61	129	60	6030
15.		Caucodau	57	115	40	4020
16.	Vyaghempeteh	Nalatore	127	266	115	11557
17.	Pennugondah	Marteru	20	24	24	1150
18.		Pundetavitloor	29	37	37	1552
19.		Chintaparro	22	31	31	1858
20.	Tanuku	Velpur	110	55	50	300
21.		Atteley	20	22	18	1000
22.		Tiropatepuram	26	33	26	1000
23.	Mugal Tore	Policole	110	221	221	23265
24.		Narsapore	24	24	24	2493
25.	Pithapuraam	Pitahpuram	30	30	30	2040
26.		Uppadah	203	202	214	15456
27.		Komaragiri	40	28	28	2668
28.		Rapurty	25	25	25	1625
29.	Tuni	Tuni Pettahs	230	174	192	13824
30.	Drakcharam	Angarah	68	68	83	7068
31.		Pedapudi	30	32	32	4842
32.	Rajahmundry	Rajamundri	89	89	89	12532
33.		Dollah	130	130	139	11380
34.		Cautaroo	92	59	65	7290

(*Continued*)

Table **1.8**
(*Continued*)

	Name of Estates	*Village Names*	*I*	*II*	*III*	*IV*
				1834–1838		
1.	Peddapuram	Peddapuram	206	208	253	9713
2.		Vettalapallam	52	52	52	5503
3.		Cautravoolapall	38	38	43	4188
4.	Nagaram	Chintapalli	40	50	54	2980
5.		Morey	30	36	30	1800
6.		Jaggempettah	69	69	69	3700
7.	Amalapuram	Amalapuram	60	92	86	4935
8.		Bandarlanka	50	96	97	6232
9.		Pollaccora	30	37	37	1954
10.	Coconada	Samulcotha	63	57	59	4956
11.		Beemavaram				
12.	Valugabandah	Mundapetah	157	515	159	13554
13.		Artamur	57	167	56	4774
14.	Bicavole	Vadurpaka	54	197	83	7075
15.		Caucodau	64	222	64.	5456
16.	Vyaghempeteh	Nalatore	83	291	83	7075
17.	Pennugondah	Marteru	21	24	24	1187
18.		Pundetavitloor	32	36	36	1376
19.		Chintaparro	18	21	21	763
20.	Tanuku	Velpur	150	136	136	6000
21.		Atteley	12	14	14	700
22.		Tiropatepuram	33	39	35	1500
23.	Mugal Tore	Policole	100	146	146	13567
24.		Narsapore	45	45	45	3969
25.	Pithapuraam	Pitahpuram	57	57	57	3696
26.		Uppadah	16	158	197	11900
27.		Komaragiri	20	18	18	1296
28.		Rapurty	28	28	29	1450
29.	Tuni	Tuni Pettahs	220	156	177	12420
30.	Drakcharam	Angarah	109	109	125	13390
31.		Pedapudi	28	29	29	4068
32.	Rajahmundry	Rajamundri	122	122	122	14112
33.		Dollah	131	141	141	10276
34.		Cautaroo	90	80	89	7605

(*Continued*)

Table **1.8**
(*Continued*)

	Name of Estates	*Village Names*	*I*	*II*	*III*	*IV*
				1839–1844		
1.	Peddapuram	Peddapuram	195	190	250	9612
2.		Vettalapallam	58	58	58	10771
3.		Cautravoolapall	27	27	30	2316
4.	Nagaram	Chintapalli	40	58	60	2808
5.		Morey	28	40	34	1765
6.		Jaggempettah	71	71	71	3230
7.	Amalapuram	Amalapuram	63	86	84	4122
8.		Bandarlanka	50	97	98	5259
9.		Pollaccora	30	36	36	1575
10.	Coconada	Samulcotha	67	63	62	4464
11.		Beemavaram				
12.	Valugabandah	Mundapetah	30	99	57	12590
13.		Artamur	30	99	57	4246
14.	Bicavole	Vadurpaka	64	188	89	6630
15.		Caucodau	80	276	71	5289
16.	Vyaghempeteh	Nalatore	85	291	84	6258
17.	Pennugondah	Marteru	23	27	27	1352
18.		Pundetavitloor	33	35	35	1197
19.		Chintaparro	30	36	36	2007
20.	Tanuku	Velpur	140	120	120	8000
21.		Atteley	20	21	20	1000
22.		Tiropatepuram	42	53	51	4500
23.	Mugal Tore	Policole	100	234	234	17494
24.		Narsapore	75	75	75	5532
25.	Pithapuraam	Pitahpuram	54	54	55	2460
26.		Uppadah	142	142	170	8500
27.		Komaragiri	20	16	16	960
28.		Rapurty	21	21	21	882
29.	Tuni	Tuni Pettahs	20	151	173	12362
30.	Drakcharam	Angarah	142	142	151	9601
31.		Pedapudi	35	37	37	2144
32.	Rajahmundry	Rajamundri	131	131	131	13296
33.		Dollah	131	140	140	7488
34.		Cautaroo	77	81	78	5724

Table 1.9

Textile Varieties Produced in the Northern Coromandel at the end of the Eighteenth Century

Textile Varieties Exported from Masulipatnam by Armenian Merchants to Persia				
1. Amberchas	16. Chint romals	31. Ginghams	46. Lachauck Painted	61. Romals
2. Arcachenes	17. Chint Batadars	32. Gulbundo	47. Lahagauloo	62. Painted Romals
3. Bargagies	18. Chintz	33. Hajaumaty Iamavars	48. Lungi Chintz	63. Rungapauny Romals
4. Baulbunds	19. Cajacks	34. Izari	49. Half longcloth	64. White Romals
5. Buschs	20. Chaundeny	35. Iaumymaud	50. Laufe	65. Saudies
6. Basamahs	21. Chintz painted	36. Izzarries	51. Lungeyslaw (Esala)	66. Saudies half
7. Bascahfurds	22. Chandinees	37. Painted Imarva	52. Merchays	67. Sujanaloo
8. Bacheauncys	23. Cashes amainay	38. Rungopany Imarvas	53. Mungaleeh	68. Small Saudies
9. Bargojies White	24. Chint Turbands	39. Kasaloo	54. Musmaseeloo	69. Sarasanloo
10. Carpets	25. Caun Posh	40. White Kasaloo	55. Mutarphy	70. Turbands
11. Catonars	26. Dagalahs	41. Longcloth	56. Neemah asteenus	71. Tukavars
12. Cholies	27. Dusburchas	42. Lungies	57. Patacka	72. Tucka funds
13. Cholies painted	28. Dustercawns	43. Lachaucks	58. Palampores	73. Vadaney
14. Furdies	29. Durpurdahs	44. Lungi assahs	59. White palampores	74. Vadanies
15. Caumbunds	30. Ejarvah	45. Lachauck White	60. Rajoys	75. White cloth

(*Continued*)

Table **1.9**

(Continued)

Textiles Meant for the East India Company			
Vizagapatnam	*Ingeram*	*Madepollam*	*Masulipatnam*
Longcloth ordinary	Longcloth ordinary	Longcloth ordinary (13.5 punjums)	Machilipatnam Romals (21 punjums)
Longcloth middling	Longcloth middling	(14 punjums)	Machilpatnam Romals (18 punjums)
Longcloth fine	Longcloth fine	(15 punjums)	Machilpatnam Romals
and superfine			(18 punjums 7-8 yards wide)
Salempores ordinary	Longcloth superfine	(16 punjums)	Sartracaudies (22 punjums)
Salempores middling	Dungarees	(17 punjums)	Callowpores (20 punjums)
Salempores fine	Percaules	Longcloth middling	Allegars
and superfine	18 cords long	(18 punjums)	(20 punjums)
	Percaules 24 cords long	(20 punjums)	Ginghams Red (22 punjums)
	Beteelas flowered	Longcloth fine (22 punjums)	Ginghams Blue (22 punjums)
		(24 punjums)	Romals as per musters,
		Longcloth superfine	each variety with specific
		(32 punjums)	dimensions of length
		(36 punjums)	1. 36 punjums
			2. 29 punjums
			3. 29 punjums
			4. 26 punjums
			5. 26 punjums
			6. 24 punjums
			7. 24 punjums
			8. 24 punjums
			9. 22 punjums
			10. 20 punjums
			11. 11 punjums

(Continued)

Table **1.9**

(Continued)

Exports from Godavari District				
For interregional commerce-South-East Asian market	*Textiles meant for Nizam's Territories*	*Guntur: textiles meant essentially for local consumption*	*Chay goods meant for Spanish investment*	*Callowpores New Dutch Masters*
1. Duyemrauper cloth	20. Cundooves or Uppada cloths	39. Angustums	47. Allegars	52. Salahs
2. Moories	21. Dovaty cloth	40. Cloths for the head (tala goodaloo)	48. Callowpores	53. Allegars Salahs
3. Punjum cloths	22. Fine cloth	41. Jamavaraloo	49. Romals of Soots	54. Sastracundies Salahs
4. Putchums	23. Head cloth	42. Chelaloo	50. Romals of Ventepollam	55. Matheforoes
5. Punchalacha-pooloo	24. Zaman cloth	43. Ravekaloo or cholies		56. Allegars small check
6. Seyem Rauper cloth	25. Muslins	44. Ootryaloo		57. Amberchas
7. Togaroo Romals	26. Salempores	45. Khandwaloo		58. Pallempores Kasodoo
8. Rungopauny-thawns	27. Wrapper cloths	46. Voneeloo		59. Devalgree
9. Chintz romals	28. Turbands			60. Pataches
10. Doovanaau-choo romals	29. French settlement imported into			61. Lahagah
11. Women's cloths	30. Men's cloth			62. Lungees
12. Chintz Mootarfaloo	31. Salempores			63. Laches
13. Chintz Cholies Thawns	32. Women's cloth			64. Jamavares
14. Jamavarooloo	33. Dhovates			
15. Reckala Chaupooloo	34. Punchas			
16. Angauastra-mooloo	35. Maddy Punchas			
17. Wootareyela Chaupoloo	36. Cheeraloo			
18. Dungarees	37. Budhakanies			
19. Boda Putchums	38. coarse cloths			

Source: District records and proceedings of Board of Revenue

GLOSSARY

acchhupani	to wind yarn on the frame for weaving; also, printing on cloth
adawlut	a court of justice
allegar	dyed cotton cloth, coming under the category of chay goods
amberchas	a type of *kalamkari* cloth, with black, red and green *butah*s on white background
anchu	selvage or border
angavastramu	an upper garment used along with *dhoti* and / or a *kurta*
anna	the sixteenth part of a rupee
arnatto	seeds used in dyeing
arse/ arsinam	silk cloth, also known as *madiceru*
arze	a petition
asara	wetlands dependent only on tank or canal irrigation
atchoo	a weaver's reel—a comb-like frame in a loom through which the warp threads are passed and by which the weft threads are pressed
atchooballa	the frame on which a weaver's reel is fixed and battened together
aumany	Land and weaving villages usually placed under the direct management of the Collector
aummen	officials in charge of collecting revenue from government lands
aurgooloo	a sort of coarse grain, *Paspalum frumentaceum*
avatar	incarnation
bafta	plain cotton cloth, average length 15 cubits; either white or dyed
Balija	Telugu trading caste; sub-castes include *gajula balija*s, *perika balija*s, and *dudekula balijas*
ballacheny	woven cloth variety from Bengal
banathu	a type of long cloth
Bania	a Hindu merchant, trader or money-lender
Banjara	itinerant traders
basti	a town
batta	daily allowance, in addition to regular pay, for travelling, etc.
bettelle	fine and flowered fabric
bogumvallu	dancing girls / *nautch* girls
boota parashee	a tax upon inferior castes, prevalent in Guntur district
bottadar	flowered or dot

	patterns on printed or woven fabric
buchakani	a type of woven fabric
butah	dot patterns
cadjan	dried leaves, used for writing accounts on with an iron stylus
cadokye	*Chebulic myrobalan*, *Terminalia chebula*, also called *haritaki* and *harad*
callowpore	a cheap striped or checked cloth
candi	weight measure; approximately equal to 500 lb
careedar	agent between the Company or merchant and the weaver
Caupoo	a caste, same as Kapu
chakali	washermen
chapakudu	commensalism
cheera	a woman's garment; a sari, a petticoat, a skirt or gown
chela	a kind of scarf or mantle
chidu	a skein or bundle of seven *punjums* or a hundred threads
chidudabba	an instrument for winding thread
chintz	hand-painted or block-printed cotton fabric, same as *kalamkari* or *zulum haree*
chokkayi	a coat, shirt, jacket or vest
cholie	woman's blouse, same as *ravekalu*
chop	a seal or stamp
chowki	a customs house, a toll gate
chunam	limewash
circar/ sarkar	government
.combali	a coarse woollen blanket locally made
conjee	starch used in preparing thread for the looms
coolie	wage or wage labourer
coontah	land measure
copdar	contractor for long cloths, from *kopudarudu* in Telugu
corjee	measure of quantity of cloth, 20 pieces
cosamboo pooloo	red flower used for dyes
cowle	written agreement between the government and cultivators
cundooloo	red gram, *Cajanus cajan*
cutchel	land measure, approximately equal to 25 acres
cutsherry	A revenue or police office
dadni	procurement of cloth / manufactures through the system of advances
dalali	brokerage, agency, commission, a tax on brokers
dalaty	a type of tax
darogha	native officer
Dasarivallu	Vaishnavite mendicants attached primarily to the low caste groups like Malas
deshmukh	a hereditary head revenue officer of the district
deshpandi	accounts officer
desimatra	a local expression with a special literary style

Devangas — a major weaving community

dhoni — a large boat, usually dug out of a single tree

dhoti/dhovati — a man's lower garment

Diwan Khan — office of the *subedar* of the Deccan

dorah — a local chief or ruler

dorea — fabric patterned with stripes

dowle — an estimation of revenue

dubashi — an interpreter or translator, literally "two languages"

dungaree — a coarse cotton fabric used by the poorer classes

dupatta — a woman's scarf or stole

dustack — revenue order

dvipada — a couplet, a sort of metre in poetry

dvipada kavya — composition in verse

ekabhogam — the possession or tenure of village land by one person or family, without any co-sharers

enakapalloo — short chay root

enika — a yarn of 3 or 4 threads

fanam — a unit of money, either silver or gold

Fasli — the Islamic year, also corresponding to the harvest year, reckoned from 590 A.D., the date of the Hejira. Thus, Fasli 1258 corresponds to 1848–49 (=1258 + 590). The Madras Government fixed its commencement to 12 July

firman — a royal order

foujdar — military governor of a district

gadium — practice of selling grain to non-agricultural groups at a higher price

gante/garite — a spoon or ladle

garce — measure of capacity

Gavaravallu — arrack sellers

Gentoo — the name of the Telugu country, derived from the Portuguese *gentio*, meaning a gentile or heathen

gingham — fabric with multiple-stranded warps and wefts

gintemu/gentamu — local name for gingham

Golavallu — cattle keepers

golenu — kettle, boiler

grama kharchu — village establishment charges

gumastah — agent, clerk, native accountant in the revenue or commercial department, substitute for village officers

gutambu — the roller of a loom

haveli — lands under the immediate control of the government

Huzzoor — 'the presence', respectful manner of addressing a public officer

idankai — literally 'left hand' in Tamil; a caste term

ikat — tie-and dye designs made on yarn before weaving

inam lands held rent free in hereditary and perpetual possession
izzari plain white fabric
jagir land given by government as a reward for services, or as a fee or pension
jagirdar holder of *jagir* land
jamah a long gown
jamavaru an upper garment
Jandra a major weaving caste
Jangamvallu orthodox Saivite mendicants
jati biddalu children of the community
jidda a coarse fabric
jonnaloo/cholum sorghum
kabooliyat sunned a counter agreement
kadaru a weaving spindle
kadeem tenant cultivator
Kaikola a Tamil weaving caste
kalam a pen
kalamkari painted or printed fabric
kamanadasta a large bow for cleaning cotton
kanakapillai literally, accountant; native accountant in charge of various functions at the factories: beating kanakapillai, washing kanakapillai, etc.
kande a ball or roll of thread
kanduva an upper garment, same as *angavastramu* and *jamavaru*
karnam village accountant
kasaloo a sari
khanabaddi fabric for cummerbunds, fine white material with designs
khazi/qazi a judicial officer
kist fixed revenue payment, also called *sist* or *shist*
Komati Telugu trading caste, same as banias
Koonapillavallu mendicant groups attached to the Sale caste
kota chuvvakathi a small knife used for separating the woven cloth
koti pullalu a stick fitted in a loom
kotwal the chief police officer
Kulabhikshuvu a mendicant group
kulapurana history of a caste or a community
kulayi a large vessel for manufacturing indigo dye
kulipadugulu warp threads
kullayamu a small cap
kunchum grain measure
lachauk a type of kalamkari cloth
lakakattu unfinished warp of a cloth, with pieces of wood still stuck to it
lakalu small pieces of wood used in weaving
Lambadi itinerant trader
lascar member of an army, camp or cantonment crew; a sailor
long cloth plain white cotton cloth, esteemed in Europe on account of its length
loongi/lungi a man's lower garment, similar to a dhoti, usually patterned
madi dhotis dhotis worn during auspicious or sacred occasions
madiceru silk cloth
Madiga untouchable caste specialising in leather work

madhurparkam traditional bridal dress
maggapugunta pit loom
mahanadu a council; territorial assembly
maharatu/ mutarphy a type of kalamkari cloth
maistri head workman
Mala
Muggalavallu non-traditional weavers belonging to the Pariah caste
malaverty extra assessment, increased tax demand or cess
mangalasutra a token of marriage
manium privileged land holdings enjoyed by village officials either at low or free assessment
marakal/ marakamu measure of capacity
Marga bahoolum the ninth lunar month, corresponding to the period mid-December to mid-January
masoola a wide-bottomed boat with timber tied together with coir
maund/manugiti a measure of weight
mirasi hereditary privileges enjoyed by the village officer
mirasidar a hereditary village officer
mocaum administrative unit, usually consisting of six or seven villages
mocca jonnaloo corn or maize
mookhiwara hill tribe, same as *munnavar*
mooree white base cloth for chintz making
mootah/mutah an administrative unit
moturpha tax levied on artisans, traders and other mercantile groups
muchalika a written contract
muga fabric from northeastern India, especially Assam
Mulliah chief of the Devanga caste
Munnavar a tribe of hill people
muslin the finest quality of cotton
nade a weaver's shuttle
nautch girl dancing girl
neelikadava a large earthernware vessel used in manufacturing indigo dye
neemah a waistcoat with sleeves
neeratypalloo jungle chay root
nesavu weaving; weaver
Niligaru caste of indigo dyers
nullah watercourse
nunja wetland or soil fit for cultivation of rice
nurkee regulator of prices
nuzzaranah gifts of money, from *nuzzar*, a gift or offering
ootariyalu an upper garment, same as angavastramu and jamavaru
Padega rajulu mendicant group attached to the Sale caste
Padma Sale subdivision of the Sale weaving caste, specializing in cotton fabric
padugu warp threads
pagah turban
paggamu cord or rope on which the warp is stretched
pagoda a coin long current in South India

palabhogamu	common possession or tenure of village land by its inhabitants, but each is responsible for the revenue of his or her own holding
palaka	the small bars of a loom
palempore	printed calico or chintz
paleru	bonded labour
pallaputtada	tax, same as boota parashee
pante	a weaver's whirl (not a distaff) on which the thread is wound
parah	salt measure
pargana	a portion of the district, comprising many villages
Pariah	untouchable caste; outcaste
parte	weaver's whirl
patta	revenue document given to the cultivator, stating the terms on which the land is held and the amount payable
Pattu Sale	subdivision of the Sale weaving caste, specializing in silk fabric
pattu vastram	silk cloth
payakari	cultivator
penoobanka	a type of insect that destroys crops
percaule	a high grade plain cotton cloth, especially noted for fineness and regularity of weave as well as for durability
pettah	a division of a town
picotah	traditional irrigation system
pinjamanu	an instrument for cleaning cotton, also called *dudikavillu*
pooti/putti	a measure of capacity, also corrupted into *pootey, pootie, poddie, poddy*
punchali	same as dhoti
punjum	same as long cloth
rahdari	transit
rakshasa	demon
rakta katreku koka/rakta pinjari chira	deep red colour sari
Rangirajulu	caste of painters and printers of cloth
ravekalu	woman's blouse, same as cholie
romal	linen fabric used as handkerchief or neck-cloth
rusum	commission collected by village officials and zamindars from cultivators, weavers, and other groups; a proprietary fee
ryot	cultivator
saderwareed	contingent or incidental village expenses which include periodic expenses, occasional allowances to village officials and to religious establishments, etc., borne by a village or community
Sadhana surulu	mendicants attached to the Padma Sale community
sahukar	trader/merchant, native banker and moneylender
Sale	important weaving caste

salempore	staple cotton fabric, used for block printing in England	*talukdar*	revenue collector
Samayamuvaru	mendicants attached to the Padma Sale community	*tanedar*	revenue collector
samium	a council or meeting; also a demonstration or a settled conclusion	*tappal*	postal system through relay
samudayam	occupancy rights on land held in common by village community	*tella patti*	white cotton
santa	periodic (weekly or fortnightly) village market	Tengalai	a sect of SriVaishnava brahmins
sash	muslin turban cloth, usually of fine quality, and sometimes embroidered or brocaded	Togata	caste of weavers
sastracundi	fabric patterned on the loom with the tie-and-dye technique	*tola*	a part or a division; a measure of weight
sayer	transit duty, customs toll	*ulavu*	ploughmen
senapati	leader or headman; caste of weavers	*ulkudi*	resident cultivator
shroff	money changer or broker	*uppena*	an inundation; the swell of the sea
sibbandy	irregular troops / soldiery	*ururkudi*	migratory or non-resident cultivator
Singamvallu	mendicant group attached to the Devanga caste	*valadahpadi*	black paddy
soosi	striped or checked fabric of silk or mixed cotton and silk	*valankai*	literally 'right hand' in Tamil; a caste term
subedar	provincial governor	Veeramushti	orthodox saivite mendicants attached to the Devanga and Komati castes
sunkoomdiara	one who glazes cloth	Velama	hill chieftains; a peasant caste
sunned	deed or order	Vellala	caste of cultivators
taffeta	fabric of twisted thread, both in silk and cotton	*visabadi*	a revenue system wherein lands or profits are allotted among hereditary proprietors
tahareer	fees	*viss/visamu*	weight measure
talapagah	turban, same as *pagah*	*voneelu*	half-saris
taluk	district	*vuduta*	staff used as a prop for the warp
		wallagu	upper jaw of a freshwater shark used for carding
		woogetta/ woogetty	register of a copdar's transactions
		woppandum	a contract
		yerra pattee	red cotton
		yetampalloo	a variety of chay root
		zamindar	landholder who collects revenue on behalf of the

	government
zamindari	land revenue settlement
zari	gold thread
zulum haree	block-printed fabric, same as kalamkari and chintz

BIBLIOGRAPHY

I. Official Records

Andhra Pradesh State Archives, Hyderabad

District Records, indexed (1765–1835) and unindexed (1835–58)

- Godavari District Records
- Guntur District Records
- Masulipatnam District Records
- Visakhapatnam District Records

General Reports of the Board of Revenue, 1787–1835

Mackenzie Collections: *Grama Kaifiyatlu*, 1982–90, covering West Godavari, Guntur, Kistna, Srikakulam, and Visakhapatnam zillas.

Tamil Nadu State Archives, Madras

Proceedings of the Board of Revenue 1790–1858

- Proper
- Miscellaneous
- Consultations

Commercial Department

- Consultations, 1812–40
- Despatches from England, 1786–1831
- Despatches to England (only 7 Volumes)

Judicial Department

- Consultations

Petition Department

- Consultations

Public Department

- Consultations
- Sundries

Nehru Memorial Museum And Library, New Delhi

Council for World Mission Archives (incorporating LMS) South Indian: Telugu Nos. 951 to 1000, 1817–54.

II. Books and Articles

Abraham, Meera. "A Medieval Merchant Guild of South India". *Studies in History* 4, no.1, 1982, 1–26.

Alam, S. Manzoor, and B. P. R. Vittal et al (ed). *Planning Atlas of Andhra Pradesh*. Hyderabad: Government of India and Government of Andhra Pradesh, 1974.

All India Handloom Board. *Annual Report*, New Delhi.

Anand, Mulk Raj. "Homage to Kalamkari". In *Homage to Kalamkari*. Bombay: Marg Publications, 1979.

Alvares, Claude. *Homo Faber: Technology, and Culture in India, China and the West, 1500 to the Present*. Bombay: Allied Publishers, 1979.

Appadurai, Arjun. "Right and Left Hand Castes in South India". *Indian Economic and Social History Review* 11, no.2, 1974, 216–59.

Arasaratnam, Sinnappah. "Indian Commercial Groups and European Traders 1600–1800: Changing Relationships in Southeastern India". *South Asia* 1, no.2, 1978, 43–53.

———. "Trade and Political Dominion in South India, 1750–1790: Changing British Indian Relationships". *Modern Asian Studies* 13, no.1, 1979, 19–40.

———. "Weavers, Merchants and Company: The Handloom Industry in South-Eastern India, 1750-1790". *Indian Economic and Social History Review* 17, no.3, 1980, 257–85.

———. *Merchants, Companies and Commerce on the Coromandel Coast 1650–1740*. Delhi: Oxford University Press, 1986.

———. *Maritime Commerce and English Power: Southeast India, 1750–1800*. U. K.: Varorium and New Delhi: Sterling Publishers, 1996.

Arudra. *Samagrah Andhra Sahityamu*, 10 volumes. Madras: M. Seshachalam & Co., 1966.

Baker, C. P. *Calico Painting and Printing in the East in the XVII and XVIII Centuries*. London: Edward Arnold, 1921.

Bagchi, A. K. "De-Industrialization in Gangetic Bihar 1809–1901". In Barun De, ed. *Essays in Honour of S.C. Sarkar*, 499–522. New Delhi: People's Publishing House, 1979.

———. "Merchants and Colonialism". In *Economy, Society and Politics in Modern India*, ed. D. N. Panigrahi, 1–41. New Delhi: Oxford University Press, 1985.

Banerjee, Kumkum. "Grain Traders and the East India Company: Patna and its Hinterland in the Late Eighteenth and Early Nineteenth Centuries. *Indian Economic and Social History Review* 23, no.4, 1986, 403–29.

Banerji, R. N. *Economic Progress of the East India Company on the Coromandel Coast, 1702–1746*. Nagpur: Nagpur University, 1974.

Bardhan, A. B. "Crisis in Handloom and the Misery of the Weaver". *Marxist Miscellany*, January 1970, 53–87.

Bawa, V.K. "Social and Economic Change in the Godavari District: 1851–1901". In M. E. Chaudhuri (ed), *Trends of Socio-Economic Change in India 1871–1961, Proceedings of VII Seminar*. Simla: Indian Institute of Advanced Study, 1969, 325–51.

Bayly, C. A. *Rulers, Townsmen and Bazaars: North Indian Society in the Age of British Expansion, 1770–1870*. Cambridge: Cambridge University Press, 1983.

———. *Indian Society and the Making of the British, The New Cambridge History of India II*. Cambridge: Cambridge University Press in association with Orient Longman, 1988.

Beck, Brenda, E. K. "The Right-Left Division of South Indian Society". *Journal of Asian Studies* 29, 1970, 779–98.

Benjamin, N. "Bombay's 'Country Trade' with China, 1765–1865". *Indian Economic and Social History Review* 1, no.2, 1974, 295–303.

Bernard, Kolver. "On the Origins of the Jajmani System". *Journal of Economic and Social History of the Orient* 31, no. 3, 1988, 265–85.

Bhadra, Gautam. "The Role of Pykars in the Silk Industry of Bengal, (C. 1765–1830)". *Studies in History* 3 no. 2, 1987, 1–35 and 155–85.

Bhattacharya, S. *The East India Company and the Economy of Bengal from 1704 to 1740*. London: Luzac and Co., 1954.

———."Culture and Social Constraints on Technological Innovation: Some Case Studies". *Indian Economic and Social History Review* 2, no. 3, 1966, 242–66.

Bijoy Mitra, Debendra. *Cotton Weavers in Bengal, 1757-1823*. Calcutta: Firma KLM, 1978.

Birdwood, Sir George. *Industrial Arts of India*. London: Chapman and Hall, 1880.

———. "The East India Company". *Journal of Indian Art* III, no.31, 1892.

Blitz, R. C. "Mercantilist Politics and the Pattern of World Trade, 1500–1750". *Journal of Economic History*, XXVII, no. 1, 1967.

Borpujari, J. G. "The British Impact on the Indian Cotton Textile Industry, 1757–1865". Ph.D. diss., University of Cambridge, 1969. Microfilm, Nehru Memorial Museum and Library, New Delhi.

Braudel, Fernand. *Civilization and Capitalism 15th-18th Century*. Volume I, "The Structure of Everyday Life". Translated, Sian Reynolds. London: Fontana Press, 1985.

Brennig, J. J. "The Textile Trade of Seventeenth Century Northern Coromandel: A Study of a Pre-Modern Asian Export Industry". Ph.D. diss., University of Wisconsin, 1975.

———. "The Chief Merchants and European Enclaves of Seventeenth Century Coromandel". *Modern Asian Studies* 11, no.3, 1977, 321–40.

———. "Textile Producers and Production in Late Seventeenth Century Coromandel". *Indian Economic and Social History Review* 23, no. 4, 1986, 333–53.

Brett, Katharine B. "An English Source of Indian Chintz Design". *Journal of Indian Textile History*, no. 1, 1955, 40–53.

———. "A French Source of Indian Chintz Design". *Journal of Indian Textile History* 2, 1960, 43–52.

Brown, Charles Philip. *Dictionary Telugu-English: Explaining the Telugu Idioms and Phrases with the Prononciation of Telugu Words*. Madras: Society for Promoting Christian Knowledge, 1903; reprint, New Delhi: Asian Educational Services, 1986.

Buchanan, Francis. *A Journey from Madras Through the Countries of Mysore, Canara and Malabar* 1. London: East India Company, 1807, 217.

Buhler, Alfred, Ebenhard Fischer, Marie-Louise Nabhol. "Indian Tie-Dyed Fabrics". In *Historical Fabrics of India* IV. Ahmedabad: Calico Museum, 1980.

Carmichael, D. F. *A Manual of the District of Vizagapatam in the Presidency of Madras*. Madras: Government Press, 1869.

Carr, M. W. *Andhra Lokakti Chandrika: A Collection of Telugu Proverbs*. 1868, reprint, Delhi: Asian Educational Services, 1987.

Charlesworth, Neil. *British Rule and the Indian Economy, 1800–1914*. London: Macmillan, 1982.

Chandra, Lokesh and Jyotindra Jain. *Dimensions of Indian Art: Pupul Jayakar at Seventy, Vol.1: Textile*. Delhi: Agam, 1986.

Chandra, Moti. "Indian Costumes and Textiles from the Ancient to the Twelfth Century". *Journal of Indian Textile History* 5, 1960, 1–41.

———. "Costumes and Textiles in the Sultanate Period". *Journal of Indian Textile History* 6, 1961, 5–61.

———. "Costumes Through the Ages". In *Treasures of Indian Textiles*, Ahmedabad: Calico Museum, 1980, 19–59.

Chandra Gupta, Sulekha. *Agrarian Relations and Early British Rule in India: A Case Study of Ceded and Conquered Provinces, U.P. 1801–1833*. Bombay: Asia Publishing House, 1963, 53–59.

Chatterjee, Rama. "Cotton Handloom Manufacturers of Bengal, 1870–1921," *Economic and Political Weekly* 22, 1987, 988–97.

Chattopadhya, Raghavendra. "De-Industrialisation in India Reconsidered". *Economic and Political Weekly* 10-12, 1975, 523–31.

Chaudhuri, K. N. "The Structure of the Indian Textile Industry in the Seventeenth and Eighteenth Centuries". *Indian Economic and Social History Review* 11, no.2, 1974, 127–82.

———. *The Trading World of Asia and the English East India Company, 1660–1760*. Cambridge: Cambridge University Press, 1978.

——— and C. J. Dewey (ed). *Economy and Society: Essays in Indian Economic and Social History*. Delhi: Oxford University Press, 1979.

Chaudhury, Sushil. *Trade and Commercial Organization in Bengal, 1650–1720*. Calcutta: Firma KL Mukhopadhyay, 1975.

———. "Merchants, Companies and Rulers: Bengal in the Eighteenth Century". *Journal of the Economic and Social History of the Orient* 31, 1988, 74–109.

Chicherov, A. I. *India: Economic Development in the 16th-18th Centuries: Outline History of Crafts and Trade*. Moscow: Nauka Publishers, 1971.

Chitra, V. P. and Tekumalla Viswanatham (ed). *Cottage Industries of India (Guide Book and Symposium)*. Madras: Silpi Publications, 1948.

Cohn, Bernard S. "Structural Change in Indian Rural Society, 1596–1885". In *Land Control and Social Structure in Indian History*, ed. R. E. Frykenberg, 53–123. Delhi: Oxford University Press, 1979.

Coleman, D. C. "Proto-Industrialisation: A Concept Too Many". *Economic History Review*, 2nd series, no. 36, August 1983, 435–48.

Commander, Simon. "The Jajmani System in Northern India: An Examination of its Logic and Status Across Two Centuries". *Modern Asian Studies* 17, no.2, 1983, 283–312.

Curtin, Philip. *Cross-Cultural Trade in World History*. Cambridge: Cambridge University Press, 1984.

Das Gupta, Ashin. "Indian Merchants and the Trade of the Indian Ocean". In *The Cambridge Economic History of India, c 1200–c 1700*, eds. Ray Chaudhuri Habib, 419. Delhi: Cambridge University Press in association with Orient Longman, 1987.

———. *Indian Merchants and the Decline of Surat 1700-1750*. Wiesbaden: Franz Steiner Verlag, 1979.

——— and M. N. Pearson. (ed). *India and the Indian Ocean 1500–1800*. Calcutta: Oxford University Press, 1987.

Datta, Rajat. "Merchants and Peasants: A Study of the Structure of Local Trade in Grain in Late Eighteenth Century Bengal". *Indian Economic and Social History Review* 23, no.4, 1986, 379–402.

De, Barun (ed). *Essays in Honour of S. C. Sarkar*. New Delhi: People's Publishing House, 1976.

Devangauni Gotra Nighantuu. Extracts supplied by Pinjala Somasekhara Rao, Vetapalem.

Dodwell, H. "Madras Weaver Under the Company". *Proceedings of the Indian Historical Records Commission*. Calcutta: Government Press, 1922, 41–47.

———. *A Calendar of the Madras Records, 1740-1744*. Madras: Government Press, 1917.

Donappa, Tomati. *Andhra Samsthanamulu: Sahitya Poshana*. Waltair, 1963; reprint, Hyderabad: Visalandhra Publishers, 1987.

Dumont, Louis. *Homo Hierarchicus*. Chicago: Cambridge University Press, 1970.

Dutt, Konduri Iswara. *Sasana Subdha Kosamu Andhra Pradesama (Inscriptional Glossary of Andhra Pradesh)*. Hyderabad: Andhra Pradesh Sahitya Akademi, 1968.

Epstein, T. S. *Economic Development and Social Change in South India*. Manchester: ELBS, 1962.

Fawcett, Sir Charles (ed). *English Factories in India 1670–77, 1678–84*. Oxford: Oxford University Press, 1952–55.

Ferminger, W. K. (ed) *Fifth Report of the Parliamentary Committee on East India Company Affairs, 1813*. Reprint, New York: Augustus M. Kelley, 1969.

Ferrier, R.W. "The Armenians and the East India Company in Persia in the Seventeenth and Early Eighteenth Centuries". *The Economic History Review* 26, nos.1–4, 1973, 38–62.

Forrester, Duncan. *Caste and Christianity*. London: Curzon Press, 1980.

Foster, William (ed). *The Travels of John Sanderson in the Levant, 1584–1604*. London: Hakluyt Society, 1931.

——— (ed). *English Factories in India 1622–24*. Oxford: Oxford University Press, 1907.

———. *John Company*. London: Bodley Head, 1926.

Fox, Richard G. "Pariah Capitalism and Traditional Indian Merchants". In Milton Singer (ed). *Entrepreneurship and Modernization of Occupational Cultures in South Asia*. Durham: Duke University, 1973, 24–27.

——— (ed). *Realm and Region in Traditional India*. New Delhi: Vikas Publishing House, 1977.

Fraser, R. A. "Weavers in Pre-Modern South India". *Economic and Political Weekly* 10, no.30, 1975, 1119–23.

Fryer, John (ed). *A New Account of East India and Persia, 1675–80*. London: R.Chiswell, 1909–15; reprint, New Delhi: Asian Educational Services, 1992.

Frykenberg, R. E. "The Administration of Guntur District, with Special Reference to Local Influences on Revenue Policies, 1757–1848". Ph.D. diss., University of London, 1961.

———. *Guntur District, 1788–1845: A History of Local Influence and Central Authority in South India*. Oxford: Oxford University Press, 1965.

———. "Company Circari in the Carnatic, 1799–1859: The Inner Logic of Political Systems in India". In Fox, (ed). *Realm and Region in Traditional India*, 117–59.

Furber, H. *The John Company at Work, A Study of European Expansion in India in the Eighteenth Century*. Cambridge: Harvard University Press, 1951.

———. *Rival Empires of Trade in the Orient 1600-1800*. Minneapolis: University of Minnesota Press, 1976.

Ganesh, Gamala. "Jajmani Relations in Tirunelveli District: A Case Study of the Kottai Pillaimar, 1839–1979". *Indian Economic and Social History Review* 22, no.2, 1985, 175–208.

Goody, Esther N (ed). *From Craft to Industry: The Ethnography of Proto-Industrial Cloth Production*. Cambridge: Cambridge University Press, 1982.

Gopal, Surendra. *Commerce and Crafts in Gujarat, 16th and 17th Centuries: A Study in the Impact of European Expansion on Pre-capitalist Economy*. New Delhi: People's Publishing House, 1975.

Guha, Amalendu. "Raw Cotton Trade of Western India: Output, Transport, and Marketing, 1750-1850". *Indian Economic and Social History Review* 9, no.1, 1972, 1–42.

———. "Output and Availability of Raw Cotton in India—1850–1900". *Arthavijna* 15, 1973.

Guha, Sumit. "Society and Economy in the Deccan, 1818–50". *Indian Economic and Social History Review* 20, no.4, 1983, 389–415.

Guide to the Records of Godavari District, 1750–1830 1 & 2. Madras: Government Press, 1934 and 1935.

Guide to the Records of Guntur District, 1750–1830 1. Madras: Government Press, 1934.

Guide to the Records of Masulipatnam District, 1682–1833 3. Madras: Government Press, 1935.

Guide to the Records of Visakhapatnam District, 1769–1830 1. Madras: Government Press, 1934.

Habib, Ifran. "Notes on the Indian Textile Industry in the 17th Century". In *Essays in Honour of S. C. Sarkar*, ed. Barun De, 180–92. New Delhi: People's Publishing House, 1976.

———. "Technology and Barriers to Social Change in Mughal India". *Indian Historical Review* 5, no. 1, 1978, 152–74.

———. "Potentialities of Capitalist Development in the Economy of Mughal India". *Journal of Economic History* 29, no. 1, 1969, 32–78.

———. "The Technology and Economy of Mughal India". *Indian Economic and Social History Review* 17, no. 1, 1980, 1–34.

Hadaway, W. S. *Cotton Painting and Printing in the Madras Presidency*. Madras: Government Press, 1870.

Hamilton, Walter. *A Geographical, Statistical and Historical Description of Hindostan and Adjacent Countries* 1. London, 1820; reprint New Delhi: D. K. Publishers, 1990

Havell, E. B. "The Industries of Madras". *Journal of Indian Art and Industry* 3, no. 27, 1889, 25–26.

Haynes, Douglas. 'The Dynamics of Continuity in Indian Domestic Industrial Manufacture in Surat, 1900–47". *Indian Economic and Social History Review* 23, no.2, 1986, 127–49.

Hemingway, F. R. *Madras District Gazetter, Godavary District*. Madras: Government Press, 1907.

Hjejle, B. "Slavery and Agricultural Bondage in South India in the Nineteenth Century". *Scandinavian Economic History Review* 15, nos. 1 & 2, 1967, 71–126.

Hossain, Hameeda. "The Alienation of Weavers: Impact of the Conflict Between the Revenue and Commercial Interest of the East India Company, 1750–1800". *Indian Economic and Social History Review* 16, no.3, 1979, 323–45.

———. *The Company Weavers of Bengal. The East India Company and the Organization of Textile Production in Bengal, 1750–1813*. New Delhi: Oxford University Press, 1987.

Irwin, John. "Indian Textile Trade in the Seventeenth Century, South India". *Journal of Indian Textile History* 2, 1956, 24–39.

——— and P.R. Schwartz. *Studies in Indo-European Textile History*. Ahmedabad: Calico Museum, 1966.

——— and Margaret Hall. *Indian Painted and Printed Fabrics*. Ahmedabad: Calico Museum, 1971.

———, Margaret Hall, Kalyan Krishna, and K. Talwar (eds). *The Chintz Collection: The Calico Museum of Textiles India, 1 & 2,* Ahmedabad: Calico Museum, 1983.

Jayakar, Pupul. "A Neglected Group of Indian Ikat Fabrics". *Journal of the Indian Textile History*, no. 1, 1955, 35–39.

———."Indian Textiles Through the Centuries". *Marg* XXXIII (1), 1979–80, 59–80.

Karashima, Noboru. *South Indian History and Society: Studies from Inscriptions, A.D. 850–1800*. New Delhi: Oxford University Press, 1984.

Kate, P. V. *Marathwada under the Nizams (1724-1948).* Delhi: Mittal Publications, 1987.

Kellenberg, Hermann "The Organization of Industrial Production". In (eds) E. E. Rich and C. H. Wilson, *The Cambridge Economic History of Europe* 5. Cambridge: Cambridge University Press, 1977.

Krishnamurti, Bhadriraju and Poranki Dakshinamurti (ed). *Mandaleeka Vrithi Padakosamu* 2. Hyderabad: Andhra Pradesh Sahitya Akademi, 1971.

Krupachary, Guzzarlamudi. *Telugu Sahityanika Kristavula Seva*. Guntur: Nagarjuna Viswavidyalayam, 1988.

Kumar, Dharma. *Land and Caste in South India: Agricultural Labour in the Madras Presidency during the Nineteenth Century*. Cambridge: Cambridge University Press, 1965.

——— and Meghnad Desai (eds). *The Cambridge Economic History of India II, C 1757–C 1970*. Cambridge: Cambridge University Press, 1983.

Kumar, Ravinder. *India and the Persian Gulf Region, 1858–1907: A Study in British Imperial Policy*. Bombay: Asia Publishing House, 1965.

Kurmanadudu, Gogulapati. *Simhadri Narasimha Satakamu*. Dvipada Kavya, c. 1750.

Mackenzie, Gordon. *A Manual of the Kistna District in the Presidency of Madras*. Madras: Government Press, 1883.

Maclean, C. D. *Manual of the Administration of the Madras Presidency in Illustration of the Records of Government and the Yearly Administrative Reports* 2. Madras: Government Press, 1885; reprint, New Delhi: Asian Educational Services, 1990.

Mallick, Binoy Shankar. "English Trade and Indigenous Finance in Bengal and Gujarat in the Seventeenth Century: A Study of the Dadni System and the Rate of Interest". *Studies in History* 2, no. 1 (new series), 1986.

Matsui, Toru. "On the Nineteenth Century Indian Economic History: A Review of a 'Re-interpretation'". *Indian Economic and Social History Review* 5, no. 1, 1976, 17–33.

Methwold, William. "*Relations of the Kingdom of Golconda.*" In Moreland (ed), *Relations of Golconda in the Early Seventeenth Century between 1608 and 1622 A.D.* London: Hakluyt Society, 1931.

Mines, Mattison. *The Warrior Merchants, Textiles Trade and Territory in South India*. Cambridge: Cambridge University Press, 1984.

Mohandas, T. "Economic History of Andhra, 1707–1801: Analysis of Economic Transition". Ph.D. diss. Osmania University, Hyderabad, 1987.

Moreland, William (ed). *Relations of Golconda in the Early Seventeenth Century between 1608 and 1622 A.D.* London: Hakluyt Society, 1931.

Morris, Henry. *A Descriptive and Historical Account of the Godavary District in the Presidency of Madras*. Madras: Government Press, 1878.

Morris, Morris David. "Trends and Tendencies in Indian Economic History", *Indian Economic and Social History Review* 5, no. 1, 1968, 381.

———. "Towards a Reinterpretation of Nineteenth Century Indian Economic History" in (eds) Morris et al, *Indian Economy in the Nineteenth Century: A Symposium*, Delhi, *IESHR* Association, 1969, 1–51.

Mudaliyar, Rao Sahib P. K. Guna Sundara. *A Note on the Permanent Settlement in Madras*. Madras: Government Press, 1940.

Mukherjee, S. N. "Daladali in Calcutta in the Nineteenth Century". *Modern Asian Studies* 9, no.1, 1975, 59–81.

Murthy, K. Radha Krishna. "The Economic Conditions of Medieval Andhra Desa (A. D. 1500)". Ph.D. diss., Kakatiya University, 1981.

Narasimha Reddy, P. *Telugu Sametalu, Jana Jeevanamu*. Tirupati: Sreenivasa Murali Publications, 1983.

Narayana Kavi, Ayyala Raju. *Hamsa Vimsathi*, c 1770–75. C. V. Subbanna (ed). Satavadhani. Hyderabad: Potti Sriramulu Telugu University, 1996.

Nayeem, M. A. *Mughal Administration of Deccan under Nizam-ul-Mulk Asaf Jah, 1720–48*. Hyderabad: Jaico Publishing House, 1985.

Neild Basu, Susan. "The Dubashes of Madras". *Modern Asian Studies* 18, no. 1, 1984, 1–31.

Nerallapalli, Vasanthi. "The Agrarian World of Masulipatnam District, c 1750–1850". Ph.D. diss. Department of History, University of Hyderabad, 1993.

Nightingale, P. *Trade and Empire in Western India, 1784-1806*. Cambridge: Cambridge University Press, 1970.

O'Brien, Patrick. "European Economic Development: The Contribution of the Periphery". *Economic History Review* 35, no.1, 1982, 1–18.

Palat, Ravi et al. "The Incorporation and Peripheralisation of South Asia, 1600–1950". *Review* 10, no.1, 1986, 171–208.

Pandey, Gyanendra. *Economic Dislocation in Nineteenth Century Eastern U.P.* Occasional Papers 37, no.1. Calcutta: Centre for Studies in Social Sciences, 1981.

———. "The Bigoted Julaha". *Economic and Political Weekly* 18, no.5, 1983, 19–28.

Pavlov, V. I. *Historical Premises for India's Transition to Capitalism (Late 18th to Mid-19th Century)*. Moscow: Nauka Publishers, 1978.

Pearson, M. N. *Merchants and Rulers in Gujarat*. Berkeley: University of California Press, 1976.

———. "Brokers in Western Indian Port-Cities: Their Role in Servicing Foreign Merchants". *Modern Asian Studies* 22, no. 3, 1988, 455–72.

Perlin, Frank. "Proto-Industrialization and Pre-Colonial South Asia". *Past and Present* no. 98, 1983, 30–95.

Potukuchi, Subrahmanya Sastri, *Achha Telugu Kosamu* 2, Tenali: 1979, 170–72.

Prakash, Om. *The Dutch Factors in India, 1617–1623, A Collection of Dutch East India Company Documents Pertaining to India*. New Delhi: Munshiram Manoharlal, 1984.

———. *The Dutch East India Company and the Economy of Bengal, 1630–1720*. Delhi: Oxford University Press, 1988.

Pratapareddy, Suravaram. *Andhrula Sangheeka Charitra*. 1949; reprint, Hyderabad: Andhra Sahitya Parishat, 1982.

Qaiser, A.J. 'The Role of Brokers in Medieval India'. *Indian History Review* 12, 1974, 225.

Raghavaiyangar, Srinivasa S. *Memorandum on the Progress of the Madras Presidency During the Last Forty Years of British Administration*. Madras: Government Press, 1893.

Raju, Sarada A. *Economic Conditions in the Madras Presidency 1800-1850*. Madras: Madras University Press, 1941.

Rama Rao, Nanduri Venkata Satya. *Andhra Sahityamu Sangheekha Jeeveena Pratipalamu (A.D. 1022 – A.D. 1856)*. Pentapadu: Srivaishnava Press, 1979.

Ramakrishna, V. *Social Reform Movement in Andhra (1848-1919)*. New Delhi: Vikas Publishing House, 1983.

Ramalakshmi, C. "The Acquisition of Northern Circars by the East India Company". *Andhra Pradesh History Congress Proceedings* 4, 1980, 1–9.

Ramana Rao, A. V. *Economic Development in Andhra Pradesh 1766-1957*. Bombay: Popular Publishers, 1958.

Ramaswamy, Vijaya. "Notes on the Textile Technology in Medieval South India with Special Reference to the South". *Indian Economic and Social History Review* 17, no.2, 1980, 227–43.

———. "Weaver Folk Traditions as a Source of History". *Indian Economic and Social History Review* 19, no.1, 1982, 47–63.

———. "The Genesis and Historical Role of Master Weavers in South Indian Textile Production". *Journal of the Economic and Social History of the Orient* 28, no. 3, 1985, 294–335.

———. "Artisans in Vijayanagar Society". *Indian Economic and Social History Review* 22, no.4, 1985, 415–44.

———. *Textiles and Weavers in Medieval South India*. New Delhi: Oxford University Press, 1985.

Rao, G. N. "Changing Conditions and Growth of Agricultural Economy in the Krishna and Godavari Districts, 1840–1890". Ph.D. diss. Andhra University, 1973.

———. "Agrarian Relations in Coastal Andhra under Early British Rule". *Social Scientist* 6, no.1, 1977, 19–29.

———. "Stagnation and Decay of the Agricultural Economy of Coastal Andhra". *Arthavijnana* 20, no. 3, 1978, 221–43.

Rao, K. Gopal Krishna. *Andhra Sataka Sahitya Vikasamu*. Hyderabad: Andhra Saraswata Parishattu, 1976.

Raychaudhuri, T. *Jan Company in Coromandel 1605–1690: A Study in the Interrelations of European Commerce and Traditional Economies*. Verhandelingen van het Koninklijk Instituut voor Taal-, Land- en Volkenkunde 38 ('s-Gravenhage 1962), The Hague, 1962.

———. "European Commercial Activity and the Organization of India's Commerce and Industrial Production, 1500–1750". In B. N. Ganguli, *Readings in Indian Economic History*. Bombay: Asia Publishing House, 1964, 64–77.

———. "Some Patterns of Economic Organization and Activity in Seventeenth Century India". *Second International Conference of Economic History*, Aix-en-Provence, 1962. New York: Mouton, 1965, 751–60.

———. "A Re-interpretation of Nineteenth Century Indian Economic History". *Indian Economic and Social History Review* 5, no.1, 1968, 77–100.

——— and Ifran Habib (eds). *The Cambridge Economic History of India I, C 1200–C 1700*. Cambridge: Cambridge University Press in association with Orient Longman, 1987.

Regani, Sarojini. "Anglo-Nizam Relations Pertaining to the Northern Sarkars". *Journal of Deccan History and Culture* 4, no.2, 1956, 21–58.

———. *Nizam-British Relations, 1724-1857*. 1963, reprint New Delhi: South Asia Books, 1988.

Richards, J. F. "The Hyderabad Karnatik, 1687–1707". *Modern Asian Studies* 9, no.2, 1975, 241–61.

———. *Mughal Administration in Golconda*. Oxford: Oxford University Press, 1975.

Richards, Paul. "The State and Early Industrial Capitalism: The Case of the Handloom Weavers". *Past and Present*, no. 83, 1979, 91–115.

Roxburgh, William. *Plants of the Coast of Coromandel* 1. Selected from drawings and descriptions presented to the Honourable Court of Directors of the East India Company, 1795–1819. London: Bulmer and Co., 1795.

Sankaranarayana, P. *English–Telugu Dictionary*. Hyderabad: Asian Educational Services, 1978.

Sarma, M. Somesekhara. (ed) *Bobbili Yuddha Kotha*. Madras: Government Oriental Manuscript Library, 1950.

Satyanarayana, K. *A Study of the History and Culture of the Andhras* 2. New Delhi: People's Publishing House, 1983.

Schwartberg, Joseph E. *A Historical Atlas of South Asia*. Chicago: Chicago University Press, 1978.

Schwartz, Paul R. "The Rowburgh Account of Indian Cotton Painting, 1795" *Journal of Indian Textile History* 4, 1959, 47–76.

Sen, S. P. "Indian Textiles in South East Asian Trade in the Seventeenth Century" *Journal of South East Asian History* 3, no. 2, 1962, 92–99.

Seth, M. J. *The Armenians in India from the Earliest Times to the Present Day*. Calcutta: Central Press, 1973.

Sethna, N. H. *Living Traditions of India: Kalamkari Painted and Printed Fabrics from Andhra Pradesh*. New York: Mapin International, 1985.

Sharma, Rajiv. "Weavers—Their Role and Economic Conditions during the Seventeenth Century". In *Papers on Indian History*. Aligarh: Aligarh Muslim University, 1986, 119–30.

Sherwani, H. K. *History of Medieval Deccan* 1 and 2. Hyderabad: Government of Andhra Pradesh, 1974.

Simmons, Colin. "De-industrialization, Industrialization, and the Indian Economy, 1850–1947". *Modern Asian Studies* 19, no.3, 1985, 593–622.

Sinha, A. K. *Transition in Textile Industry (A History of Textile Industry in Bihar, 1783–1833)*. New Delhi: Capital Publishers, 1984.

Sitapathi, P. and V. Purusotham (eds). *Enugula Veera Swamy's Journal (Kasiyatra Charita)*. Original compiled in 1941 by Komaleswarapuram Srinivasa Pillai. Hyderabad: Andhra Pradesh Government Oriental Manuscripts Library and Research Institute, 1973.

Specker, Konrad. "Madras Handlooms in Nineteenth Century". *Indian Economic and Social History Review* 26, no.2, 1989, 131–66.

Srinivasachari, C. S. "Right and Left Hand Caste Disputes in Madras in the Early Part of the 18th Century". *Indian Historical Records Commissions*, 1929, 68–106.

Stein, Burton. "The South". In Raychaudhuri and Habib, *Cambridge Economic History*, 203–13.

———. "Circulation and Historical Geography of Tamil Country". In his *All the Kings Mana: Papers on Medieval South Indian History*. Madras: Oxford University Press, 1984, 90–117.

———. "Integration of the Agrarian System of South India". In *All the Kings Mana*, 128.

Styles, John. "Embezzlement, Industry and the Law in England, 1500–1800". In Maxine Berg et al, *Manufacture in Town and Country before the Factory*. Cambridge: Cambridge University Press, 1983.

Subrahmanyam, Sanjay. "Persians, Pilgrims and Portuguese: The Travails of Masulipatnam Shipping on the Western Indian Ocean, 1590–1665". *Modern Asian Studies* 22, no.3, 1988, 503–30.

———. "Rural Industry and Commercial Agriculture in Late Seventeenth Century South-Eastern India'. *Past and Present* 126, 1990, 76–114.

———. "Staying On: The Portuguese of Southern Coromandel in the Late Seventeenth Century". In his (ed) *Improvising Empire: Portuguese Trade and Settlement in the Bay of Bengal 1500-1700*. Delhi: Oxford University Press, 1990, 216–40.

———. *The Political Economy of Commerce: Southern India 1500-1650*. Cambridge: Cambridge University Press, 1990.

Sudhir, P. "Colonialism and the Vocabularies of Dominance: The Conquest of Telugu, c 1600–c 1850". In Tejaswini Niranjana et al (ed), *Interrogating Modernity Culture and Colonialism in India*. Calcutta: Seagull, 1993, 334–47.

——— and Swarnalatha Potukuchi. "Textile Traders and Territorial Imperatives: Masulipatnam, 1750–1850". *Indian Economic and Social History Review* 29, no.2, 1992, 145–69.

Sundaram, Lanka. "The Revenue Administration of the Northern Sarcars, 1769–1786". *Journal of Andhra Historical Research Society*, 7–15, 1946.

Susheela, T. *Andhra Dwipada Sahitya Charitra.* (A study of dvipada kavyas in Telugu literature till the end of the 18th century.) Hyderabad: Pragati Books, 1979.

Swarnalatha Potukuchi. "The Agrarian Structure of Godavari District, c 1800–1840". M.Phil. diss. University of Hyderabad, 1986.

Temple, Sir Richard C (ed). *The Travels of Peter Mundy in Europe and Asia, 1608–1667* 1–5. Cambridge: Hakluyt Society, 1907–1936.

——— (ed) *Diaries of Streynsham Master (1677–79)*. London: John Murray for the Government of India, 1911.

Thurston, Edgar. *Castes and Tribes of South India* 1–7, Madras: Government Press, 1909; reprint, New Delhi: Cosmo Publications, 1975.

Torri, Michelguglielmo. "Ethnicity and Trade in Surat during the Dual Government Era, 1759–1800". *Indian Economic and Social History Review* 27, no. 4, 1990, 377–405.

Varadarajan, Lotika. "Saga of Indian Textiles". In R. C. Mazumdar (ed), *Indian Heritage*. Bombay: Air India, 1981, 93–99.

———. "Towards a Definition of Kalamkari". In *Homage to Kalamkari*. Bombay: Marg Publications, 1979, 19–22.

Venkataramanayya, N (ed). *Cuddapah Silasasasanamulu*. Madras: Tamil Nadu Government Oriental Manuscripts, 1974.

Visaria, Pravin, and Leela. "Population: 1757–1947". In Kumar and Desai, *Cambridge Economic History of India* II, 463–69.

Wallerstein, Immanuel "Incorporation of Indian Subcontinent into Capitalist World Economy", *Economic and Political Weekly* 21, no. 4, January 25, 1986, 28–39.

Washbrook, David. "Land and Labour in Late Eighteenth Century South India: The Golden Age of the Pariah?" In Peter Robb (ed), *Dalit Movements and the Meanings of Labour in India*. Delhi: Oxford University Press, 1996, 68–87.

Watson, Ian Bruce. *Foundation for Empire: English Private Trade in India, 1659–1760.* Delhi: Vikas Publishing House, 1980.

Yule, Henry and A. C. Burnell. *Hobson-Jobson: A Glossary of Colloquial Anglo-Indian Words and Phrases* (ed W. Crooke). London: Murray, 1903.

A Note On Currency, Measures and Weights

Currency

In the northern Coromandel, the currency in use till 1820 was the Madras pagoda.

One Madras pagoda = 4 rupees

One rupee = 20 fanams

One fanam = 4 dubs

The East India Company's rate of exchange was 1 Madras pagoda = 192 dubs (1 rupee = 12 fanams). The shroffs and renters varied the rates of exchange of the fanam to the rupee.

Measures

Cloth Measurement

In the northern Coromandel, the local measurement of cloth by the cubit was determined by the length of the arm, rather than by the yard.

4 finger breadths = 1 bettaloo

2 bettaloo = 1 span

2 spans = 1 cubit

2 cubits = 1 arm's length, measured from the tip of the finger to the middle of the chest.

4 cubits = 1 bara

This was essentially followed for measuring local cloth as well as imported long cloth. But other varieties—such as China and other silk satins, broad cloth, and blankets—were measured by the yards, inches, and gerahs. A gerah was equal to one-sixteenth of the yard or 2¼ inches.

A punjum was a skein of 60 or 120 threads, and the quality of the cloth depended on the number of punjums in it. There were standard specifications, such as 14-punjum cloth, 18-punjum cloth, 22-punjum cloth, 36-punjum cloth.

20 pieces of cloth = 1 corge

The number of corges a bale contained varied, depending on the measurement of a variety.

Grain Measurement

1 pooty = 20 tooms = 960 seers
1 toom = 4 mercals= 48 seers
1 mercal = 12 seers
1 ara mercal (½ mercal) = 6 seers
1 pavoo mercal (¼ mercal) = 2 tuvus= 3 seers
1 manika = 2 tuvus = 3 seers
1 tuva = 2 solas = 1 seer
½ sola = 2 giddas = ¼ seer
1 gidda = ⅛ seer
½ gidda = 1/16 seer

INDEX